Confessions of a Catholic School Dropout

Patti Lavell

DEDICATION

To Dougie for allowing me to escape the nine-to-five rat race and relocate to Paradise. You'll always be my hero. To Zak, you are fearless and uncompromising in your approach to life and your wit is unmatched. To Lauren, you have a strength and depth of character beyond your years and never fail to impress me. To Mom, I hope you laugh..

1 MISSING PENIS

I think if my brother Timothy hadn't died my parents wouldn't have had any more children. They had always wanted four boys and that's exactly what God blessed them with. But die he did so they decided to have one more. Having four boys means you can send them up the aisle to Communion by two's. That's how Noah did it; two by two.

Baby number five was due and he was to be named Patrick Gordon in honor of my Dad's older brothers. Irish Catholics always name their kids after fathers and uncles and saints. That's why every generation ends up having the same damn name. Patrick was a no-good drunk who couldn't hold a job for love of the drink. Never had two pennies to rub together but always smelled of whiskey. Some might say my parents were tempting fate, naming a child after such a man, but they were Irish Catholics and his name was to be Patrick Gordon come hell or high water.

On a cold, grey January day in 1968, in the hospital of a small western New York town, my parents discovered a problem with their family plan. I was a girl. Patrick Gordon tossed aside like an empty bottle, they decided to name me Patricia Anne Elizabeth, which still gave a wink and a nod to Uncle Patrick. Dad's mother was named Anne and his only sister, Elizabeth. A solid Irish Catholic name to be sure and one tainted with whiskey. Each of them, at one time, found it damn near impossible to pass a roadhouse without parting with a week's worth of wages and yet they decided to saddle their only baby girl with three names doused in booze. I've done my best to keep with tradition.

To further tempt the gods, Patrick and Elizabeth were chosen to be my Godparents. Irish Catholic Godparents take their spiritual role quite seriously and promise to help guide their godchild through life's struggles with The Devil. Proud of their responsibilities, they jump on every opportunity to remind their godchild of the burden placed on their weary souls.

On the day of my baptism into the One, Holy, Catholic and Apostolic Church, Patrick began nipping at the bottle long before he'd scrubbed his face or washed his arse. Apparently, he was disappointed at having a niece as a namesake instead of a nephew, and went on a three-day bender to cope with the embarrassment. Whatever his excuse, he arrived at Church quite late. My parents were already on the altar dressed in their Sunday best, standing by the baptismal font with my Godmother who was decked in one of her signature, ridiculously large hats. Elizabeth's hat was so grandiose, she had to stand several feet from the font so the brim didn't take out Father Lyntz's eyeball.

Patrick stumbled into the vestibule, banging the heavy wooden door against the grey stone wall. "Where's the ugly thing that's to carry me name?"

The family and friends gathered at Nativity of the Blessed Virgin Mary turned in unison to look back at the source of commotion. They saw Patrick leaning on a pew, taking a nip from his pocket flask. He'd apparently not made use of a looking glass before leaving the house, because his shirt was buttoned incorrectly and coming mostly untucked from his trousers, which were so wrinkled they looked like he'd slept in them for a week. Those gathered for the happy occasion looked in disbelief at the less-than-fashionable outfit he'd assembled to cover his thin frame; tan shirt, brown trousers and white socks with house slippers visible beneath his overcoat.

2

Wiping his mouth with the back of his hand and running it through his unkempt hair, he made his way up the aisle. He lowered his head and whispered to relatives as he passed them on his way to the altar. Between the acoustics of the old church and his level of alcohol consumption, his whispers were heard by all.

"Shame really, 'tis the ugliest thing I've ever seen...If Timothy had lived, I wouldn't be 'ere in this monkey suit... Never saw such a homely lass...Your wife's hat is nearly as big as her arse...Where's the jax? I've gotta rid meself of a pint or two."

Patrick stumbled through the nave and up to the altar. He tipped his invisible hat to Father Lintz. "How do, Monsignor?"

My mother questioned her choice of husband while my father considered the murder of his older brother. Somehow they made it through the christening with only minor embarrassment. When asked to make a profession of faith on my behalf, Patrick farted and laughed.

"Never in me live long days 'ave I heard sech a wee baby make sech a powerful racket!"

The day of a child's baptism into the Church is a monumental day in the life of an Irish Catholic parent. Mine were no exception and invited everyone back to the farm for the requisite reception. Corned beef and cabbage, baked ham and peas, potatoes and corn, cakes and pies were laid out in abundance. Not ones to break with tradition, there was also plenty of Irish whiskey.

With full bellies, my family passed me around the room, each person taking their own mental notes regarding my homeliness. When my Godmother got hold of me she called for a toast.

"Raise yer glass to Mac and Betty. Sech a pretty thing. Just look those eyes. Irish eyes to be sure."

Patrick most heartily disagreed with Elizabeth as he glared down at me

3

and said, "Ah hell, she looks a wrinkly mess and smells of piss. Never laid eyes on a bigger bucket o' snots."

"Shet cher bloody cake hole, ya drunken dosser! Ye've had more 'n enough whiskey to know what yer talking about! Why in the hell Mac asked ye to be this wee doll's Godfather is a mystery to us all."

"Hold yer tongue, ye old hoor! No one asked ye. If yer brain was half as half as big as yer arse, I'd be able to talk some sense into yer noggin. As it is, yer as useless as a lighthouse on a bog!"

No one batted an eye as brother and sister pissed back and forth at one another. It was normal family banter and very much expected until Patrick began to cough and choke. He grabbed his chest and sat down hard.

"That's Arthur's Guinness showing right there! Nothin' wrong with ye that a bath and a bed won't cure," chastised Elizabeth.

Patrick continued to cough and clutch his chest. My Mom called for an ambulance as Elizabeth continued to berate Patrick, calling him an eejit and a louse for ruining such a blessed day. My Godfather went quiet. He sat on the floor beneath me as I lay cradled in my Godmother's arms, a glass of whisky still clutched in his hand.

"Oh feck, he's shit his cacks," complained Elizabeth.

As far back as I can remember, all my relatives tell the story about Patrick being so disappointed with me as his namesake, his heart seized until he croaked. I killed my Godfather Patrick and took a good man from this world. Funny how when people talked about Patrick in any context except my christening day, they used words like "eejit, bad egg and wanker." But when they talked about how I killed him, they said "saintly, honest as the day is long, jolly and cracker."

I grew up with a clear understanding my gender was a great disappointment to most of my family. I killed Patrick because I didn't have a penis.

Only my Dad didn't seem to mind I was without male parts. In fact, I think he liked the idea of having a little girl to spoil, but Mom wouldn't allow it. She didn't believe in spoiling little girls with ruffled, pretty things. That wasn't practical. She realized that, although she wanted four boys, things hadn't worked out that way. Betty was from solid German stock and Germans make do with what God provides.

Rather than girly clothes, I wore my brothers' hand-me-downs. I called myself "Patti" but my family called me "Pat", even though they knew I hated it. Even Santa was against me. I wrote him a letter asking for black patent leather Mary Jane's but he brought me a pair of work boots instead.

I knew my Mom wanted to send another son to Nativity School and I could feel her disappointment in my gender building daily. I looked in the mirror at my long auburn curls and hated them. They made me look like a girl even though I was wearing patched blue jeans and an old flannel shirt.

"Mom, can I get a haircut before Kindergarten starts?"

Without looking up from the ironing board she asked, "What kind of haircut?"

"I want short hair."

The words were no sooner out of my mouth than she yanked the iron's cord from the wall. Within seconds, she was standing at the door with her purse in one hand and the car keys in the other. "Let's go," she said.

Wow. That was easy.

We drove to the "beauty parlor" and Mom asked the fat woman who was eating a Snickers bar in front of the TV to give me a pixie cut. By the time she finished, my hair was shorter than any of my brothers'. I didn't recognize my reflection, but judging by the grin on my Mom's face, I looked like the boy she'd hoped for.

When we walked into the house, my Dad's mouth dropped open. He stared without comment.

"Well? Do you like it, Daddy?"

He didn't answer right away. "Umm...do you?" he replied.

"I guess so." I didn't know whether I liked it or not. My head felt lighter and I wasn't used to feeling cold air on the back of my neck. I found my reflection thoroughly shocking. Mom hadn't stopped smiling since my curls hit the beauty parlor floor.

"I'll be back in a few minutes, Betty," Dad mumbled as he went out the back door.

I thought I saw a tear roll down his cheek and I wondered if he was sick. Hearing the family station wagon start, I wondered where my Dad was going. Normally when my parents made a trip into town, they announced it to the family so all of the errands could be done at once. A short time later, he returned with my curls in a plastic bag.

"I just couldn't part with these beautiful curls, Patti Anne," he said as he held up the bag and looked lovingly at the contents.

"For Pete's sake, Mac. What the hell are you gonna do with those damn things?"

Dad just looked at her and smiled without saying a word. He kept those curls in the top drawer of his dresser, where they stayed for the rest of his life. It must have really pissed off my Mom because shortly after he died, she threw them in the trash. I suspect they made her feel guilty.

With my hair cut short I looked like the boy my parents had prayed for and that seemed to ease the tension in the house. My Mom wasn't so quick to snap at me for small infractions and my brothers seemed to almost like me. I started walking like a boy and I practiced peeing while standing up. I learned to spit and burp from the diaphragm. I climbed trees, aimed at birds with my slingshot and swore like a sailor on the playground.

I remember how proud I was when the checkout lady at Wegman's called me "young man" and my Mom looked down at me with a great big smile on her face. She was so pleased she bought me a Reese's Peanut Butter Cup. There were only two times I could remember Mom buying me candy, and they were when our dog Shep was killed by a motorcycle and when Grampa George died. I was a lot more upset about our dog.

2 HUMBLE BEGINNINGS FOR CHURCH FOLK

My Dad's parents, Pete and Anne, emigrated from County Mayo, Ireland, to western New York with four small children. When they arrived, they bought a small chunk of land. They'd been farmers in Ireland, and because it was the only life they knew, they continued to farm in the new country with hopes for better crops and prosperity. Their new farm sat dead center of the four major attractions in my hometown; the Erie Canal to the north, the B&O railroad tracks to the south, Mt Olivet Catholic Cemetery to the west and the village dump to the east. Location, location, location.

Dad was raised in extreme poverty and Pete was a heavy handed patriarch who made clear education was a waste of time. Yanking my Dad and his siblings out of school to pick potatoes or finish the spring planting was a way of life; farming always took precedence over their studies.

Pete didn't actually do any of the farm work. He sat in a rickety, old wooden chair barking out orders to his slaves, I mean children, while he emptied one whiskey bottle after another. Once good and plastered, he'd start belittling and chastising them. Frequently, it became physical and Pete didn't just knock his kids around. He'd often push Anne to the floor and slap her in front of their children.

"Nothin' but a used up hoor. Ain't good fer nothin' no more." Ah, love is grand.

The old clapboard farmhouse was heated with a secondhand pot-bellied stove that did little more than warm the kitchen and the first floor sitting room. Dad woke up plenty of mornings to find a light dusting of snow covering his feather tick because the roof had gaping holes that let in the elements. Before making a breakfast of homemade bread and bacon grease for her family, Anne had to fight off the snakes that had wrapped themselves up near the stove to stay warm.

Not surprisingly, Dad's siblings couldn't get away from that hell-hole fast enough. His brothers joined the service at very young ages just to escape their impoverished surroundings and predictable sad futures. His sister decided anything was better than the life she was living and married the first boy she dated. My Dad, however, felt obligated to stay on the farm and help his aging, ailing parents. Diagnosed with a brain tumor, Pete had undergone a botched surgery that left him unable to perform even the simplest of chores. By some miracle, the surgery eliminated his taste for whiskey, which drastically improved Anne's quality of life.

While working two jobs and providing for his parents, my Dad somehow managed to build up a fairly successful dairy farming operation. He was almost thirty years old when he met the love of his life; my mom Betty.

After only two months of dating, Dad proposed and she immediately said yes. They married a few months later and, against Mom's wishes, they moved into the farmhouse with her in-laws. Somewhere between working two jobs and operating the dairy farm, Dad found time to start building a house for him and Mom. She knew they couldn't afford to live in an apartment of their own, but she resented having to live with her in-laws. Anne never thought my Mom was good enough for her son and she didn't try to hide it.

"Ach, Mac, couldn't ye have made a better choice of wives? This one can't make a proper cuppa tea to save her life."

Opposite the farmhouse on the other side of the drive, Dad built a modest one-and-a-half story, four bedroom house. It had small rooms and narrow doorways and sat on top of a cinder block, walk-out basement. Tensions eased a bit when Mom and Dad moved into their new home, but Anne's health was going downhill and Mom spent most of her days caring for both of Dad's aging parents. In spite of my Dad's repeated invitations to move out of the farmhouse and into his newly built home, my Grandparents refused. They were too proud. They weren't particularly appreciative of their caregiver either.

"Away with ye! All ye want to do is yank at me poor bones. Why don't cha try makin' a decent cuppa tea and give me head some pace?"

Ten months after the wedding, the Irish Catholic stork began delivering babies to my parents every eighteen months. Right on schedule.

"Aye. I guess she finally found somethin' she's good at." That was Anne's assessment of my mother's worth.

Before the birth of my oldest brother, Pete died and my parents moved Anne to the village nursing home. Although the staff predicted she'd live only a few months, she flourished and grew healthy and strong. Had the doctors realized the state in which she had been living, they probably would have realized what a warm bed, three squares and much needed rest would do for her. Anne lived happily with her roommate, Mrs. Gracie, for eight more years.

Shortly after Anne was safely settled, Dad stopped milking cows. He'd landed a job as a blue collar worker at the Eastman Kodak Company, and the farm was converted from dairy to beef. We grew crops that provided food for the cattle he raised for slaughter and had an enormous garden from which we harvested much of what my family consumed. With increased wages, Dad purchased a few lots surrounding our farm and together, he and Mom owned one hundred and thirty acres. That was more wealth than they had ever dreamed of achieving.

With Pete six feet under and Anne thriving in the village nursing home, there was no need to keep the old run-down farmhouse.

My Dad blew his nose in typical foghorn fashion before saying, "Well Betty, I think it's time to tear down the old house. I really hate to do it, but between the snakes and the rats that have infested the place, it's gotta go."

"Be my guest, Mac. I've always hated that deathtrap."

"Betty, that deathtrap was my home for many years and it's full of memories."

"But are they happy ones, Mac? Are they really?"

Dad remained silent with a nostalgic look on his face.

"Honestly Mac, you'd keep used Kleenex because of the memories of the events happening around you when you were blowing your nose if I let you. Tear that damned thing down and let's move on."

A few days later, I was forbidden to leave the house while my Dad and my brothers went to work on the dilapidated old farmhouse.

"Why can't I help too, Daddy?"

"Because it's man's work."

"Well, I'm one of the boys. Why can't I help?" I asked, putting my hand in his.

My mother cleared her throat, which by then I recognized as a warning signal someone was nearing forbidden territory. Pushing on, I ignored her warning. "Daddy, please? I can help."

"No, Patti Anne, you can't. I know you're trying very hard to be tough like your brothers but the truth is," he said as he glanced at my mom, "you're a girl and you don't belong out there."

Mom slammed the cupboard door with a loud bang.

No one had called me a girl in so long it shocked me. *Am I really still a girl after all this time of acting like a boy?* I didn't think so. My brothers certainly didn't act like they thought I was girl and neither did my Mom. "I don't wanna be a dumb old girl. I wanna be a boy. I am a boy!"

Even though I was trying to help him, my poor Dad looked very sad. "No honey, you're not a boy. You… are … not … a … boy."

My Mom cleared her throat again. "Mac!" Dad changed the subject.

"The house is full of snakes and rats and I don't want you to get hurt. Your brothers are older and stronger. You have to stay inside and that's final."

"Snakes?" I knew how scared my Dad was of snakes and I was genuinely worried for him. My Dad wasn't afraid of anything in the world except snakes.

"What about you, Daddy? I don't want one of those nasty things to bite you!"

He laughed as he picked me up and reminded me nothing could hurt him. He was the Daddy and Daddy's don't get hurt. I promised to stay in the house to protect my Mom while the boys were out doing their work.

I watched from the kitchen as my brothers and Dad fashioned a harness of heavy chains around the exterior of the old house, which they connected to the back of my Dad's Allis Chalmers-B tractor. Equipped with shovels, my brothers backed away from the house and Dad gave his favorite old tractor the juice. Straining for a few moments, looking like the front tires might come off the ground, the tractor finally proved stronger and the house succumbed to its power.

The holey roof was the first to buckle and gave way in the middle, crashing to the floor. The weathered and worn walls just laid down on top of it as if they were tired of holding in all those years of sick and hungry people. It reminded me of the way shirt boxes from JC Penney folded up. The sides and the top folded in until it was flat. Then came the snakes.

Peeking between my fingers as my hands covered my eyes, I watched in horror as hundreds of snakes came slithering out from the rubble. The boys formed a circle around the wreckage and sliced through the reptiles with shovels as they tried to escape through the grass. Terror stricken, I watched in disgust from the kitchen as my Dad and the boys hacked away at masses of slithering bodies. My brothers looked like they were enjoying themselves, but my poor Dad was whiter than I'd ever seen him and his hands appeared to be shaking. It looked like he may have wet his pants, but I tried not to notice. I wanted to help him, but I was too afraid to move from my window vantage point. Like my Dad, nothing scared me as much as a snake.

After what seemed like hours of hacking and chopping, the boys used their shovels to fill wheelbarrows full of snake pieces. When one of the wheelbarrows was full, two of them would walk it down the driveway, across the one lane gravel road to the Eric Canal and dump its contents down to the watery depths. Removing the evidence of the carnage that had taken place only hours before, they filled and emptied the wheelbarrow until the yard was barren of snake bodies.

I was in shock not only from the sight of the battle with the snakes, but that my brothers were allowed to go near the banks of the canal. From the day we could walk, we were forbidden to even think about going near those waters. My Dad had a powerful fear that one of us would drown. I can honestly say that's the one, and probably only, rule I never disobeyed. That might have had something to do with the fact the damn thing was in our front yard. There was no chance of getting near it without being seen, but let's just give credit where credit isn't due.

Perhaps some of my Dad's fear of losing a child to drowning stemmed from the memory of his crazy sister attempting to baptize their mother in the canal. Elizabeth found Jesus shortly after I killed Patrick, and wanted to save her poor mother's soul from Eternal Damnation by dipping her in the healing waters of the Erie Canal. Not quite the River Jordon, but it's all my little town had to offer. Anne was in her seventies at that point and had never learned to swim. She nearly drown and the memory haunted my father for many years.

To say Elizabeth found "Jaysus" doesn't do it justice. She was half baked. She spoke out loud to Our Lord and Savior as if He stood right next to her. I guess that's not much different from praying, but she would ask Him what He wanted for dinner and if His cacks needed to be washed.

She bought every statue and crucifix in the county and planted them all over her yard. Every surface in the house was filled with statues of Jesus, Joseph, Mary, and their band of saintly friends. My Godmother had a Nativity scene in the front yard that was a permanent fixture all year long. For Halloween, she carved crosses into pumpkins and put them around the manger. At Easter time, she decorated it with baskets of plastic eggs. Jaysus loves Easter eggs. Other than nearly drowning Anne, my Godmother's newfound religion never hurt anyone, so I didn't let it bother me.

It irritated the hell out of my mother, which was comical considering she was Ms. Holy Catholic, Church-Goer, Obeyer-of-all-religious-holidays. You'd think Mom would have appreciated my aunt's love of Her Maker and shared in her joy of God. Instead, she thought the woman was mad as a hatter.

Elizabeth was very demonstrative and vocal about her love of Jaysus. She'd belt out a "Hallelujah" for whatever made her happy. The only time my Mom used that word was during Mass, when it was appropriate. Loud praise for God outside of Nativity put a twist in her church knickers. My Mom praised God in typical Catholic fashion by mouthing the words to church hymns and reciting prayers too quietly to be heard by others. She certainly never shouted things like "Praise God!" When Mass was over, she'd gossip about her fellow church goers as soon as her feet hit the parking lot. That's how Catholic folk do it.

Demonstrative praise for God made Mom uncomfortable. She'd become irritated when someone who'd won an award or an Olympic medal thanked their maker out loud on TV.

"Why do you do that? Do you think God had anything to do with it?"

I guess it never occurred to her there are people in this world who believe something bigger than themselves is at work. Mom couldn't relate to people who were sincere when they thanked God for whatever happened in their lives. From her perspective, God only had time for important things like making sure the rain didn't ruin the crops, keeping Dad employed at Kodak and making sure no blacks or Puerto Ricans moved into our town.

Ours was a very prejudiced home. We were taught black people aren't as smart as whites. They're dishonest, they steal and they'll shoot you for no reason. The word nigger was as common and benign to me as the word pancake. We never said "black people" or "African American." We always said nigger, in school and church. No matter.

My brothers were more creative than my parents when it came to name calling. They taught us new ways to describe my family's favorite racial targets. 'Mom back. As in "come on back," something a blue collar worker might say to help a driver back up. We said mo tea. As in, "would you like more tea?" Spear Chucker. Jigaboo. Porch Monkey. We called each other Mammy, Kunta Kinte, Chicken George and Kizzy. I remember my family watching Roots on TV and never once do I recall a discussion about the cruelty, the tragedy or the crime. All I remember is making fun of the way the slaves spoke and how stupid they were.

We weren't just prejudiced against Blacks. No sir. We were equal opportunity bigots. We gave every nationality their due; spics, chinks and gooks, dagos, wops and spaghetti benders. One of my favorite sayings was "Italian tires: when dago down the street, dago wop, wop, wop."

After going to church, we'd spend Sunday afternoon playing rummy and making up more hurtful names. To us, that was just normal, everyday fun. What an exemplary church-going, Catholic Family. We should have been the poster family for the Bishop's Catholic Outreach Program.

3 BROTHERLY LOVE

None of my brothers were normal and I consider myself lucky to have turned out as socially acceptable as I am. While certainly not a model citizen, I'm pretty much okay with where I find myself in comparison.

George was eight years older than me and slow, which was the nice way of saying he was mildly retarded. Our parents joked about the fact that George didn't roll over until he was eight months old and didn't walk until he was damn near two. George was so much older, I didn't spend much time with him except for meals and church. Middle school boys don't want to spend a lot of time with a little sister, at least that's what Aunt Elizabeth told me. Whenever I'd complain George wouldn't teach me how he flicked his finger on the inside of his cheek to make a loud popping sound, Aunt Elizabeth reminded me, "Ye think yer big brother wants to mess with likes of ye? Not 'til you can stick a feather in the ground and grow a hen." *Whatever that means.*

My middle brother, Scott, was six years older with the typical eighteen month spread between him and our oldest brother. Irish Catholics crank out babies every eighteen months, that's how our stork operates. Scott was cunning and nasty, taking every opportunity to trip or run me down with his sled. Sitting on my head and farting, Scott would make clear he wouldn't move until I sniffed it all up. He was never my favorite brother.

Peter was four years older and the youngest of the boys. Because my older brother Timothy died before I was born, Peter and I lacked the standard, eighteen-month gap. Our four year spread was a constant reminder to my family of the boy they really wanted, but lost. God played a dirty joke on my parents by taking Tim to Heaven and sending me a year or so later as a less-than-adequate replacement. I grew up knowing if Tim had lived, my parents wouldn't have needed me.

Peter let me tag along when he went sledding and allowed me into his tree fort in the western forest. My job was to stand guard while he read comic books and ate cookies stolen from the Tupperware container on top of the fridge. Peter taught me a little bit about constellations and we sometimes sat on the roof of the old milk house, looking for the big dipper and Orion. Like all brothers, Peter teased me a little, but he only got nasty when Scott was around. Self preservation, I suppose.

While playing under the ancient catalpa tree in the backyard, I heard Scott call my name. I was with my German Shepherd, Rex, who was far better company than Scott, so I pretended not to hear. The catalpa was my favorite because the grass growing in its shade was thick and cool under my bare feet. Every fall, the tree grew bean pods and when they opened, the seeds flew away on two, veined wings. My brothers and I called them helicopters, and Rex liked chasing them on their flight to earth almost as much as I did.

When Scott shouted, Rex and I'd taken a break from chasing helicopters so I could teach him to speak, but he didn't have much to say. I heard Scott call again. "Pat! Do you wanna know a secret?"

"Are you talking to me?" I was almost afraid to ask, in case it was a trick. Scott had never shared a secret with me before and I should have been more suspicious.

"Is anyone else named Pat? Duh. Do you wanna know a secret or not?"

What kid doesn't? Especially from a big brother who's never been anything but nasty. "Yeah, I love secrets!"

"Well, I've got a great one. Come on," he said, as he waved me toward the kitchen door.

Rex and I chased after him, through the thick, cool grass. Rex got there first, but I didn't mind because he was always faster. We followed Scott through the kitchen, which was unusually quiet, and to the living room. Putting a finger to his lips, he shushed me and started upstairs to the two bedrooms my three brothers shared. He motioned for me to follow.

"Mom says I'm not allowed up there!" I whispered. I was only allowed to go upstairs when we wrapped Christmas presents for our parents. Other than once or twice a year in mid-December, the upstairs bedrooms were off limits.

"She's not gonna know. Do you wanna be in on the secret or not?"

Of course I do, you big dummy. I followed him, excited to be allowed in a normally, off-limits zone.

"Don't let Rex come. He's gotta stay downstairs."

"Why? He's my best friend!" Rex went everywhere with me except to church. I would have taken him there too, but I didn't want to torture him. He was lucky to be able to stay home and chase helicopters in the grass while I had to sit in silence, pretending to pray.

"If you wanna know the secret, then he's gotta stay down there." Scott turned and walked upstairs, out of sight.

Promising to tell Rex the secret when I came back down, I gave him a big hug and told him to stay. He looked suspicious, but I went upstairs anyway and into the room Scott shared with Peter. It was bigger than George's room and had dips in the ceiling to accommodate the dormers on the front of the house. Sparsely furnished, the room still seemed cozy with two single beds, a couple of dressers, a red lava lamp and a low table the boys used for playing Rock'em Sock'em Robots and

Battling Tops. In spite of the Dallas Cowboy Cheerleaders poster taped to the closet door, it seemed like the coolest room in the world.

"Holy Toledo!" I pointed to the poster. "Does Mom know you have that? I'm not allowed to put tape on my walls!"

Rolling his eyes, he said, "Don't be dope. She doesn't come up here."

I stared at the poster, wondering how much trouble Scott would be in if Mom knew he had a poster of girls showing off their boobies. He'd probably be in even bigger trouble when she realized he'd used scotch tape. As I imagined her reaction, I heard the bedroom door close.

"So, what's the secret?" I asked, eyes wide.

"Hold your horses, I'm getting to it. Take off your pants and lie down on the bed," he said, in a hushed voice.

Without embarrassment or fear, I did so without question. Four-year olds are easily manipulated. While I struggled with the snap on my hand-me-down jeans, Scott took off his pants and underwear. He pointed to the bed and I sat down on the edge, trying to pull my pant legs over my work boots.

"You're such a clod," he barked, yanking off my boots and jeans with one, frustrated tug.

Well, you're a zit face.

"Lie down and be quiet."

I lay back on the bed wondering when Scott would get around to telling me his secret. He cocked his head as if listening for sounds of people downstairs and got on top of me.

"What are you doing?" *Whatever you call this, it's weird, and I don't think Mom would approve.*

"Be quiet, Snotsy! Close your eyes and don't talk," he barked.

Something jabbed between my legs and pushed them apart. It hurt and I didn't like it. It kept going further and further until I screamed. Scott covered my mouth with his hand and told me to shut up. I was having difficulty breathing because of his weight on my chest and his hand over my mouth, so I bit him. Hard.

"You little snot!" he hissed, jumping off of me. "Why'd you bite me?"

"Cuz you're hurting me and I can't breathe!" *Duh. Why do you think I bit you, dumbass?*

"It only hurts the first time, you idiot! This is a really cool game I was gonna let you play, but if you're gonna be a brat, I'll play with somebody else. For your information, Patsy Swine, I was gonna ask Mom and Dad if you could come to the fair with me when I go with the 4-H Club. But forget it now. Go downstairs and don't ever talk to me again!"

The fair? He was gonna take me to the fair? I love the rides and the smell of waffles and corndogs! I didn't like Scott's game, but I wanted to go to the fair more than I'd ever wanted anything. It was sort of like having to eat peas and carrots, which made me gag, so I could have dessert.

"I'm sorry. I won't bite you again, I promise. Can I go? Please?"

Scott had me right where he wanted me. I would have agreed to anything in order to go. "I'll think about it, but you better do whatever I tell you or I'm telling Mom you snuck up here to watch me undress, and I won't let you come to the fair."

He shoved me out of his bedroom and slammed the door behind me. I didn't know if I was more afraid of playing that game again or being tattled on for something I didn't do. I was tempted to tell Mom what Scott had done, but was too afraid. Scared it would somehow be my fault and I wouldn't get to go to the fair, I kept my mouth shut. I wished for parents that would believe and protect me. I could almost hear my Godmother Elizabeth saying, "Wish in one hand an' shit in the other.

See which one fills up first."

Stringing me along with promises of going to the fair, in addition to threats of drowning Rex in the canal, Scott kept me silenced and cooperative. Between the desire to ride the Ferris Wheel and the love of my faithful dog Rex, I did whatever Scott asked. On more than one occasion, that meant putting his nasty boy thing in my mouth.

"Suck on it like it's a baby bottle," he commanded.

I thought I was gonna puke all over his baby bottle, and I gagged on it more than once, but he'd whack me so hard on the ear, it rang for hours afterward. I learned to concentrate on the fair or ice cream until it was over.

Undressing for my Saturday night bath, which I took while my parents watched the *Lawrence Welk Show* so I could be done in time to watch *Emergency*, I made an announcement. "Mom, it hurts when I pee."

She looked away and asked, "Have you been touching it?"

That's a weird question. Why would I touch where I pee? Gross. "No, I haven't, but Scott's been getting naked and lying on top of me. He put his thing in there." I didn't mean to tattle, but the words were spoken before I could stop them.

"Well, here," she said, handing me a jar of Vaseline, "wipe some of this on the parts that hurt."

She closed the bathroom door, leaving me to bathe. *Huh, that's weird. I guess she's not mad about the yucky game Scott makes me play. I wish she was really mad so she'd tell him we can't play it anymore. There's no point telling her I gag every time he makes me put his thing in my mouth.*

4 THE CATHOLIC FOUNDATION

After I killed Uncle Patrick, my parents became more devoutly Catholic. My earliest memories are of ten o'clock Mass at Nativity of the Blessed Virgin Mary. More than a mere obligation, Mass was something my parents truly enjoyed but, then again, they didn't get out much. Cattle need to be fed every morning and every night. It's no surprise what goes in the front end of every Holstein eventually comes out the back end and someone has to clean it up. Sunday Mass was a social event for my parents and although I never shared their exuberance for the rigors of Catholicism, it never stopped them from pounding those ideals into my head.

Our lives revolved around Sunday Mass, Holy Days of Obligation, Lent, Advent, Pentecost, and perhaps others I've managed to wipe from my memory. For me, Mass was a time of extreme boredom and hunger, but as my Mom frequently reminded me, I was always hungry. Unlike parents today, mine didn't let me color while snacking on Cheerios. I had to sit quietly without fidgeting and talking or I'd get the death stare followed by a smack on the ass. When I was young, parents spanked their children in public without offending other adults or answering to the cops. My parents subscribed to the church's "spare the rod, spoil the child" way of thinking, which was fully endorsed by the nuns of the parish.

What a wonderful discovery I made, finding the church bathroom, and it became my favorite way to alleviate the boredom of Sunday Mass. All it took was a quiet whisper to my Mom that I had to go potty, and she would lead me by the hand down the side isle to the single holer in the back vestibule. I loved the long walk under the high, arched ceiling past the beautiful stained glass windows depicting biblical scenes and portraits of saints. The clickety-clack of my Mom's heels and the thud of my work boots on the cold tile floor still resonate in my head.

I climbed on the back of the toilet to look out the window and down onto Main Street. Kids who were a whole lot luckier than me were out riding bikes and shouting at the top of their lungs about going to Tastee Freeze instead of kneeling and praying. After wishing I could escape out the little hand-cranked window, I'd climb back down and cram the john full of paper towels to see how full I could get it and still make it flush. On a few occasions, the water backed up and came over the lip of the bowl, spilling onto the floor. Before it could leave evidence on my work boots, I'd run out and close the door behind me to find Mom waiting impatiently in the vestibule.

"Are you alright? You were in there long enough."

"I'm okay. I had to poop."

For several months, I was able to break up the monotony of Mass by screwing around in the bathroom. Unfortunately, one Sunday Mom demanded I leave the door to the john open. *I know what you're doing, you old witch.* She stood in the doorway and listened, to make sure I actually did something in the potty. When it became apparent that I didn't have to go, she yanked me out of there faster than the parishioners in the back pews dash out of church after the final blessing. The next time I whispered I had to go potty, she told me the bathroom was broken. My own mother lied to me. In church. Given how strictly Catholic she is, I don't think that was wise and it should count against her on Judgment Day.

Like my Dad and his brothers, my brothers and I went to our church's elementary school. The priests would visit our classroom every once in awhile, which was very exciting because I thought they must really like us and want to help us get into Heaven. I now realize they were probably just scouting for young boys to recruit and take under their vestments, I mean wings.

My first introduction into the wonderful world of masturbation came in Kindergarten at Nativity of the Blessed Virgin Mary. Odd perhaps, but since Mary was a virgin she probably masturbated so I guess it's only fitting I should first witness the act within those hallowed halls.

Unable to fall asleep during our mandatory naptime, I heard some weird sounds and rolled over to look at the mat next to mine. Catherine's dress was rising further and further up her scrawny, white legs until her grey undies were showing. Nosy little Chrissy slipped off her mat and tip-toed over to our teacher, Mrs. Keystone. I heard her whisper, "Catherine's doing something."

Mrs. Keystone walked Chrissy back to her mat and then knelt down between me and Catherine. "Catherine," she said in a hushed tone. "Please stop that. Right now."

Catherine must not have heard because she kept at it. Mrs. Keystone spoke a little louder and said, "Catherine! Stop that."

When it became obvious she wasn't going to stop, Mrs. Keystone picked Catherine up under her arms and tried to stand her up. That's when the rest of us saw Catherine had one of her hands in her crotch! She was rubbing it and would not stop. Unable to believe what we were seeing, everyone began to whisper until the room buzzed with noise.

"Silence!" shouted Mrs. Keystone, as if we were the ones rubbing our crotches. "Lie down and be quiet, or else!"

Or else what, I didn't know. Maybe the Virgin Mary would come down from heaven and spank us or something.

Our teacher was visibly shaken as she carried Catherine out of our classroom and into the hall, but Catherine didn't stop rubbing. The door closed behind them and whispering began once more. We never knew what took place out there, but it was clear whatever had happened, it wasn't enough to make Catherine stop.

My classmates and I were subjected to the same scene again and again. Without fail, someone would tattle Catherine was "doing it again" and Mrs. Keystone would be on her like Father Lyntz on the leftover wine at Communion. Catherine didn't seem to care who saw it, and she never stopped rubbing herself until she finished whatever it was she was doing.

I knew Catherine had to be onto something worthwhile or she wouldn't keep doing "it" in plain sight. Even though she knew someone would tattle and then she'd be in trouble with Mrs. Keystone, she did it almost every day. Curiosity got the best of me, and in the privacy of my bedroom one afternoon, I decided to give it a whirl. *Wow. Catherine is absolutely brilliant.* I bet we were the only six year olds who knew how to climax. Thanks Catherine, it's a skill I devoutly revered. You, me and the Virgin Mary; Madonnas of Masturbation.

5 A LITTLE SISTER AND A BIG BEATING

Near the beginning of first grade at Nativity, my parents announced our family was about to grow. I thought my Mom was pregnant but it was actually worse.

"You're getting another brother, named Max, and an adorable little sister named Heidi. She's the cutest thing you've ever seen. She's very tiny."

What? A sister? A cute and tiny sister? I don't like her already. "Are we using Top Value stamps to get them?" I asked, "'Cuz if we are, there's a dirt bike I'd rather have."

I didn't like the idea of wasting books of stamps on two kids I didn't even want. It took several trips to the grocery store to get enough Top Value stamps to fill just one book, and several books to buy my Mom a dumb old iron. Imagine how many books it would take to buy two stupid kids!

Shooting me a nasty look, Mom elaborated. "Heidi is a precious little girl, the same age as Pat, who needs a Mommy and Daddy and her older brother Max needs us, too. They're foster kids, which means their parents can't take care of them right now. They'll live with us until their parents are back on their feet and you goons better treat them better than you treat each other. Or else!" I wasn't happy but no one asked

27

me.

Expecting Max to be taller than me because Mom said he was three years older, I was surprised to see we were the same height. He wore thick brown glasses that seemed to be stuck at the end of his pointy nose and he was painfully thin. Of course, next to my chunky frame, most kids looked painfully thin. He held an old, brown suitcase in one hand while clutching a stack of comic books to his chest with the other.

Arriving with a cardboard box full of toys and a blue suitcase of clothes, it appeared Heidi intended to stay for awhile. She was indeed tiny, but I couldn't understand why my Mom said she was the 'cutest thing.' With mousy brown hair and dark brown eyes, I didn't see what was so special about her. Eyeing the toys piled inside her cardboard box, I was impressed to see Heidi had a Weebles tree house and an Easy Bake Oven. I'd asked Santa for an Easy Bake Oven last year, but I got a Hot Wheels race track instead.

Maybe she's not so bad after all. "You wanna go see our room and make some cake?" I asked, pointing at her Easy Bake Oven.

Before Heidi could answer, Mom snapped, "You don't need anything more to eat, Pat. I don't care if you guys make cake but you better let Heidi eat the whole thing. She's too skinny."

When we got to my bedroom, which was now 'our' bedroom, Heidi said she wasn't hungry and didn't want to make cake. I couldn't understand that at all and figured she must be some sort of weirdo. All she wanted to do was lie on her bed, facing the wall.

"Are you just gonna lie there all day?" I asked, without any tenderness whatsoever.

"I don't know," came her reply.

Wow, not only is she weird, she's dumb too. "Do you wanna go out to the barn and see our cats? We've got a bunch of mommy cats and tons of kittens. They keep mice and rats out of the silo."

Heidi didn't answer, so I left our bedroom to tell Mom she'd gotten a dud.

"Hey, Mom? There's something wrong with that girl. She's just lying on the bed and won't talk. Maybe you should send her back."

"She's scared and no doubt misses her Mom. Try to be nice and imagine how you would feel," suggested Mom, as she formed hamburgs for Dad to grill outside. "Just leave her alone for now. Please go set the table for supper."

"How come she doesn't have to help?"

"Don't be sassy, just go do it. Heidi can lie down until it's time to eat."

What a creep! Not only does she just lay there like a lump on a log, but she doesn't have to do chores either? Hell, if that's what being a foster kid is like, then sign me up.

My parents did their best to make suppertime fun that night. In addition to hamburgs, Mom made french fries, which she'd never done before. Dad told stories about practical jokes his brothers used to play on each other after Grampa passed out from too much whiskey. My brothers were laughing and teasing each other, Max was smiling and asking Dad questions about the farm.

The only one who seemed unhappy was Heidi. She barely touched her food, so I asked if I could have her fries.

"No, Pat, you may not! You've eaten more than your fair share and can barely fit in the school clothes you have now. We can't afford to buy new ones just because you can't control your eating! Whatever Heidi doesn't eat will be refrigerated and heated up for her again tomorrow," chastised Mom.

Lying in bed that night, listening to my stomach rumble, I couldn't understand how Heidi could be sleeping. I'd eaten everything on my plate as well as a few fries from Heidi's that I'd taken when Mom was in the kitchen getting coffee, but I was still hungry. My belly was grumbling so loudly I couldn't sleep. Heidi had hardly eaten anything, but her tummy didn't seem to notice. That was all the confirmation I needed that this kid was indeed a weirdo.

After a bowl of Cheerios the next morning, Heidi seemed more normal and interested in playing. We headed outside to spy on the boys who'd talked about building tree forts. While sneaking through the woods to the west of the house, in search of the boys, we realized we had to go to the bathroom. Running back to the farm, we jockeyed for the door to the only bathroom in the house. I hip-checked her skinny butt out of my way and ran to the toilet. Heidi was in tears because she had to poop. I only had to pee, but I wanted to make her suffer.

"Go get the box you brought your toys in and poop in that." She stood there looking at me like she didn't understand English. "Go get the box. If you poop in your pants, Mom will kill you."

I guess she sensed the truth in that because she dashed away with her little butt cheeks clamped together. Heidi came back with the box, put it on the bathroom floor and closed the door. She stood there looking at me with tears in her eyes, but I refused to move. In desperation, she dropped her drawers, straddled the box and walked forward as she pooped an enormous turd in to it.

I couldn't believe she actually did it. I laughed so hard I almost fell off the john. That thing was almost as big as she was and laden with peanuts. Then came the big question. How do we get rid of it? There was no way on God's green earth we could get that monster down the crapper. I thought about trying to flush it anyway and blaming it on Peter, because he was notorious for plugging the toilet, but since he had just given me his old slinky and some silly putty, I decided against it.

I made Heidi carry the box outside and we tossed it into the burning barrel, which was a fifty-five gallon drum used for burning trash. Living outside the village boundaries, we didn't have trash pickup so everything that could be burned was disposed of in the burning barrel. She dropped the box and we ran before it grew arms and legs and came after us.

Within the hour, Mom questioned us about a mysterious poop in a box. We played stupid.

"Poop in a box?" I asked with feigned surprise. "I saw the boys carrying poop in a box." Having brothers finally came in handy.

Within just a few days of her arrival, my brothers started calling Heidi cute little nicknames like "Heidi McHigh" and Hydrox McDrox," while they called me "Snotsy," "Fatty Patty" and "Patsy Swine." They came up with a very clever nickname for Max, too. They called him Dildo. To make that even more ridiculous, my parents called him Dildo, too. No one ever called him Max anymore and he happily told people his name was Dildo when introduced.

For Dildo's ninth birthday, he asked my parents to take us to Friendly's for ice cream. I couldn't believe my ears when Mom said yes, because whenever I asked, she said we couldn't afford it. Parking the station wagon in the shade, my parents waited in the car while sending all of us to the take-out window. Repeating everyone's order to the lady in the window was George's privilege because he was the oldest. The rest of us stood there waiting impatiently. Peter and Dildo got bored and sat down at one of the picnic tables in the grass to read Mad Magazine.

"Dildo! Dildo!" George was yelling at the top of his lungs. "I forgot what you want."

Suddenly, I had the impression everyone within ear shot was staring at us. George and Scott laughed so hard they coughed.

"What's so funny?" I asked.

"Mind your own business, Pasty Swine. Go find out what Dildo wants," Scott managed to say between snorts of laughter.

"Dildo!" I screamed as loudly as I could. "What kind of ice cream do you want?"

I guess Mom lost her patience because she leaned out her window and shouted, too.

"Dildo! Clean the taters out of your ears and tell your brother what you want. Do you hear me, Dildo?"

While waiting for Dildo to answer, I watched a policeman walk toward my parent's car. There weren't any other cars parked in the shade, so it was obvious that's where he was headed. I snuck over to eavesdrop.

"Excuse me, Sir. Are those your children at the take-out window?"

"Yes, is there a problem?"

"And the ones at that picnic table?" He pointed to Peter and Dildo. My father nodded.

Behind the station wagon, I sat on the bumper and listened.

"Sir, I can't tell you how to raise your children, but to call one of them by such an inappropriate name, and to do so in public, borders on abuse."

"What are you talking about?" asked my mother.

"I heard several members of this family, including you, Ma'am, refer to one of your boy as 'dildo'. That's what I'm talking about!"

"W-Well..I'm lost," said Dad.

"Don't play dumb with me. I'm trying to offer you a little friendly advice but if you wanna give me an attitude then..."

Before he could continue, my Dad interrupted, "Officer, I don't understand what the problem is. What's wrong with 'Dildo'?"

I peeked through the back window and saw the look on the cop's face change from irritation to confusion.

"You really don't know what I'm talking about do you?"

"No, I really don't," said Dad.

"Well, this is awkward. A dildo is, well, it's a plastic replica of a penis that, um, well, women use to satisfy themselves."

What? What the hell does that mean?

"You've gotta be kidding me." Dad sounded like a confused little kid.

"No sir, I'm not kidding. Now you know why I felt compelled to say something to you."

"Yes, I do. I'm so sorry. We didn't know."

My Dad sounded embarrassed but I didn't understand why. "Wait a minute. I don't get it. What's wrong with Dildo?" I asked as I walked out from behind the station wagon.

The cop turned to look at me and then looked back at my Dad. "Enjoy the rest of your day, Sir." He walked away.

"Patti Anne, go get your brothers and tell them to get in the car right this minute."

"But Dad, what was the cop saying about Dildo?"

"Do as you are told!"

Take it easy. You're the one the cop was lecturing, not me.

I ran to the take-out window and George handed me mint chocolate chip on a wafer cone with chocolate sprinkles. In between licks, I told them Dad wanted us in the car on the double and that a cop just talked to Dad about Dildo's name.

When we piled into the car, the air was so thick I could cut it with my Play Doh knife. Dad's stern voice interrupted the uncomfortable silence. "When we get home, I want George and Scott in the barn dressed for chores."

I knew what that meant. We didn't do extra barn chores on Sunday because it was Dad's day to rest in the hammock and grill hamburgs outside. My brothers were clearly in deep shit, but I didn't know why. George and Scott looked at each other and then down at their laps.

My two older brothers worked in the barn all afternoon, getting frequent visits from Dad to make sure they weren't goofing off or harassing the barn cats. Scott had been punished a few months earlier for swinging one of the cats by its tail and throwing it through a barn window. He did extra barn chores for weeks to pay for a replacement.

As Heidi and I read a Winnie the Pooh book in the living room, I heard Mom calling from the kitchen. "Pat, please set the table, but you don't need to set places for George or Scott."

Oh man, they're in big trouble. They're not getting dinner. "Hey Mom? What did George and Scott do to get into so much trouble?"

"Mind your own bee's wax and set the table." Mom wasn't very helpful.

After we'd eaten in virtual silence, we cleared the table and did the dishes. While setting the table for breakfast, which we did each night to make things easier for Mom the next morning, Dad walked in with George and Scott.

"Listen up, everyone," said Dad. "Your brothers have something to say."

George and Scott apologized to Max for calling him Dildo, and told him they'd never do it again. Dad made it abundantly clear to the rest of us if we ever called Max by the name Dildo again, we'd be in deep shit.

"I don't understand what's going on. Why can't we call him Dildo anymore?"

George and Scott broke into maniacal laughter, and within seconds my Dad had them by the scruffs of their necks. He dragged them back out to the barn and when Heidi and I crawled into bed that night, the lights in the barn were proof my brothers were still out there working. I took the hint and decided even though I didn't understand why, Dildo was a bad word and I would never say it again.

On a chilly fall afternoon, Heidi and I were playing "Go Fish" in front of the fireplace, talking about Christmas. Shocked after hearing she didn't really believe in Santa because Dildo, I mean Max, told her Santa was a made-up story used by adults to make kids behave, I assured her Santa was indeed real and he came to our house without fail.

"Let's start making our Christmas lists!" I suggested.

I grabbed the JC Penney catalog out of the magazine rack with both hands. The damn thing was so heavy, I could barely lift it. We lay on the floor, flipping pages and looking for the toy section. We never found it because we stumbled upon pictures of men. In their underwear. We were very curious.

"Look at that guy's lump. It's huge."

"What's that poking out?" Heidi asked, as she pointed to a close-up crotch shot.

"That's his thing, you dummy." *What do you think he has in his underwear? A Pez dispenser?*

"Well, then, what's that roundish part down there?" she asked.

Good question. It looked like the guy rolled up his thing and crammed it into the front of his undies. Curious and confused by the pictures, I tore out the underwear pages and hid them in my closet for further study. I decided to take them to school to show my best friend, Barbara Ann, who had two older sisters. They each had boyfriends and for all I knew, they talked about underwear when they were out on dates. Maybe Barbara Ann's sisters taught her stuff my brothers hadn't taught me and she would be able to explain what those guys had in their crotches. I swore Heidi to secrecy.

"Barbara Ann, I gotta show you something," I whispered during religion class.

"Pat! No talking."

"I'm sorry, Sister."

Sister Constance Joseph was a nasty, nasty nun who looked like a man. She had a full blown mustache, for Christ's sake. So fat she couldn't stand for more than a few minutes without sweating, Sister perspired so severely it dripped in her eyes and she couldn't see who she was yelling at. Her poor feet had to be tired of dragging around all that blubber for so many years, and judging by the wrinkles on her face, she had to be at least a hundred years old. Besides looking like an old fat man, she was meaner than a wasp shaken in a pop bottle.

I pretended to pay attention to her monotone litany about Praying The Rosary for a few minutes and then whispered to Barbara Ann.

"You're not gonna believe what I have to show you."

"That's it! Pat, you march your little motor mouth right on up here!"

Oh crap. I slowly peeled myself out of my chair and up the aisle towards mean old Sister Constance Joseph.

"Stop right there! Are you trying to litter in my classroom?"

What the hell is this crazy old bat talking about? Her habit must be getting too tight.

"John, pick up whatever it is Pat dropped on the floor and bring it to me. She doesn't have the good sense God gave a Schafer bug."

I turned around and looked behind me, horrified to see that a page from the JC Penney catalog had fallen out of my pocket.

Oh crap! I don't want Sister to know I look at pictures of men in their underwear! She'll find a way to call it a sin and God will be angry. Jesus probably had a similar bulge under his loin cloth, so he won't be sympathetic when he finds out I've been staring at men's crotches.

I rushed to grab it, but missed. John held it over his head and pranced up to Sister's desk with it in his greasy little hand.

"Thank you, John. You may take your seat."

When Sister unfolded the page from the catalog, her beady, black eyes bugged out of her fat face. "What in God's Holy name is this?"

I didn't answer. Apparently she'd never seen men in their underwear if she had to ask. *Of course! Nuns don't get to see men in their underwear and that's why she's confused. She honestly doesn't know.*

"It's from the JC Penney catalog, Sister. It's just some pictures of men in their underwear. Ya know, the things they wear under their pants?" I thought I'd educate the dumb old woman just a bit.

Sister Constance Joseph's rolls were shaking, making it very hard to concentrate on what she was saying. All that flesh giggling back and forth made me car sick.

"I know full well what this filth is!" she hissed.

"Oh, well then, why did you ask me?" I was confused. *Does this old bat know what she's looking at or doesn't she?*

"How dare you bring this dirty trash into my classroom! I knew you were gonna be trouble from the get go. You killed your saintly uncle and now you've brought pornographic materials into my classroom!"

Pornographic? Is that some sort of record player?

Sister Constance Joseph hefted her enormous bulk out from behind the desk and grabbed the yardstick that was never far out of reach. I started to cry.

"Don't you start the water works with me, Missy. If you're old enough to want to look at men in the altogether, then you're old enough to pay the price."

She turned me around and began spanking my butt with her wooden yard stick. I tried to get away from her, but she had my arm in a vise-like grip that kept me right in the line of fire. Sister hit me again and again while I cried and struggled to break free. Embarrassed my classmates knew I looked at pictures of men in their underwear, and ashamed they were watching Sister beat me, I begged her to stop.

"Please, Sister! Please stop! I'm sorry!" I choked through my tears. I hated her for letting my classmates see me cry and I hated myself for begging her to stop.

"Go sit in the hallway until I come for you and don't make a sound or you'll get the yardstick again!"

Trying to run away from her toward the door, I slipped in the droplets of perspiration Sister SweatMonster had dripped all over the tile floor during her great exertion. I fell backwards and landed on her swollen, angry looking feet.

"You stupid clod!" she snarled, and leaning on a desk for support, she used one of her fat feet to push me away. "Get outta here!" she growled as I continued to cry.

My ass was on fire as I stood in the hall thinking about how much I hated that old bitch. I hoped she'd slip and fall in her sweat puddle like I did, but then realized it probably wouldn't work. She was so fat she'd bounce like Tigger on his tail. Instead, I prayed she'd choke to death at Communion.

The day went downhill from there.

"Pat got a beating from Sister Constance Joseph today," Heidi announced during supper that night.

I shot her a look that would have signaled "shut up" to anyone with half of a brain. She kept talking.

"It was a bad one, too. Sister probably whacked her twenty times with a yard stick!"

"Impressive, Snotsy. What'd you do?"

"Shut up, Scott, you toad-faced jerk!" I wanted to call him a dickhead but my butt was already covered in bruises and I didn't want Dad adding to them.

"Tell us, Pat. What happened?" Mom was more interested than I liked.

"I was whispering to Barbara Ann and it made Sister mad. Everything makes that fat old goat mad!"

"Excuse me? Your father and I expect you to show respect for your elders."

I wanted to roll my eyes or stick out my tongue at her, but again my beaten backside managed to keep my mouth shut.

"That's not all she did," added Heidi, between bites of spaghetti.

I shot Heidi another death stare but she was oblivious.

"She had a page from the catalog with pictures of men in their underpants in her pocket and Sister took it from her!"

No one except Mom says underpants, you moron, and shut your mouth already before you get me into more trouble. What the hell is wrong with this kid anyway?

"Oh, my god! Patsy Swine is a pervert!" snorted Scott, slapping his hand on the table.

Dad shot Scott a look that was more effective than the ones I gave Heidi, because Scott stopped talking and looked down at his plate.

"Is that true, Patti Anne?" Dad was the only one in the house who called me that.

"I guess so."

"What is wrong with you? Who carries underpants pictures around in their pockets?" asked my mom, thoroughly disgusted.

Well, Mom, obviously I do. Hello? Haven't you been paying attention?

"Sick freaks, that's who!" laughed Scott.

Dad put an end to my brother's laughter. "Scott, you're now finished with supper. Clear your place and go to your room. Don't come down until morning chores."

Good! I won't have to put up with his crap for the rest of the night.

"Well, I don't see how another spanking is going to help. Do I have to tell you how much trouble you'll be in if you do anything like this again?" asked Dad.

"No." I looked down at my plate, wishing I could shove it right down Heidi's throat.

"Clear your place and go to your room. You can stay there until breakfast."

I picked up my place setting and shot Heidi a look that told her to be very afraid to close her eyes that night. I went to our room and plotted my revenge, but I never had the chance to carry it out.

I came home from a sleepover at Barbara Ann's the next weekend to find Heidi and Max were gone. All of Heidi's things were gone from our room, her clothes missing from our dresser and the pictures she'd drawn were no longer covering our bedroom walls.

"Where's Heidi? All her stuff is gone."

"Heidi and Max are gone. They've gone back to live with their mother," said Mom as she peeled potatoes at the kitchen sink.

I thought I might have seen a tear on her cheek, but I'd never seen her cry so I had my doubts. "Are you crying?"

"Don't be silly. Please go set the table."

"But I didn't get a chance to say goodbye to Heidi. Can we call her? Can she come back to play?" Now she was gone, I realized I liked her and wanted her back.

"No, we can't call her. The social worker said it would be best for Heidi and Dildo, I mean Max, if we made a clean break and didn't contact them at all," said Mom, turning her back to me.

"What's a social worker?"

"The person who brought them to live here in the first place. Please go set the table."

"Well, then, that person is a lunatic! How can it be good for us not to talk to each other? She's my sister!"

My mother slammed down the potato peeler and spun on her heel to face me. "This is the last time I'm going to say this. We will not call Heidi or Max. Ever. We will not see them again. Ever. We will not speak of them again. Ever. Do you understand?"

She was shouting and I was sure I saw a tear in her eye.

"Why are you mad at me? I didn't take them away. And why are you crying?"

"Go set the table!"

I recognized a useless cause when I saw one, so I set the table as I cried for Heidi and for me. I hoped her mom would be able to take care of her until she was grown up and if she couldn't, then I hoped she could come back to live with me.

We never heard from my foster brother or sister again. Max told his mother during their last monthly visit Scott was playing a game with him very similar to the one he played with me. The only difference was he didn't put his nasty boy thing in Max's mouth. Scott put it in his butt.

6 MY FIRST HOLY COMMUNION

My second grade teacher, Sister Mary Margaret, was a wonderful nun who wore a traditional habit and headpiece. Soft spoken and kind, she was the complete opposite of Sister Constance Joseph. I wanted to be Holy and perfect just like her.

I thought if I said Mass at home, I could become more Holy and therefore more like Sister. To help me with the difficult passages during the Consecration and whatever those other parts were called, I stole a missalette from church. I wasn't worried my theft would send me to Hell because I stole it to be closer to God. Since I hadn't made the Sacrament of Reconciliation, I didn't have to worry about Confession. No one needed to know. Looking back, I should have committed more sins before the fourth grade because I never would have felt obligated to confess them to a priest.

My bedroom was the altar, the same place I masturbated, and my pulpit was the box from my GI Joe Headquarters play set. I placed a clear glass bowl for Holy Water on a table beside my door so I could bless myself as I entered and exited. It was only tap water, but I'd given it a lovely blessing and was convinced it was Holy. One afternoon, as I was about to bless my grape juice and saltine crackers for Communion, my maternal Grandmother stuck her head into my room.

"What the hell are you doing?"

"Saying Mass. Why don't you come in and bless yourself? I'll start over." I was serious.

"You're off your rocker. I warned them about letting that loony tune Elizabeth be your Godmother." Gram went to the kitchen and told Mom to get me some help, ASAP.

Sister Mary Margaret was helping us prepare for our First Holy Communion and it was a very exciting time for me. I was tired of staying in the pew, knelt in prayer, while my parents and brothers had the privilege of walking up the aisle to receive The True Body and Blood of Jesus Christ.

"The Sacrament of Holy Communion is the third Sacrament of Initiation. These Sacraments bring us closer to God. Can anyone name the other two?" asked kind Sister Mary Margaret. A few hands went up and Sister called on Tommy.

"Baptism and Confirmation, Sister," he answered.

"Very good. We know each of the Holy Sacraments produces its own special kind of grace, right? If they all gave the same kind of grace, then only one Sacrament would be necessary, but we know Jesus gave us seven different ones.

When we receive the Holy Eucharist, our sins are forgiven. Think about what Father says during Mass when he transforms bread and wine into the body and blood of Christ:

'Take this, all of you, and eat it:

for this is my body, which will be given up for you.

Take this, all of you, and drink it:

for this is my blood,

the blood of the new and everlasting covenant,

which will be shed for you and for all men

so that sins may be forgiven.

Do this in memory of me.'

Whoever takes the body and drinks the blood is forgiven of their sins. That's a very powerful Sacrament, don't you think?" Sister said.

I loved the sound of Sister's voice. Her gentle way of speaking and sweet disposition could make me believe anything.

"The Sacrament of Baptism involves water to cleanse away original sin. The Sacrament of the Holy Eucharist involves bread and wine, which are spiritual foods. Spiritual foods do for the soul what physical foods do for the body. Does anyone know what that is?"

A few hands were in the air and Sister called on Debbie.

"To make us lose weight?" Debbie was a porker who'd been put on a diet by her parents when we were in Kindergarten. That girl would eat cheese doodles off the floor and old cough drops that had been through the washer and dryer a few times. She was always hungry.

"Well, not exactly, Debbie. But you're on the right track." Sister Mary Margaret never told us we were wrong or made us feel stupid, even when we were. She was the best nun in the whole wide world.

"The very act of eating the Holy Eucharist makes us One with Christ."

Wow. That was exciting and confusing all at the same time. *Jesus is God's Son and if I'm gonna be One with Him after eating the Holy Eucharist, does that mean I'll be God-like? Maybe I'll be able to make blind people see and bring dead people back to life.* I wondered if I could bring back my Godfather, Uncle Patrick, who I'd accidently killed right after my first Holy Sacrament. The timing seemed right. Kill him after the first Sacrament and bring him back to life after the second.

Lost in thought, I realized Sister was talking to me. "Are you listening, Patti Anne?"

"I'm sorry, Sister. I didn't hear what you said because my brain was talking louder than you were."

"Oh, I see. What was your brain saying, if you don't mind me asking?"

"I don't mind. My brain was talking about how if the Holy Eucharist will make me One with Christ, then if I eat enough of those little thingies, I'll probably be able to do stuff like Jesus did. You know, like make deaf people hear and stuff like that."

There was laughter in the room, but Sister continued to smile sweetly as if everything I said made perfect sense. "I understand how you might think that but unfortunately, partaking of the Body and Blood of Jesus Christ doesn't make us able to perform miracles. What a wonderful world we would live in if that was the case! Just think of the kind things people could do for each other."

"I would make you rich, Sister, so you could afford a car with a heater. I know you took a vow of poverty, but I'd make you very rich because you'd probably give most of it away after you bought a better car."

Sister Mary Margaret beamed at me while I thought of the many times I'd seen her scraping ice off the outside and inside of her car windows. I wanted her to be warm, even if she had to be poor to be a good nun.

"You are a very sweet girl, Patti Anne, and I thank you for thinking of me, but Our Lord provides all I need. Now, let's get back to the Holy Eucharist. When I said it makes us One with Christ, I meant it brings more of him into our souls. Receiving the Sacrament of Holy Communion strengthens our spiritual growth. Does everyone understand?"

I still didn't understand what Sister was trying to say, but I didn't want to hurt her feelings and make her feel like she was a bad teacher, so I shook my head yes.

While riding the bus home, I replayed what Sister Mary Margaret said about communion and tried to make sense of it. Loud shouting in my ear brought me out of my private thoughts. Stevie Hayes was barking in my ear.

With flaming red hair and an enormous butt, Stevie Hayes was one of my least favorite people. He had the biggest butt I'd ever seen on a boy. When Dad talked about a woman with a big butt, he'd call her "Chicken Ass Mary" or describe her as 'having an ass like a harvest frog'. I didn't know from Chicken Ass Marys or harvest frogs, but I knew Stevie had a huge nigger woman butt.

"You're an idiot. You actually thought eating a Jesus cookie could give you superpowers? You're such a retard!"

"What you say is what you are," I snapped back.

"Good come back, you little twit! What did you think you were gonna do? Bring back that uncle you killed?"

"You shut up and mind your own business!"

"You shut up! Everybody knows you killed him because your drunk aunt blabs it all over town. Why does she talk so funny, anyway? Didn't she go to school? Or is she just stupid like you?"

"You shut up, Stevie Hayes, or else!"

"Or else what? Are you gonna eat the Jesus cookie and turn into Underdog or something? Huh, are you?"

"If you don't shut up, I'll kick you right in your fat nigger ass! Your ass looks like one of those nigger mamas in Roots! I've never seen a boy with an ass as big as yours!"

The other kids laughed and someone started to chant "Stevie has a nigger ass! Stevie has a nigger ass!" The whole bus chanted and Stevie's freckled skin turned bright pink.

"I'm gonna teach you a lesson, you little Irish bitch! You're gonna be sorry!" snarled the boy with the big butt.

Grabbing me by the straps of my backpack, Stevie threw me to the floor in the center aisle. My head bounced off the dirty, black rubber cushioning and I thought I might pass out. The other kids stopped chanting about Stevie's big ass and broke into something new.

"Fight! Fight! A nigger and a white! Come on nigger, beat that white!"

That sent fat-ass Stevie into a rage. He lifted his leg high to step on my stomach or my throat, I didn't know which, but he didn't get the chance. Aiming right between his freckled legs, I kicked him as hard as I could. He screamed like a girl and fell into the seat he'd just yanked me out of. The bus went wild as he doubled over in pain. Someone raised my arm up in the air to signal I'd won the fight, but I wasn't through with that fat ass. Not yet.

I grabbed Stevie's flaming orange hair with my right hand and jerked his head back. With my left, I punched him in the face and shoved him to the floor.

"Don't you ever say anything about my Uncle Patrick again or next time you'll get it worse."

Making my way up the aisle to the front of the bus to wait for my stop, I shook from the surge of adrenaline. The driver never blinked an eye throughout the entire debacle and didn't seem to notice Stevie lying in the aisle with his hands wrapped around his bald, little nut sack. Stevie Hayes never bothered me again.

For the next several months, Sister Mary Margaret worked hard to get us ready to receive Holy Communion. I had some lingering doubts and questions about why we were going to eat Jesus Christ, but I wanted to please Sister and walk up the aisle like the big kids.

"Let's take a minute to talk about appropriate attire. Boys, you must wear dress slacks, dress shirt and a tie with a jacket. Girls, you must wear a dress. I know many of you want to wear the traditional white dress and veil but it's not necessary. Any nice, clean dress will do just fine," Sister assured us.

Every girl in my class wanted to wear a white dress and veil with matching gloves, the ones that reminded me of miniature wedding dresses. I would have killed for a dress like that, but I knew my parents couldn't afford it. Aside from the monetary hardship, I knew Mom didn't want me to wear girl clothes because I was a substitute son, but I hoped she wouldn't make me wear my brothers' First Communion hand-me-downs. I had to wear a dress. Sister said so.

"Hey, Mom, what am I gonna wear for my First Communion?"

"I'm making you a dress, remember? You picked out the fabric."

Whew. "I did? I don't remember that."

"Well, you did," she said. We bought the pattern and the fabric in Grants a few months back."

I had no memory of it and considering how much my First Holy Communion weighed on my mind, I was pretty sure I would have remembered it. "Can I look at them 'cuz I don't remember anything about it."

"Honestly, Pat. I'm trying to make supper and don't have time to listen to you complain. Go set the table, please."

"I'm not trying to complain. I just wanna know what it's gonna look like."

"Well, it's too late to change your mind. You made a decision and that's what you're getting. Now please set the table."

I did as I was told, but secretly I suspected her of picking out both the pattern and the fabric without me. There's no way I would have forgotten, but I wasn't gonna argue with her because she just might make me wear my brothers' old trousers and dress shirt. Then I'd really die of embarrassment. Even if the dress was ugly, at least it would be a dress.

The day I was to receive my First Holy Communion, Mom announced she wanted me to try on The Dress so she could make any last minute adjustments. Finally! The anticipation was killing me. I hoped by some miracle, Mom had actually gotten white fabric and sewn a miniature wedding gown.

She walked into my bedroom carrying a cantaloupe-colored dress with a pattern of tiny daisies. Telling me to stand still, she held The Dress up to me. With short puffy sleeves and a hem that went clear to the floor, it was the prettiest thing I'd ever been given.

"Oh Mom! I love it!"

"Well, I'm happy to hear that because this is what you're wearing. Let's slip off your shirt and see how it fits."

Pulling off my John Deere T-shirt, I hiked my bare arms high in the air. As Mom slipped the opening over my head, I aimed my hands at the arm holes. The Dress slipped down over my waist and fell to the floor. Wearing a dress felt so strange…I felt like a girl!

"It's so pretty, Mom. I love it! Thank you."

"You're welcome. Let's take it off before you ruin it."

"Can we hang it in my closet, please? I promise not to touch it," I begged, jumping up and down.

"I guess so, but paws off."

I was on cloud nine, lying across my bed and gazing at The Dress. *God will be so pleased when he sees how pretty I look, he'll be happy to let me eat and drink His Body and Blood.* Panic set in as I realized the dress might not cover my work boots. *Am I really gonna traipse up the aisle in a beautiful, girly dress and work boots? Everyone will laugh at me and I won't get any of God's Grace.*

I was still worrying about shoes when Dad got home from Kodak. His daily routine after work was the same; he walked into the kitchen, kissed Mom and changed into his barn clothes to do evening chores before supper. I was surprised when his head popped into my bedroom.

"Hi, honey. What're you doing?"

"Oh, hi Daddy. I'm just looking at The Dress Mom made for my First Holy Communion. Isn't it beautiful?"

"It sure is. I have a surprise for you," he said, wearing a great big smile.

"A surprise? For me?" I hopped off the bed.

"Yep, just for you."

"What is it? Tell me what it is!" I jumped, grabbing at his arm as he pulled out a box from behind his back. It had a picture of a little girl and her dog and read "Mary Jane."

Could there really be Mary Jane shoes in this box? I'd asked Santa for a pair, but he brought me work boots instead. Since that Christmas, I'd given up on the idea.

"What's in here, Daddy?"

"Open it up and you'll see."

I lifted the cover to find black patent leather shoes. They were girl shoes and they were simply the most beautiful things I'd ever seen.

"Oh, Daddy! Girl shoes! Thank you so much." I jumped up and wrapped my pudgy little arms around his tanned neck.

"I'm glad you like them, sweetheart. I've gotta get the chores done or I'll be late for supper."

"Don't do that, Daddy. Mom will yell at you and you won't get dessert."

He laughed and was gone. I slipped on the new shoes and walked around my room, pretending I was walking down the aisle for Communion. Fascinated by the clickety-clack sound they made on the wood floor, I realized they sounded like Mom's church shoes. More importantly, they didn't thud like work boots.

"What's that racket?" asked Mom as I clickety-clacked into the hall.

"The new girl shoes Daddy gave me! Just look at them!"

"Heavens to Murgatroid!"

I didn't know who Murgatroid was but my Mom mentioned him a lot. She stormed past me, into her bedroom where Dad was taking off his Kodak shoes. I knew he was in trouble by the way she was walking, but I didn't know why. It was pointless for her to close their door, because I could hear everything being said through the thin, plasterboard walls.

"Why in God's name did you buy her those shoes, Mac?"

"Were you planning to let Patti Anne wear work boots with her dress? Come on, Betty. It's time to dress her like the girl she is."

Uh oh, he's gonna be in big trouble.

"We can't afford those shoes and you know it."

"This isn't about money," Dad said. "Honey, Patti Anne's not a boy and I'm putting my foot down. That's the end of the conversation."

My Dad walked out of their bedroom and to the barn. I'd never heard him stand up to Mom. He wasn't a doormat but avoided confrontation and did what he could to keep peace. Judging by the look on her face, she wasn't very happy and I suspected she would send him to bed without supper or make him wash and dry the dishes by himself.

While Dad was still doing chores in the barn, Aunt Elizabeth arrived wearing one of her gigantic hats. It was so big she had to tip her ear to her shoulder so the hat could squeeze through the back door. I held back a giggle. Elizabeth was sensitive about her hats, and I'd taken more than one tongue lashing for laughing at her headwear. I didn't want to ruin this perfect day by pissing her off.

"Hi, Aunt Elizabeth! I'm making my First Communion today!"

"Aye, I know child. That's why I'm here. As yer Godmother, 'tis me duty to be there when ye partake of Holy Communion for the first time."

"Wait 'til you see the dress Mom made and the beautiful shoes Daddy bought for me. I've never worn anything so pretty!"

"Tha's cuz yer mum's crazy as a loon and dresses ye like yer one of the boys," said Elizabeth, rolling her eyes.

"Come see my dress!" Grabbing my Godmother by the hand, I pulled her to my room. She couldn't fit through my door with her hat on so she looked in from the hallway.

"Look! Aren't they beautiful?" I asked as I pointed to The Dress and my new Mary Jane's.

"Boys a dear, she actually done it then! She's dressin' ye like a girl. I'm cut to the onions with her dressin' ye like yer brothers. 'Tis a disgrace, it is."

"I'm so happy I get to wear a dress today. I wanna wear it every single day," I said as I danced around my room.

"I've a mouth on me. Let's go see what yer mum is burnin', then."

"I'm starving too. We're having my favorite; spaghetti!"

"Boilin' water is all tha numpty knows how to do, and yet she can't make a decent cuppa tea!"

Suppertime that night was perfect. My whole family was talking about my big day while eating my favorite meal. Soon I'd put on The Dress and shoes and be ready to eat a piece of Jesus Christ.

"While yer mum's getting the afters ready, I have something for ye to open."

"A present? For me?"

"Duh, Snotsy, didn't you hear what she just said?" Scott always had to jump in where he wasn't wanted.

"Houl yer wheest, ya hooligan. Now wee doll, go ahead and take a peek." Aunt Elizabeth handed me a small box wrapped in pretty silver paper with a red ribbon.

"Oh man, it's too pretty to open."

"Well, I haven't heard of that in all me puff," laughed my aunt.

I tried to open the package without tearing the paper, because I wanted to save it. My presents were usually wrapped in newspaper or paper bags from Wegman's. It was the most beautiful wrapping I'd ever seen. When I finally opened one end, I looked inside and saw a white box.

"What is it, Aunt Elizabeth?"

"You are such a dork, Pat. Just open the stupid thing, will ya?"

"Scott, ye make one more sound outta that gob and I'll bust ye on the dial, I will," said my Godmother making a fist and shaking it at my brother. "Go ahead, my love. Give it a rip."

I managed to slip the box out of its wonderful wrapping as Mom came out of the kitchen with my favorite dessert; homemade Boston Crème Pie.

"Oh, thanks Mom! That's my favorite."

"The afters can wait 'til ye've opened the box. Now git busy."

I lifted the lid and found a black velvet pouch, its drawstring tightly pulled. I opened the velvet bag and dumped the contents into my hand. Out slid a beautiful Rosary made with pearly white beads. They were linked together by an intricate silver chain and the Crucifix at the end was nicer than any jewelry my Mom owned. I was absolutely speechless. My Mother was not.

"Elizabeth, you shouldn't have spent so much on a Rosary for a child her age! She's careless and she'll probably lose it by next week."

"Wise yer bap and give me head pace!"

That was one of Elizabeth's ways of telling Mom to shut her mouth and leave her alone. I loved to hear her say it.

"Oh, Aunt Elizabeth! It's beautiful and I love it! Thank you. Can I take it to First Communion tonight?"

"Aye."

I got up from the table, wrapped my arms around my Godmother and whispered, "I'm so glad you're my Godmommy."

"A've got a throat on me. Where's the whiskey, Mac?"

The hands on the clock seemed stuck in place while we cleared the table and did the dishes. As I hung my dishtowel to dry, Mom said I could get dressed for church. Those were the words I'd been waiting to hear all day.

I quickly dressed and looked at my reflection in the mirror. Except for the hair, I thought I looked very much like a girl. I walked into the kitchen, new Rosary in hand, to show everyone how pretty I looked in The Dress.

"Ach, give us a twirl then. Aw, yer done up like a dog's dinner."

"You're right, Elizabeth. She sure does look pretty," agreed my Dad. "Alright, time to go. Everyone in the car."

Aunt Elizabeth had to drive her own car because there wasn't enough room for both her and her hat in ours. She followed us to church and we all walked in together.

Sister Mary Margaret was waiting in the vestibule to greet her students as they arrived. When she saw me, her face lit up like an Advent Wreath and she held out her arms. I ran to hug her as tightly as I could without wrinkling The Dress.

"You look absolutely lovely, Patti Anne."

"Thank you, Sister! Look at these." I lifted the hem of my dress to my knees so she could see my fancy shoes.

"Oh, they are beautiful," she said as she tugged my dress back where it belonged.

"Are you nervous?"

"A little bit," I said, "but I know you worked really hard to get us ready to be One with Christ, so I'm trying to ignore the butterflies flying all around my tummy."

Sister smiled her perpetually patient smile. "You're ready and I know you'll do just fine." She hugged me one last time and as she did, she whispered, "I love you, child," in my ear.

"I love you too," I said, and for no reason at all I began to cry.

"What's wrong, dear?" she asked.

I felt my face turn red and was embarrassed. "No one's ever said that to me before."

The look on Sister's face went from one of concern to one of heartache. She drew me to her tightly. "Well let me assure you, Patti Anne, you are worthy of being loved. You're a good girl and both Jesus and I love you very much."

She released me from her embrace and rose to look at my parents standing behind me.

"We don't have to say it in our family," Mom said. "All of our children know how we feel about them."

"I agree with the look on yer gob, Sister," chuckled my Godmother. "Betty's head's a Marley."

Sister smiled and gestured us into church. I sat in our pew thinking about what just happened. Never in my life had anyone told me they loved me. I heard Ma and Pa Ingalls say it to Laura, but that phrase had never been uttered in my house.

This day couldn't possibly get any better. A new dress, fancy girl shoes, a beautiful Rosary, Sister loves me and I get to eat The True Body and Blood of Jesus Christ. I felt luckier than Bobby Brady when he pretended he was dying so he could meet Joe Namath.

Mass went by more slowly than usual and I tried to pray extra hard. I wanted something very special to happen to Sister Mary Margaret and I hoped I didn't burp on Jesus while chewing Him.

When it was our pew's turn to get up and walk up the aisle to receive Communion, my Dad stepped out in the aisle to let my Mom go first. Waving me toward him, he took my hand in his and walked next to me. His hands were huge and mine was lost somewhere inside his great, big bear paw. Looking down, he smiled and gave my hand a little squeeze.

As we approached Father Lyntz, Dad let go of my hand and gestured toward the altar. I was very nervous about sticking out my tongue to a priest. It seemed like a bad thing to do, but Sister Mary Margaret assured me it wasn't rude to stick out your tongue if you're doing it to receive Communion.

Father Lyntz held up a round white wafer over a gold chalice. He looked me in the eye. "The Body of Christ," he said.

"Amen." I opened my mouth and stuck out my tongue.

Father smiled just a bit as he placed My First Holy Communion in my mouth. I made the sign of the cross and walked back to the pew. *Holy crap!* Jesus was stuck to my tongue and He tasted like cardboard. I wanted to open my mouth and pick Him out, but I was afraid to touch Jesus' body with my fingers because it had been almost an hour since I'd dipped them in Holy Water.

I knelt down knowing I should pray, but all I could think about was Jesus stuck to my tongue. I didn't like the way He tasted at all. I expected the "Jesus cookie" to taste like a cookie not like an old cereal box. Unable to resist another minute, I picked God off my tongue, but He got stuck on the roof of my mouth. I kept digging at Jesus until I finally got Him down.

I waited. Surely, I'd feel the Grace of God enter my soul now that I'd eaten The True Body of Christ. I waited but didn't feel any differently. I tried wiggling my nose like Samantha on Bewitched to make Stevie Hayes' pants fall down. He was in the pew in front of me and had completely ignored me during the Offering of Peace. Nothing happened.

I probably need to eat more of Jesus before I'll have enough Grace to notice any changes. "Dad, can I go back up for more Communion? I'm still hungry."

"No. You only go once."

"Why? Father just shoves whatever's left in his mouth anyway. Can't I go get another hunk of God?"

"Shush." Mom was giving me her look.

I leaned back so she couldn't see me and whispered to Dad again. "Why can you only go once?"

"I don't really know. It's just the way it is, now stop talking."

I decided if I was ever going to become One with Christ, I'd have to ask Father to put three or four pieces of Jesus on my tongue each time I went to Communion. The one-bite-at-a-time strategy would take too long. I wanted to be full of Grace as soon as possible so I could work miracles like Jesus or at least get Sister Mary Margaret a new car.

7 JESUS ON STAGE

My third grade teacher, Miss Redman, wasn't nearly as special as Sister Mary Margaret, but since she'd never beaten me with a yardstick she was among my favorites. It was obvious Miss Redman wasn't a nun or had taken a vow of poverty, because in sharp contrast to Sister's thin, willowy frame, Miss Redman's shape resembled that of Mrs. Claus.

In predictable Mrs. Claus fashion, she had boxes of cookies stashed in just about every cupboard of our classroom. When my graded papers were returned, they almost always had chocolate smudges on them, but I didn't mind. I figured the cookies made her happy, and a happy teacher grades papers more leniently than a hungry, cranky one.

The best thing about third grade at Nativity was we weren't making a Sacrament. Holy Communion was behind us and the Sacrament of Reconciliation was off somewhere in the distance. Preparing for Communion had taken several months of hard work and I was still trying to comprehend the logic behind it. I didn't want to deal with another Holy Sacrament until I understood the last one.

Exactly why we ate the body of Our Lord and Savior continued to be mystery and I spent a good chuck of my free time thinking about it. My brain hurt from puzzling, so I decided to forget about it for awhile and think about it later in the year. Until then, I needed a distraction. Oddly enough, it came in the form of Jesus on stage.

The faculty announced they were putting on a production of Jesus Christ Superstar, and tryouts were open to any of Nativity's parishioners. My brother Peter brought it up during supper and said he was going to audition.

"I'm happy to hear that, Peter. You're a natural." Mom beamed.

With a nasty snicker, Scott said in a stage whisper, "They'll probably dress you in a tutu 'cuz you're such a fruit."

"Scott, knock it off," warned Mom. "I heard Jan Redman and Bob Elderberry are the directors. Is that true, Peter?"

He nodded "yes" because his mouth was full of creamed corn, and we were sent away from the table if we spoke with our mouths full. Like me, Peter was a chunky monkey and didn't want to risk losing his food.

"I wanna be in it too!" I announced.

I knew nothing about being in a play, all I cared about was getting near Mr. Elderberry. He was Nativity's sixth grade teacher and I had an enormous crush on him. Driving a big, orange Chevy van, he looked so handsome with his long sideburns and wide gauge corduroys.

"Pat, if you want to sing so badly, you can join the Folk Group at church," Mom said without even looking at me.

Up your nose with a rubber hose, Mom. I don't wanna sing in church with a bunch of old ladies who smell like gardenias. I wanna be with Mr. Elderberry. I crossed my arms under my invisible boobs, straightened my back to make me appear taller and asked, "How come Peter gets to do everything?" I knew I was pushing it.

"Quit whining, Snotsy. Mom already told you no. You couldn't sing your way out of a paper bag," Scott snorted.

"That's enough! I don't want to hear anymore bickering," grumbled Dad, who probably wished they'd stopped at one kid.

The rest of supper was silent and the house remained that way while we did dishes. Shooting Scott nasty looks every time he glanced in my direction, I tried using my Grace from being One with Christ to make him drop and break a plate so he'd get in trouble. Obviously, I hadn't eaten enough hunks of Jesus because nothing happened.

I doubted I'd ever have the kind of Grace I wanted. If I'm not getting Grace from eating so much of Jesus, where is it going? If it was being pooped out with the rest of my food, God must be really pissed off watching Father Lyntz turn bread into His Son's body just so we could poop Him out. I wondered if I should write a screenplay about that; *Jesus Makes Us Regular.*

Because our school was small, play practice was held at the Newman Center on the town's college campus. Commonly known as Newman, it was built as a casual place for college kids to go to Mass and do other Holy Things instead of drinking beer and making out. Some of Nativity's parishioners were jumping ship to attend Mass at Newman because things there were a little more laid back compared to the rigidity of Main Street. Just the name "Newman" sent my Mom into a religious tizzy.

"Good. Let them go to Newman! We don't want their kind anyway," snapped Mom, as we pulled out of Nativity's parking lot. "They want to call themselves Catholics, but they want to wear dungarees to Mass. I heard they have a band with an electric guitar. That's disgusting!"

"Why can't you play church music with an electric guitar?" I didn't remember reading in the Bible that electric guitars were sinful.

"I wasn't talking to you, Pat, but if you must know, Mass is supposed to be a quiet and solemn occasion not a rock and roll show."

"Maybe that's why people are going there. It's probably more fun than

Nativity." *Opps, I probably shouldn't have said that.*

"You watch your mouth! Church is not supposed to be fun!" admonished Mom, while Dad nodded his head in approval.

"I think God likes fun or he wouldn't have created Steve Martin. You know? The guy who sings King Tut? He's hysterical."

"Steve Martin is a boob and anyone who plays loud music in church isn't really interested in God. They're only interested in having a good time," Mom said, shaking her head.

"Hmm. You'd think God would want people to have fun in church so they'll keep coming back and putting money in the collection basket. If I were God, I'd want church to be so much fun people would want to go every single day."

Mom shot me a look that told me to shut my mouth because I didn't know what I was talking about. I sat quietly in the back seat wondering why God was anti-fun.

The next morning during breakfast, Mom announced I would go with Miss Redman to play practice after school. She had some sort of doctor appointment to go to, so I could hang out at play practice until she came to pick up me and my brother. *Yes!*

When school was finally over, Miss Redman walked me out to her blue Volkswagen Beetle. I wanted to give her a "punch buggy", but I didn't think I should punch my teacher and resisted the urge. She had purple, fuzzy dice hanging from the rear view mirror and bottles of bubbles on the front seat. When Miss Redman told me I could blow some while she drove, I thought she was trying to trick me into doing something bad. My parents would have crucified me if I'd even thought about blowing bubbles in our station wagon.

Insisting she was serious, Miss Redman opened a pink bottle and handed it to me. As we pulled out of the parking lot and headed for

Main Street, I blew bubbles and filled the space between us. I tuned toward the open window to share some with the neighborhood and realized we missed our turn.

"Um...Miss Redman? You missed the turn to Newman." *Geez, I thought she was smarter than that.*

"I know. We're making a stop first. Are you hungry?"

"Yeah, but Mom says I'm always hungry and shouldn't eat so much."

"Well, I'm hungry too. We're going to McDonald's."

"McDonald's? I've never been there before!"

"You've never been to Mc Donald's? You're joking."

"Nope. The only restaurant I've been to is Lums. My parents take us there every year after Thanksgiving when we drive into the city to do our Christmas shopping. They make the best grilled cheese sandwiches in the whole world!"

"Well, you can't get a grilled cheese at McDonald's, but they have the best cheeseburgers and french fries ever. Just you wait," promised Miss Redman.

I was the happiest I'd ever been. This was even better than the new dress and shoes for First Communion. Riding in a beetle with the windows down and blowing bubbles while Miss Redman drove through town on the way to McDonald's would have been enough to make it an amazing day. It's about to get even better, because soon I'll be at play practice with Mr. Elderberry. I don't think Heaven could be any better than this!

Waiting in the car to guard the bubbles while Miss Redman went inside to get food, I couldn't stand the excitement and was afraid I was gonna pee my pants. I bounced my legs up and down but I couldn't hold it any longer. Opening my door and looking around, I decided the parking lot was empty. I squatted down in front of Miss Redman's punch buggy and peed.

Back inside the car, I felt much better. Miss Redman appeared at the driver's side door, holding a bag and some sort of cup holder thingy I'd never seen before. I leaned over and opened the door, anxious to dig into some fries.

"Thank you, Patti Anne. Hmm, I don't remember parking in a puddle," said my teacher, suspiciously eyeing the water collecting under her door.

Uh oh. "Um...that's not water, Miss Redman. I really had to pee and couldn't hold it anymore, so I did it in front of your car. I'm sorry. I didn't know you were gonna step in it." I felt my cheeks and ears burn red with shame. This lady let me blow bubbles in her car and brought me to McDonald's for the first time in my entire life and she was standing in my piss.

"I hope you're joking." She looked at me with a very serious expression. "Oh, man, you're serious! Alright, don't worry about it, but next time just tell me you have to go to the bathroom. We aren't on the farm anymore and it's not okay to tinkle wherever you want."

"I'm sorry, Miss Redman. I really am."

"It's okay. Let's eat."

My kind and understanding teacher opened a styrofoam box and laid it across my lap. I thought I'd never smelled anything better until she dumped some fries into the lid of the box.

"Oh, my God, this smells better than anything in the world!"

"Please don't take the Lord's name in vain, Patti Anne."

I popped a couple of fries into my drooling pie hole. "Sorry. Oh, my gosh, these fries are way better than Lums!"

Miss Redman opened a styrofoam box identical to mine and laid it across her lap. She dumped the rest of the fries into the lid and started the car. To my complete amazement, she drove while she ate. *I didn't know you could do that!* Trying to picture my Mom eating fries from her lap while driving made me laugh so hard I choked.

Miss Redman handed me a cup with a straw and told me to drink. I sipped, but nothing happened. I looked at my teacher, hoping to get a clue.

"Keep sucking. It's a chocolate shake and it's hard to get started."

I kept sucking and was rewarded by a thick and delicious chocolate ice creamy thing. I couldn't stop drinking. *Forget the burger and fries, this is the best damn thing I've ever tasted.*

"Take it easy," warned my teacher. "You're gonna get an ice cream headache."

"What's that?" About five seconds later, I figured it out. Bam! My brain was frozen and screaming bad words at me.

"It'll go away in a few minutes. If you drink it more slowly, that won't happen," Miss Redman explained.

"It's worth it! I've never had a shake before and I think it's the best thing I've ever had!"

Miss Redman looked like she felt sorry for me, but I didn't know why. I didn't really care. I went back to the manna from Heaven in my lap and didn't think about anything except how much I loved Ronald McDonald.

As we pulled into Newman's parking lot, I thanked Miss Redman from the bottom of my heart, telling her it was the best day of my life. She gave me the look again and handed me the rest of her shake.

"Here," she said, "I'm too fat. You can have this."

"You are the coolest person God ever created, Miss Redman. When I finally eat enough of Jesus' body to be full of His Grace, I'm gonna do some really great things for you."

She stopped walking and turned to look at me. "I don't think I want to know what that means so I'll just say thanks and pretend I never heard it."

Miss Redman walked me into Newman where we were surrounded by teenagers. Most I recognized from Nativity, but there were a few unfamiliar faces. She told me to keep out of trouble and went off to do whatever it was directors do.

I sat in the audience watching Mr. Elderberry work with some kids on stage. My brother Peter was among them and I was consumed with jealousy because he stood so close to the man of my dreams. After giving the kids some directions, Mr. Elderberry walked into the audience to watch while they rehearsed the scene. I waved at him eagerly and he waved back. My heart skipped a beat. He walked over and sat down next to me. My heat almost stopped.

"Hello, Bob," I said, in what I hoped was a sexy voice.

"I'm Mr. Elderberry to you."

"Oh, sorry. I thought since we were out of school that, well..."

"Sorry, Patti Anne. You still have to call me Mr. but it doesn't mean we can't be friends."

Friends? I don't wanna be your friend, you moron. I want to be your girlfriend. I want you to pick me up for school in your orange Chevy van and hold my hand.

"Okay," I said, smiling sweetly. What else could I say? I couldn't tell him how much I loved him if he wouldn't let me call him by his first name. Who calls their boyfriend "Mr."? So much for becoming Patricia Anne Elizabeth Elderberry.

I turned my attention toward the stage and fell in love again. The kid playing Jesus was hotter than a two dollar pistol and obviously a lot closer to me in age. I suddenly realized it never would have worked out with Bob. He was probably fifty years older than me and I'd end up pushing him around in a wheel chair while I was still young and cool.

"Who's the kid playing Jesus?" I asked Bob.

"Lance Peterson. He's a sophomore."

Patricia Anne Elizabeth Peterson. It sounded better than Elderberry anyway. The kids on stage messed up and Bob got up to tell them what they did wrong. I moved closer so I could get a better look at my new crush.

Lance was a beautiful creature and put old Bob to shame. Then he started to sing. *Holy crap!* Not only was he more handsome than Bob, but he could sing better than Elvis. I was ready to send out the wedding invitations. The only problem was, Lance didn't know I existed.

I waited until practice was over and joined Peter and my husband-to-be on stage.

"Hey, Peter, guess what? Miss Redman let me blow bubbles in her car while she drove us to McDonald's. I had the greatest food ever."

I hoped Lance would be impressed I was hanging out with a cool teacher and eating fries from my lap.

"Is there anything left? I'm starving," asked Lance.

"Oh, sorry. We ate it all."

"Lance, this is my little sister, Pat."

"I'm not little. I can drive our Dad's tractor." Why did I say that? Like he's gonna be impressed by a third grade tractor driver. I tried sticking out my boobs, but I didn't have any so it was uncomfortable.

"Why are you standing like that? What's wrong with your back?" asked Peter.

"I'm not standing like anything." *Mind your own business, Peter. I'm trying to get Lance to fall in love with me and you're not helping.*

"Whatever. We better go out and wait for Mom."

I didn't want to go. I wanted to stay with Lance for the rest of my life, but he walked away to talk with his high school friends.

During supper that night, I relayed the details of my exciting day to my family. Everything except the part about my new crush.

"Miss Redman asked me to be her helper at play practice. She said I can ride with her every day after school." *Where did that come from?* That big ole lie was out of my mouth before it even had time to form in my brain.

"What does she need you to do?" Mom wanted to know.

Good question, Mom. I have no idea what she'd need from a third grader. "Um…I don't know. Maybe take attendance or pick up trash? I don't know but I wanna do it anyway."

"I guess it's okay but if you start acting up, you're not going back, do you understand? No funny business. It'll get you out of my hair for a couple of hours and I'll be able to get something done."

I knew what that meant. She'd be able to sit on the davenport and watch The Guiding Light while eating ice cream without anyone knowing about it. I'd walked in after school a few times and caught her watching that stupid show with a big bowl of cookies and cream in her lap. I guess she'd lost track of time because when I walked in, she jumped up to turn off the TV. It was a stupid show about people kissing and lying in bed together. I didn't know what the big deal was, but I knew she didn't want anyone to know she did it.

Before morning prayers at school the next day, I eagerly told Miss Redman if she needed a helper at play practice, my Mom said I could go with her every day. She looked a little surprised, but she finally said she could use my help. I promised to be the best helper in the whole entire world, but all I really cared about was making Lance fall in love with me.

As the days went by, I spent more and more time near Loverboy Lance. I knew his lines and solos by heart. He was nice to me, at least nicer than my brothers were, but he treated me like a little kid. I needed to show him even though I was a third grader who didn't wear a bra, I was almost a woman.

Deciding a letter was the best way to let Lance know how much I loved him, I found a quiet corner and collected my thoughts. Once he knew how I felt about him, Lance would realize he loved me too, and we could hold hands during play practice. I thought I'd seen it work on The Brady Bunch, so I wrote the letter.

"Dear Lance,

I know you think I'm just a kid but that's not true. My aunt always tells me I'm mature for my age. I think you are so cute and I love everything about you. You have the best voice in the whole wide world. I want to be boyfriend and girlfriend and kiss just like Joanie and Chachi. If you want to be my boyfriend, meet me after play practice in the basement.

Love,

Patti Anne"

Perfect. I folded it until I couldn't fold it any smaller and set off to find my true love. He was at the drinking fountain with some other kids. I handed him the letter.

"Mr. Elderberry asked me to give you this," I lied, passing the folded paper to Lance.

Turning from the group of teenagers, I ran as fast as I could to the

his hand in the cookie jar. "Oh, God...Patti Anne." I expected Bob to say he would ask my Dad for my hand in marriage. After all, we'd just kissed. It was the right thing to do.

"Bob, I love you and can't wait to be your wife," I crooned as I wrapped my arms around his neck, ready for more passionate kisses.

"Get off me!" he barked, sidestepping me and running his hand through his wavy, brown hair.

Huh? That's not what he's supposed to say. "Bob, what's wrong?"

"Don't call me Bob and don't ever lay your hands on me again! You're only a child and I'm a grown man. I'm sorry to hurt your feelings, but this is gross!"

Gross? Kissing me was gross? I concentrated real hard, trying to muster up all of my Grace from being One with Christ, determined to make Bob's heart ache for me.

"Um...you look like you need to go to the bathroom so this is a good time for me to get the hell outta here," Bob managed to stammer before he dashed out the door.

What's that supposed to mean? I looked in the mirror and I could see how Bob interpreted my look of extreme concentration as one of severe constipation. No wonder he ran out so fast. Who wants to kiss a girl with backed up poop?

I knew the only solution was to get my parents to take me to Mass three or four times a week so I could eat a lot of Jesus. His Holy Body would not only erase the look of constipation that scared Bob away, but it would fill me with His Grace and I could use it to make my true love fall in love with me. Just like a Tootsie Pop, Jesus was two treats in one.

8 THE SACRAMENT OF RECONCILIATION

Fourth grade was going to be a big year. I knew we'd spend most of it getting ready to receive the Sacrament of Reconciliation, which normal people call Confession. We talked a lot about sin and forgiveness. We learned only God can forgive our sins and we can't go to Heaven unless we're truly sorry for all the bad things we've done.

"However," my teacher, Miss Butt pointed out, "being sorry isn't enough. God tells us that although we must first be truly sorry for what we've done, we must then confess our sins to a priest."

What? I have to tell Father Lyntz what I do in my bedroom at night after watching The Fonz on Happy Days?

From what I gathered, if we confessed to Father, he'd put in a good word with God to hopefully get us off the hook because he had a direct line to Heaven. Since Father Lyntz was so Holy, God probably like him a lot and would grant his wishes, even though he wore an ugly black dress most of the time.

"But it's more complicated than that. Being sorry and confessing your sins aren't enough to guarantee your place at Our Lord's Heavenly Table," explained Miss Butt. "You must atone for your sins by performing a penance, which might include reciting prayers or going through the Stations of the Cross. If you do these three things; have a contrite heart, confess your sins and perform your penance, then Father Lyntz has authorization directly from God to absolve you of your sins."

I was confused. I understood people have to apologize to God for doing bad things. That made sense. *But why do we have to tell a priest and why does he get to decide what we have to do to make up for our sins? How come I have to go through a priest to get to the Pearly Gates? Why isn't saying a sorry prayer to God good enough?*

"Miss Butt?" I asked with my pudgy, freckled arm raised high in the air.

"Yes?"

"Where in the Bible does God tell us we have to tell our sins to priest before He will forgive us?" I asked.

"What?"

Since when did this fat, old crow have a hearing problem? Not five minutes ago she heard Tommy squeak out a small fart from the back corner of the room. "I want to read the part in the Bible where God tells us we have to confess our sins to a priest."

"Are you questioning the quality of this schools' ecumenical teaching?" asked Miss Butt, with an unpleasant scowl.

I had no idea what the hell that meant, so I didn't answer.

"How dare you question Our Faith! How dare you question Our Lord!" My teacher was pissed, but I didn't know why.

"I'm not questioning Our Lord, Miss Butt. I just don't remember ever reading that anywhere. When we were preparing to receive our First Holy Communion, Sister Mary Margaret told us our sins are forgiven when we receive the Holy Eucharist."

"Oh she did, did she? Well, then she needs to loosen her headpiece. She was wrong," spat Miss Butt.

That stung. No one said bad things about Sister Mary Margaret. I made a mental note to use my powers on Miss Butt as soon as I'd eaten enough of Jesus to be full of God's Holy Grace. "She was not wrong. She's the greatest nun that ever lived!"

"Just because you managed to fool her into thinking you're a nice kid doesn't make her a great nun," Miss Butt said, rolling her eyes. "She was completely wrong and your sins are not forgiven just by taking Communion."

"What about the words Father uses when he changes bread and wine into The True Body and Blood of Christ? You know these ones:

'Take this, all of you, and eat it:

for this is my body, which will be given up for you.

Take this, all of you, and drink it:

for this is the cup of my blood,

the blood of the new and everlasting covenant

which will be shed for you and for all men

so that sins may be forgiven.

Do this in memory of me.'"

"How dare you disrespect me! Do you honestly think you know more about our religion and God's Ways than I do? Get out of this classroom right this instant! Go sit in the hall and think about your behavior and don't move until you're told to do so!" barked Miss Butt, pointing at the door.

I was angry at her for saying bad things about Sister Mary Margaret and confused about what I'd done wrong. Had I sinned by asking where God tells us we have to confess our sins to a priest? I kept a list of all my sins so when I made my First Reconciliation, I wouldn't forget to tell any of them to Father. I needed to know if asking Miss Butt that question belonged on my list.

If I forgot to confess one little sin, then I could be doomed to Purgatory for Eternity. Or worse. I could wind up being tortured by Lucifer in the fiery bowels of Hell until Jesus comes again. I didn't even believe Jesus was coming again. I mean, why would he? The last time he came to Earth, his ass was nailed to a cross. I wouldn't come back and I was betting he wouldn't either, which meant if I wound up in Hell, I'd be there forever and ever amen.

I stood up and knocked on the classroom door. With lightening speed, Ms. Butt's ugly mug looked down through the glass window near the top of the door. She yanked it open so hard, I thought it might come off its hinges.

"Haven't you interrupted this class enough, young lady?"

"I'm sorry, Miss Butt. I just wanted to know if asking you where God tells us we have to confess our sins to a priest was a sin. I'm trying to keep track of them and I don't wanna leave anything out, in case God remembers it," I tried to explain. "And by the way, who does Father Lyntz confess to? He can't tell himself his sins, so who gets to hear about all the bad stuff he does and who gets to decide what his penance will be?"

Miss Butt's face turned a brilliant shade of purple and I thought her earrings might pop off because she was pressing her lips together so tightly her ear lobes appeared to be swelling. The gold crucifix around her neck trembled and she shook her fat, sausage-like finger at me. She was so ugly you wouldn't ride her into battle.

"Take yourself to the Principal's Office right this minute and tell Sister what you've done!"

Miss Butt slammed the door in my face, leaving me more confused than ever. *Was it a sin or wasn't it? Did I just commit another by asking if my question about confession was a sin? And now I had to tell the Principal, too? Maybe I should just take out a full page ad in the Penny Saver Newspaper to let the whole damn town know about my sins.*

I took my time going to Sister Carol Fatass's office because she was famous for the huge paddle hanging on her wall. Stories of her beating kids with that paddle were plentiful and legendary, so I wasn't in a big hurry to be in its company. She was almost equally famous for the thick, black mustache covering her upper lip.

I was in Kindergarten the first time I saw it and was so distracted that when Sister asked my name, I said "mustache." It earned me a whack on the knuckles, the first of many. Two years later, I still hadn't grown accustomed to the hairy mess below her nose.

Although the door to Sister Fatass' office was open, I knocked and waited in the hall. We were taught early in our Nativity career we never spoke until spoken to, and the only appropriate way to get the attention of someone in an office is a light tap on the door. Sister continued reading the paper in her hand for a bit, just to keep me sweating. Finally she looked up over the top of her old lady glasses that were shaped like cat eyes.

"May I help you?"

That last thing I need is your help, you fat cow. "Miss Butt sent me."

She didn't answer. She just continued to glare at me over the tops of her glasses, well aware she was making me damn near piss myself. She glanced up at the paddle on her wall and then back at me. The old bitch was enjoying herself.

"I don't think she got enough sleep last night because she's a little cranky," I explained, hoping to put some of the blame on Miss Butt for losing her temper.

Sister didn't reply. She and her mustache just kept staring at me, burning holes through me with their nasty glare.

"I asked her some questions about Confession. I guess they upset her."
I guessed? No shit, they upset her. That's why my chunky ass was
standing on Hell's doorstep.

"What questions?" Sister finally spoke.

"Ummm, well, just about telling the priest our sins." That was
technically a true statement, just an incomplete one.

"What exactly did you ask? Don't leave anything out."

Oh hell. "I asked why we have to tell our sins to a priest because I don't
remember reading it in the Bible and I reminded her about something
Sister Mary Margaret taught us. I guess it made Miss Butt mad, because
she sent me to the hall. After I was out there for a couple minutes, I
knocked on her door to find out if I'd sinned by asking about telling our
sins to a priest. I'm making a list and I don't want to leave anything out.
Oh, and I wanted to know who Father Lyntz tells his sins to and who
gets to decide what his penance will be."

"I see. Well, aren't you something? A little wise cracker like your
brother, Scott? I know how to fix that."

She stood up and lovingly took down the paddle from her wall. It was
ginormous. Coming out from behind the desk, Sister Fatass put her
gnarled hand of crooked fingers on my shoulder and spun me around.

"March!" she barked.

Sister steered me into the main office where her secretary, Mrs.
Weddle, was making copies. I loved the smell of papers fresh off the
ditto machine. They were a little cool to the touch and the smell of the
purpley-blue ink was so delicious.

"Mrs. Weddle, please get on the PA and tell everyone to gather in
Bolger Hall at once. I want all students and faculty there in less than

five minutes," said Sister Fatass. The PA was what Mrs. Weddle used to make announcements. She spoke into a big microphone and could be heard in every room throughout the school.

Mrs. Weddle stared at Sister, then at the paddle and then at me. A nasty little smile started to form at the corners of her lipstick-caked mouth. "Of course, Sister, right away," she sang.

Once again, Sister used her nasty, crooked fingers to steer me out of the office. She was poking into a spot between my shoulder blades and it was beginning to hurt. Sensing my discomfort, she poked harder and did so all the way to Bolger Hall, which was used as both the gym and auditorium. Marching me to the far end, she shoved me up the wooden stairs onto the pathetic little stage we used for the annual Christmas Pageant.

"Sit down in the middle of the stage and don't you dare move a muscle!"

The only muscle that was moving was my sphincter. It was all I could do not to foul my britches.

It didn't take long before teachers funneled their students into Bolger Hall. Each class walked single file in silence behind their teacher. Kindergarten and first grade sat in the very front, each class on a separate side leaving a large aisle down the center. The older classes walked in silently and filled in behind. I saw my classmates near the back and my eyes locked with Barbara Ann's. She mouthed "sorry". I was sorry. Very sorry.

After everyone was seated, Sister Fatass spoke. "Thank you everyone for coming so quickly and quietly. I'm sure you're wondering why I called you here today," she said, as she waddled down the aisle toward the stage. "I am very sad to share with you that one of our very own students has been saying some truly ugly things about the Holy Sacrament of Reconciliation."

There was a gasp from some members of the faculty.

"Our purpose on earth is to follow in Jesus' footsteps. As Good Catholics, we are obligated to do His will and share His love with those around us. Sometimes people make fun of what they don't understand. But sometimes people make fun because they're bad eggs and they listen to Satan. Those kinds of people need to be punished and that's why you're here today."

What the hell? Is this crazy lady gonna beat my ass in front of the entire school?

Sister Fatass slowly walked up the creaky stairs and paused when she reached the top. She looked out at the students and faculty with a look that expressed her sincere sadness at the task at hand. *Bullshit!* Sister was in the spot light and cherishing the thought of punishing me for all to see.

She slowly waddled to where I sat on the floor. "Get up," she said sweetly, as if gently waking me from a winter nap.

I stood up and backed away. Sister grabbed me by the elbow and shoved me against the wall.

"Put your hands on the wall and your feet shoulder-width apart!"

Apparently, there's a proper stance for a public beating. Who knew? I stood glued to the floor, looking at the crowd of kids and teachers, waiting for someone to come to my rescue. Surely, at least my Kindergarten teacher still loved me and wouldn't let Sister go through with this. I tried to make eye contact with Mrs. Keystone, but she quickly looked away the moment our eyes met. If Sister Mary Margaret were still teaching, she'd never let this happen. Unfortunately, she'd been reassigned to another parish and I was on my own.

No one moved. There wasn't a sound to be heard except the wicked, fast beating of my heart. It pounded in my ears and I was sure everyone else in the room could hear it, too.

"Do it, NOW!" barked Sister Fatass, as I trembled and choked back tears.

Should I make a run for it? Where the hell would I go and how much more trouble would I be in? I'll never get to Heaven at this rate.

Tears rolled down my face as I put my hands on the wall. I was sweating like a pedophile in a Mickey Mouse costume.

BAM!

I screamed from the shock and pain of her enormous wooden paddle connecting with my ass. Humiliated and angry, I spun around and put my back to the wall. Sister grabbed me by my hair and forced me to turn back to the wall. Holding me in place with her left hand, she continued to whack me with the paddle in her right. I struggled to break free and sometimes the paddle connected with my hips, sides or hand. I don't know how many times she hit me before it was finally over.

"Boys and Girls? I hope you've learned a valuable lesson. This is what awaits anyone who questions God's ways."

I couldn't take it anymore. Pride and dignity stripped away, what else was there to lose? "I don't remember reading any Bible stories about Jesus beating little kids," I hissed. "But I do remember Jesus getting beaten by a bunch of Roman soldiers and they went straight to Hell!"

If I thought the room had been silent before my paddling, it was like a morgue after that little announcement. No one dared breathe, except me. I panted and shook, but I wasn't done.

"You're nothing but a bully and I feel sorry for you because you can't say enough Hail Mary's and Our Fathers to save your fat ass from the fiery kiss of Satan!"

Wow. It was out of my mouth before I knew what happened. I

wouldn't have been at all surprised if Sister Fatass fashioned a cross and nailed me to it right then and there.

Quickly turning her back and walking offstage, Sister marched down the center aisle between students who were too afraid to look at her as she passed. Most looked down at their lap or in the direction of their teacher, in search of a clue about what was happening. Sister Fatass quietly conferred with Mrs. Weddle who watched the spectacle from the back of Bolger Hall, no doubt with a smile upon her weasel face. As Sister whispered, Mrs. Weddle shook her head hard enough to make her cheeks jiggle back and forth. Sister Fatass walked out of sight.

"Teachers, please take your students back to your classrooms. The lesson is over," announced Mrs. Weasel, I mean Weddle.

I'd never seen kids line up so quickly. Everyone seemed to want to get away from Bolger Hall as fast as possible. Before long, Mrs. Weddle and I were the only two left in the room.

"Collect your things from your classroom and then come immediately to the office," the ass-kisser said before she walked out the door.

She turned and walked out of sight, leaving me alone in Bolger Hall with only my shame for company. I cried and was shocked by the agonizing, awful sounds escaping my mouth. I was unable to stop them and felt disjointed from the disturbing noise I heard myself make.

Humiliated and drained, I realized as I walked offstage my hips and ribs hurt far worse than my ass from where the paddle had missed its mark. With an ass the size of mine, how could that idiot miss? The large, purple bruise growing on my hand, illustrated where Sister hit me as I tried to protect my backside. With a throbbing head and a burning throat, I walked to the girl's room wishing I was home in bed.

Surprised by my reflection, I washed my face but it didn't change my puffy eyes and bright red color. I waited a few minutes, hoping my appearance would return to normal before I faced Miss Butt again.

When I walked into the classroom, I couldn't get anyone to look at me. I tried whispering to Barbara Ann, but my evil teacher grabbed me by the arm and told me to stop disrupting her class. I gathered my things and walked to the office in a daze. Mrs. Weddle was on the phone, so I waited by the door.

"Your mother is on her way to get you. You may wait outside the front door," she said, after hanging up the black monster-sized telephone on her desk. She didn't even look at me when she spoke.

Still crying when my Mom pulled up, I opened the passenger door, crawled in and sobbed. I tried telling her what happened but she couldn't understand me.

"I am not driving anywhere until you stop crying and tell me what the devil is going on!"

I wanted her to hug me and send my Dad to kick Sister Fatass in the face, but I couldn't stop crying so she finally drove home. Mom sent me to my room to pull myself together.

"When you stop crying, you can come out and tell me what happened."

The tears finally ended and I told Mom every detail I could remember. I expected her to go ape shit crazy but she didn't. My parents never questioned the actions of our Church's leaders. She did, however, take me to the doctor who x-rayed my hand and discovered three broken bones. When he asked how I hurt myself, I told him my principal spanked me with a paddle in front of the entire school. He stood with his mouth hanging open like some kind of human fly catcher.

Turning to my mom, the doctor asked with great interest, "What did you do about it?"

She told him to mind his own business.

9 A PARTIAL CONFESSION

Back at school the following Monday, Miss Butt continued her efforts to prepare us for Confession.

"The Sacrament of Reconciliation is sometimes called the Sacrament of Penance or Confession. They all refer to the same Blessed Sacrament, which is one of seven. Who can name the other six?"

Determined to put Friday's humiliation behind me, I raised my chubby hand high in the air. I wasn't going to let Miss Butt or Sister Fatass keep me from getting to the Pearly Gates. No matter how high I raised my arm or how fast I waved it, Miss Butt refused to look at me. Instead, she called on her beloved pet, Debbie.

Sitting in front of me, Debbie looked like a miniature Miss Butt and I didn't like her one bit. She was a tattle-tale with waxy ears that made me sick every time I looked inside them. My Mom was a stickler for checking our ears before we left the house, to make sure they were 'tater free' and it made me wonder what the hell was wrong with Debbie's mom. Debbie's ears were just plain disgusting.

Debbie smiled at Miss Butt as she answered, "The other Sacraments are Baptism, Holy Communion, Confirmation, Marriage, Holy Orders and....um...," she couldn't remember the last one.

"Anointing of the Sick," I blurted out without raising my hand. I didn't mean to say anything, it just came out.

"You will raise your hand if you wish to speak in my classroom, young lady! Or do you wish to repeat Friday's lesson?"

I turned what I'm sure was a lovely shade of red while everyone stared at me. I hated Miss Butt and hoped when she got home from school, her dog would bite her face.

"The seven Holy Sacraments were instituted by Christ. In the case of Reconciliation, He appeared to His Disciples on Easter Sunday, after His Resurrection. Jesus breathed on them and said, 'Receive the Holy Spirit. For those whose sins you forgive, they are forgiven; for those whose sins you retain; they are retained'. And boys and girls, that's why the Catholic Church performs the Sacrament of Reconciliation."

Well, that was as clear as mud. Jesus' breath must have stunk like crazy because he'd been dead for a few days. I wouldn't want a dead guy breathing on me, but aside from that, how do you get "tell your sins to a priest and he'll decide what you have to do to make up for them" out of "for those whose sins you forgive" nonsense? *What a load of crap. Jesus didn't say people have to tell their sins to anyone. Priests must be nosy old creeps with nothing better to do because they can't get married and have kids to keep them busy.*

"The Sacraments are an outward sign of our inward grace. In the case of Reconciliation, the outward sign is absolution. Absolution is what Father grants after you confess your sins. It means forgiveness. The inward grace is our reconciliation with God. When you sin, you deprive yourself of God's grace and once you've done that it becomes easier to sin again," said Miss Butt, reading from her secret teacher's workbook. "The only way out of the vicious circle of sinning and losing grace, sinning and losing grace, is to be mindful of your sins, repent those sins and ask God's forgiveness. During the Sacrament of Reconciliation, grace will be restored making you stronger and more able to resist the urge to sin."

Miss Butt looked directly at me. "At least, for most of you. Some of you are rotten to the core and you'll never have your grace restored. For some of you, there is no hope."

Well, if there's no hope, then I might as well sin as much as I want, right? If there's no hope, then I've got nothing to lose. I wanted to point out to Miss Butt her little Jesus story made no sense and the Catholic Church must be run by a bunch of morons if they could take the Easter morning story and turn it into God telling us we have to confess our sins to a priest. Did they think we were all stupid? I had a brain and I could see right through that Confession bullshit. Not really up for another beating, my broken hand convinced me to keep my mouth shut.

Miss Butt seemed disappointed when I looked away from her and down at my workbook. I think she was hoping for another public display of Catholic Intolerance. I was glad to disappoint her. Debbie raised her hand and I was thankful for the distraction.

"How often does God want us to go to Confession?"

"That's an excellent question," said Miss Butt, flipping pages in her workbook. "Jesus tells us we must receive the Sacrament of Reconciliation whenever we commit a mortal sin."

Our teacher was reading straight from her book and it made me wonder if she really knew any of this crap or if she just spewed out whatever the book told her to say.

"However," she continued, "even if you don't commit a mortal sin, the Church tells us we should go to Confession at least once a month."

"What's a mortal sin?" Debbie was scoring as many suck-up points as she could.

"Another excellent question! A mortal sin is one of a very serious nature. It's committed by someone who knows it's a very serious sin but commits it anyway. Mortal sins cut us off from God and remove Him from our hearts." Miss Butt read from the book again. "A mortal sin is more serious than a venial sin, but someone who commits venial sins is likely to collapse into mortal sin if they continue in their evil ways."

I wanted to ask if beating a child publically for asking an innocent question was a mortal sin, but it didn't seem like a good time. Fat little Debbie's hand shot in the air for the third time in five minutes.

"Wow, Debbie!" said Miss Butt. "You sure are going to be ready for the Sacrament of Reconciliation, aren't you? I'm so proud of how dedicated you are to learning all about what Jesus wants of us. Now, what's your question?"

"What are mortal sins, exactly? I mean like, is swearing a mortal sin? Or burping in church?"

Miss Butt looked down at her workbook and flipped pages back and forth. She seemed to be having trouble finding what she was looking for. Putting the book aside, Miss Butt glared at her little pet in a way I'd never seen before. She looked like she wanted to smack Debbie and her waxy ears right out of the chair. *What a turn of events!* I wanted Debbie to raise her hand and ask more questions.

"Are you mocking me?" Miss Butt asked a confused, fat little Debbie.

"No, Miss Butt. I just want to know what kinds of things are mortal sins so I don't do any of them. I want Jesus to stay in my heart."

Normally, Miss Butt loved that kind of garbage but not today. She was pissed off about something and wasn't doing a very good job hiding it. Maybe her little teacher's workbook, from which she'd been reading all morning, didn't actually describe mortal sins. Maybe Miss Butt didn't know her ass from a hole in the ground and she was just regurgitating what the teacher's workbook told her to say. Maybe she didn't know any more about getting to Heaven than we did.

I poked Debbie in the back and whispered, "Ask her again." I wanted to see Miss Butt turn the same brilliant shade of purple she'd been on Friday.

"Umm...Miss Butt? Don't you know what mortal sins are?" asked Debbie.

Perfect! That sent Miss Butt and her fat turkey neck right over the edge. Her color started to change and I wouldn't have been surprised to see her head spin around followed by green barf spewing from her mouth.

"Get out of my classroom this instant! Take yourself to the Principal's Office and don't you dare step one foot in my classroom until you apologize for what you've done!"

I grinned ear to ear. I thought that would be the end of it, Debbie would wobble out of our classroom in tears and Miss Butt would go back to reading from her cheat sheet, I mean teacher's workbook. But that's not what happened at all, and I never saw it coming. I didn't know fat little Debbie had it in her.

"You don't know the answer and you're taking it out on me. That's not fair!" Debbie was almost shouting.

I couldn't believe my ears. This was the same little snot rag who'd been sucking up to Miss Butt since we were in kindergarten and now she was calling her out? As much as I didn't like to admit it, I had a new respect for Debbie.

"How dare you! You have no idea what kind of trouble you're in, Missy!" Miss Butt walked over to the black receiver on the wall and waited for Mrs. Weddle to answer. "Mrs. Weddle? Please tell Sister Fatass to come to my room right away. I have a student that needs to be removed. Thank you."

Miss Butt replaced the mouthpiece, opened our classroom door and went into the hall. Closing the door behind her, she was out of sight.

Debbie began to cry. I really didn't like her, but I whispered to her anyway.

"Miss Butt is such a bitch and I think you're right. She didn't know the answer to your question and that's why she's sending you to Sister Fatass."

"I don't wanna get beaten like you." She cried harder.

"It wasn't that bad. Don't worry, you'll be fine." I got a glimpse of her wax filled ear and almost puked my Frosted Flakes all over her back.

For several minutes, neither Miss Butt nor Sister made an appearance. We sat whispering until I couldn't take the suspense any longer. Tiptoeing to the door, I peeked out and saw our teacher and the principal standing in the hall. They appeared to be arguing. I couldn't hear them but Sister made big arm gestures, reminding me of what my Dad said about dagos. 'Dagos talk with their hands and if you tie their arms behind their back, they go mute.' I guessed this is what he meant, because Sister's arms were flying all over the place, and Miss Butt kept stepping back to avoid losing an eye.

Finally, Miss Butt turned and walked away from our classroom, out the double doors to the foyer. Sister watched her walk away and then spun on her heel, headed toward our classroom. Racing my fat ass back to my desk, I prayed Sister hadn't seen me in the window.

"Hello, boys and girls."

"Good Morning, Sister Fatass," we all sang in unison.

On our very first day of Kindergarten at Nativity of the Blessed Virgin Mary, we learned to stand up next to our desk and greet whoever walked into our classroom in unison. We said "Good Morning" or "Good Afternoon", in a slow monotone, as if retarded. We did that every day for seven years.

"Miss Butt told me she was having a little trouble this morning. I'm disappointed to hear one of you may have been trying to upset her and make her feel unappreciated. Miss Butt works very hard to help you become better Christians."

Horse hockey. I raised my broken hand.

"Yes?" I was surprised she called on me.

"It wasn't Debbie's fault, Sister. She wasn't being mean at all. Miss Butt just got mad because she didn't know the answer to a question." *Whoops.* I realized I probably shouldn't be talking, but as usual, my mouth was way ahead of my brain.

"And who asked you for your opinion? I don't care what you think. You're a trouble maker and a sinner who will likely never meet Jesus Christ face to face. Go wait in the hall," Sister said, in a very calm, quiet voice.

Oh shit. Here we go again. I was not going to take another beating. If I had to bash her head in with that ridiculously large crucifix she wore around her neck, then that's what I'd do, but I'd be damned if I was going to submit to more abuse from a woman who looked like Chef Boyardee.

Finally, Sister walked out of the classroom and stood so close to me, I could smell the leftover pasta and sausage she'd eaten for breakfast. She had a five o'clock shadow and needed a good shave. Sister bent down until her face was so close to mine, I was afraid she would turn into a monster and eat my face off. Instead of ripping into my flesh, she squinted her black eyes and poked me in the chest with her gnarled finger.

"This is your last warning! Do not test me again or you'll get a real beating and I'll personally see to it you can't get into any college in these United States of America! Do I make myself perfectly clear?"

Her breath could have gagged a maggot and she had BO like she'd been working the farm without the benefit of a shower since my beating last week. I'd agree to anything just to get away from her putrid breath and rancid pits. "Yes, Sister."

"Good, now get back to your desk and don't let me hear your voice again until you graduate."

As I turned to go into the classroom, she smacked my butt with her big, manly hand. My ass was so bruised from last week, her half-hearted spank brought tears to my eyes. I hated that woman and promised myself someday I would repay her for the years of torment she and her Band of Mustached Amigos put me through.

The Big Day finally arrived and I managed to avoid any additional beatings or undue attention from the Warden of Nativity. As usual, my parents and I arrived at church several minutes early. Sitting in same pew we did for Mass, we waited for things to get started. Sister Fatass came out of the vestibule and at first glance I thought we had a new priest. She looked even manlier than she had a few hours ago. She still hadn't shaved.

The mustached old bat walked up to the pulpit and turned on the microphone. "Good Evening. Welcome parents and students. Tonight we will participate in the Blessed Sacrament of Reconciliation. You have all worked very hard and I'm sure I speak for Father Lyntz when I say the entire Church Community is very proud of each and every one of you."

A nun. Lying in church. This was possibly worse than my own mother lying to me in church when she told me the shitter was broken. I looked at the ornately carved ceiling, expecting God to send it to crashing down to squash Sister for lying in His house but, unfortunately nothing happened.

"I'd like all of my fourth graders to come forward and sit in the first three empty pews that have been reserved."

As I stepped over my Mom and Dad to exit our pew, my Dad smiled and whispered, "Don't be scared." He knew I was shitting a brick because I hadn't been able to eat any supper. I was always hungry and could eat regardless of the situation, except that night. I was so nauseous and worried about what I was going to tell Father, I'd left my supper untouched.

I made my way up the center aisle and sat next to Barbara Ann. She looked a little worried, which made me feel better because I knew I wasn't alone.

"Are you scared?" she whispered.

"Very scared. I feel like I'm gonna barf."

"Me too," she confessed. "Do you know what you're gonna say?"

"Yeah, I memorized my list of sins but I'm afraid I'll forget something. I know Sister said I probably can't get into Heaven, but I'm gonna try anyway."

Miss Butt appeared out of nowhere and shushed us. She and Sister Fatass led kids from the first pew to the Confessionals near the side chapel. There were four enormous wooden booths with intricate carvings on the doors. Each Confessional contained a priest just waiting to hear our dirty little secrets, and I felt annoyed I had to tell one of those guys my sins. That stuff was between me and God.

It seemed to take an eternity for our pew to be called, and during that time I silently recited my list of sins and the Act of Contrition. I was sweating and uncomfortable because I had to pee. I shook my leg to keep it contained.

"Stop fidgeting!" warned our teacher.

How does Miss Butt keep appearing out of thin air? I stopped shaking my leg and hoped I didn't baptize God's house with piss. My list of sins was long enough without adding to it.

Debbie stepped out of the Confessional looking like she may have shit her pants. Going directly to the closest pew, she knelt and bowed her head. I turned away before I got another glimpse of her revolting mound of ear wax. That's all I needed. My stomach was already threatening to empty itself, and I knew one brief look at her green wax ball would be all the encouragement it needed.

Sister Fatass motioned me to the Confessional door. I opened it and stepped in. Great. There sat Father Lyntz; Grumpy Old Fart. I'd hoped to find Father John or one of the other, younger priests. Father Lyntz was probably around when Jesus walked the Earth and he was so grumpy, he'd no doubt make me carry a wooden cross around town for a week once he heard my list of sins.

He was mostly visible behind an elaborate, wooden screen, so we were separated only by delicately carved scrollwork. I knelt in front of the dark wooden barrier. "Bless me Father, for I have sinned. This is my First Confession and my sins are ...um...well, they're not too bad. At least most of them."

Father Lyntz raised an eyebrow and motioned for me to continue. This was even harder than I imagined.

"Am I supposed to confess every single sin I can remember for my whole life or just the recent ones?" I was trying to speed things up, because if I had to confess everything bad I'd ever done, we'd be there all night.

"Patti Anne, you must confess everything that keeps you from being close to God. Look into your heart and it will tell you what to do."

My heart wasn't telling me shit and I was beginning to worry this whole Confession thing might not be scam. *What if it's true? What if God really did say we have to tell our sins to a priest or he'll keep Heaven's door locked and we'll be without a key?* It was a chance I didn't want to take. I really wanted to go to Heaven to see Uncle Patrick and meet my brother, Tim.

"I fight with my brothers, I don't always honor my mother and father, I stole a peppermint patty from Gretzinger's, I lied to my Mom about who pooped in a box, I call Debbie names behind her back, I farted in church and blamed it on my brother, I took cookies from the Tupperware container on top of the fridge after my Mom said I couldn't have any...and... um," I stammered.

Father Lyntz didn't seem to be listening. His head was slightly bent down toward his chest and I realized, with great happiness, he'd fallen asleep. *Perfect.* I could still confess my two biggest sins but he wouldn't hear them because the old geezer had passed out.

"And I killed my Uncle Patrick and touch my privates," I whispered, but since I said it out loud, the confession still counted. I waited a few moments but nothing happened. I coughed, which did the trick. "For these and any sins I may have forgotten, I am truly sorry." That was the cue to Father I was done.

"I want you to say three Hail Mary's, two Our Father's and an Act of Contrition. I absolve you from your sins in the name of the Father, the Son and the Holy Spirit."

"Amen," I said, as I made the sign of the Cross.

"Go forth in peace."

"Thank you, Father. Have fun listening to everyone's sins." The words were out before I could stop them, but Father didn't seem to mind. He tipped his head slightly and looked like he was trying not to smile. Priests aren't supposed to smile during Confession because God would think they're not taking their job seriously enough and that could mess things up for everyone.

I walked into a pew and knelt down to say my prayers and wait for everyone else to finish tattling on themselves. I didn't feel any differently and was a little worried. *If I'd been absolved, shouldn't I feel a sense of relief? What if it didn't count I'd confessed two great big sins while Father was asleep?* Feeling sick again as I looked around at my classmates, I realized they all had the same look of serenity and peace. I was not feeling the least bit serene or peaceful, and I worried I may not have been absolved from two of the biggest sins a kid can commit.

It was now or never. Jumping up off the kneeler, I headed straight for Father Lyntz's Confessional. Sister Fatass pounced on me and grabbed my arm before I touched the door.

"What sort of hijinks are you up to? You've already had your turn. Trying to listen in on someone else's Confessions?" she accused.

"No, Sister, I'm not. I didn't know anyone was in there. I remembered two sins I didn't confess and need to see Father again."

"Now, you listen here! It's bad enough I have to put up with your shenanigans in school all day, but don't make me put up with you in church, too!" I don't think Sister realized she wasn't using her church voice and several heads turned to see what was going on.

"Sister, this is serious! I need to see Father again!"

The door to the Confessional opened and Father Lyntz stepped out. "Is there a problem, Sister?"

Yeah, there's a problem. Sister Fatass is the fucking problem.

"There's no problem, Father. I'm just keeping this one from causing any further trouble." Sister was trying to turn me around and send me back to the pew.

"Father, I forgot to tell you two sins. Two big ones. I really need to see you again." I didn't care who heard me. This was serious business.

"I'm not going to tell you again!" Sister Fatass said, again too loudly for church.

"Sister, let the child come to me. Don't you see how troubled she is?

Come, my dear." Father motioned me into the Confessional.

I smiled sweetly and thanked him. As I stepped in, I glanced back and wrinkled my nose at Sister who looked like she'd just been slapped in the face. Father took his place behind the screen and I started the speech once again. "Bless me Father, for I have sinned. It's been fifteen minutes since my last Confession. I need to confess three sins."

"I thought you said you forgot to tell me two sins," Father said, eyebrows raised.

"Well, that was a lie, so that's the third thing I have to confess. I lied when I said I'd forgotten to tell you two sins. I actually told you, but you feel asleep and didn't hear them. I was afraid it didn't count and I don't wanna go to Hell. Even though Sister said I probably won't get into Heaven, I wanna do everything I can, just in case there's a chance."

"What do you mean, Sister said you won't get into Heaven? Why would she do such a thing?" he asked, looking very disturbed.

"Oh, she says lots of things like that. She told me I'm a sinner and will probably never meet Jesus face to face. She really hates me."

"I hope that's not true. Sister shouldn't hate anyone. I will speak with her myself about that. Now, let's get back to the matter at hand. I encourage you to always tell the truth, and while I realize you lied so no one would know I'd fallen asleep, I can't condone the behavior."

"Yes, Father," I replied, fearing I was now in bigger trouble with Our Lord.

"However, I appreciate your kindness nonetheless. It was a gracious thing to do and it shows me you have a kind heart. Tell me child, why do you look so scared? Do I frighten you?" Father asked, leaning forward slightly, almost pressing his face to the screen between us.

"Oh no, Father, not at all. You're way nicer than my teachers, it's just that, well...those sins you didn't hear were pretty big ones."

"Big ones, eh? Well, technically, you already confessed them and I absolved you of the sins you confessed aloud. The fact that I may not have heard all of them doesn't change the fact that you were sorry and confessed. God knows you kept your end of the deal. In His eyes, you have done the right thing. Fear not, my child. Go in peace."

I went home very relieved I'd been absolved and Father Lyntz didn't make me confess my really big sins twice. Realizing I really liked the old priest, I decided during my next Confession I needed to ask forgiveness for all of the times I called him an old fart or made fun of him for wearing a dress.

As I drifted off to sleep with a clear conscience, I remembered Father said he would talk to Sister about telling me I'd never get to Heaven. No one had ever stood up to Sister Fatass on my behalf and I was touched. I prayed Father would beat her bubble butt with her very own paddle during ten o'clock Mass.

10 DO AS I SAY, NOT AS I DO

Toward the end of my sentence at Nativity School, Father John became assistant pastor. He was a little porky fellow with flaming red hair and an enormous Mr. Pringles moustache. I think we kids liked him because he was fairly young, at least compared to Father Lyntz, and he wore lay people's clothing, making him seem more approachable. Apparently, I wasn't the only one who considered him so.

Father Pringles frequently presided over ten o'clock Mass, which was my parents' time slot of choice because the music was a little more lively than the traditional organ music played at other Masses. Although I'd only been to one funeral, I always associated organ music with the extreme sadness and desperate grief of funerals. Rather than dreary organ music, the ten o'clock Mass was graced by acoustic guitars, a flute and voices of the Folk Group.

The musical group consisted of parishioners who volunteered their time and talent to lead the congregation in hymns and musical prayer. My Mom nicknamed one of the members "Bellybutton" because she often wore midriff tops that showed her, well, her belly button. I didn't remember this being mentioned as a no-no in the Ten Commandments, but my Mom must have read it somewhere because it really pissed her off. She and Dad were decidedly against Bellybutton and her inappropriate dress, as were many others of the congregation. It didn't matter she volunteered at least two hours a week to sing praises unto Our Lord, all that mattered was what she wore. Isn't that how Jesus did things?

Apparently, Father John rather liked "Bellybutton's" navel showing while he said Mass, because instead of looking at the congregation or the Bible, he mostly looked at her. Our congregation noticed the two of them out in public. Together. Alone. You know that means, right? I didn't, although I suspected maybe they held hands and Father talked about her belly button while they prayed the Rosary. Apparently, there wasn't much praying going on but allegedly, they were having sex and word got 'round to our Bishop who had the good sense to move him to another parish. Bellybutton stopped singing in the Folk Group and the congregation felt justice had been served.

"Did you notice who was missing from Folk Group this morning, Mac?" my Mom asked in a voice that sounded like she'd just proven someone wrong.

"How could I not notice?" he replied.

"I guess she learned her lesson. That's the end of Bellybutton, thank God," Mom said, straightening the pleats of her skirt. "Let that be a lesson to the rest of 'em. We won't stand for trampy behavior, inside or outside of our church!"

What's wrong with Father John holding hands with Bellybutton? Why can't priests have female friends? Jesus did. He let Mary Magdalene wash his feet, which seems a little trampy. If she was kneeling at his feet, she probably peeked up his dress and saw his thing.

"Hey, Daddy, do think Jesus wore underwear under his dress?" I asked. Since Dad was a man like Jesus, he'd probably know.

My Mom turned around to look at me, wearing an odd expression. I couldn't tell if she was angry or trying not to laugh. "What did you say?"

she asked.

"I asked Daddy if he thought Jesus wore underwear," I answered.

"Why do you ask, Patti Anne?" said my Dad, looking at me in the rear view mirror and wearing a big grin.

"Well, I wondered what Bellybutton did that was so bad, because all I know is she showed Father John her tummy. Since Mary Magdalene washed Jesus' feet, she might have seen his privates if he didn't wear underwear, which would be way worse than what Bellybutton did."

"This conversation is over. I don't think God wants us talking about his privates," said my Mom, turning away. Dad continued to smile until Mom whacked his arm, telling him not to encourage me.

"Mac, did I tell you Ellen's going to be an altar server?" asked Mom. I knew she purposely changed the subject.

All three of my brothers were altar servers and I was jealous. They could sneak through the back passages of the vestibules, go on weekend retreats and carry delicious smelling incense during midnight Mass on Christmas Eve. I wanted to be an altar server too, but our priests weren't interested in female altar servers, they only recruited young boys. In fact, as soon as my brothers reached a certain age, they were removed from the serving schedule. Our pastor seemed to prefer boys who were between eleven and thirteen years of age. *I wonder why?*

Father Cornhole was the pastor of a neighboring town and uninterested in boy servers. Much like Father John, he liked to talk to girls and was one of the first pastors to support the idea of female altar servers. The congregation and parish superiors praised him for his forward thinking and sense of equality. I overheard George and Scott talking about Father Cornhole's affinity for female altar servers.

"The guy's a creep," claimed George. "Have you even seen the way he looks at every girl's boobs during Communion?"

"Yeah, I don't know why the adults don't see what a perv he is," agreed Scott.

"Everyone says he's so cool because he lets girls serve but all he's doing is making it easier to dip his crucifix," said George, as he and Scott laughed.

Dip his crucifix in what? Altar wine? Why would he need girls for that?

My cousin, Ellen, was thrilled when given the opportunity to be an altar girl. She quickly became the star server of her parish and Father Cornhole sang her praises, making me quite jealous. He ensured Ellen served every Mass over which he presided and attended every retreat he led. The two seemed almost inseparable and not just with church stuff. Father Cornhole tutored Ellen in the rectory every day after school for the better part of a year until one day, she refused to go.

While doing homework at the kitchen table, I overheard my parents whispering.

"Ellen said he's been forcing himself on her since she was eleven years old! Do you think she's telling the truth, Mac?" asked my Mom.

"I agree, it's hard to believe but why would she lie, Betty?"

Father Cornhole forced himself on Ellen? Forced her to do what? Eat more Communion? Pray the Rosary? I knew by their whispering, my parents didn't want me to know what has going on so there was no point asking. I walked out to the barn, where my brothers were doing chores.

"Hey, guys? What did Father Cornhole do to Ellen?" I knew they'd tell me, especially if it was disgusting because they loved to make me wanna puke.

"None of your business, Pat. Go back to the house," said George. He gave Scott and Peter a look I didn't understand.

"Why won't you tell me? How come I'm the only one in this entire family who doesn't know what's going on?" I asked, angry at my brothers for keeping secrets.

"Because you're too young," explained George, "so go back in the house."

I stayed put, hands on hips, and put on the biggest scowl I could muster. "Let me tell you something, Mister, I know a lot more than you think I do. So you better tell me what's going on before I come over there and kick your butt!" I tried to look bad-ass tough, like Sylvester Stallone in Rocky.

"You're such a twerp, Snotsie!" teased Scott, "You think you're some sort of tough guy? Gimme a break."

I turned, pretending I was going to leave and when Scott turned back to shoveling shit, I lunged at him from behind and sent him face first into the gutter full of cow dung. "Now who's a tough guy, asshole?" I shouted. I knew Dad allowed the boys to swear but only in the barn.

Before Scott could tear me limb from limb, George stood between us and held my angry brother back. "You fucking little brat! I'm gonna kill you!" screamed Scott.

"Just simmer down, Scott," said George, sounding exactly like Dad. "You had it coming." Looking at me, George explained, "Ellen quit serving, refuses to go to church and doesn't want to see Father Cornole ever again."

"Why?" I asked, trying to ignore my shit-covered brother who glared at me from behind George's back.

"Because he forced her to have sex with him. I guess it's been going on for a few years and she's a little messed up. Don't you dare tell Mom and Dad I told you."

I know how she feels. At least she can get away from Father Cornhole and he doesn't live in her house. "I won't. I'm going back to the house and I promise not to tell Mom and Dad," I assured him.

"Watch your back Snotsy, 'cuz I'm coming for you!" warned Scott.

"You just try it and I'll tell everyone what you've been doing to me!" I threatened, sounding braver than I felt. George and Peter looked at Scott in horror. Without waiting to see what happened, I turned and ran to the house, into my bedroom and shut the door. *Holy shit! What have I done?*

At breakfast the next morning, Scott had a black eye and split lip. When Mom asked how he'd gotten hurt, he said he tripped and fell down the cellar stairs. I looked at George and saw him fight back a smile. *I wonder what the Confessions of Father Cornhole and Scott sound like.*

Father Cornhole's cousin was my fifth grade teacher. Although she was reportedly female, she looked more manly than he did. Sister Mary Joseph Cox was a short, fat nun who resembled a pig. Her nose turned up at the end, forcing you to look into both nostrils. It was very distracting.

Almost as distracting, was the furry caterpillar living right below it. Her upper lip wasn't quite as hairy as Sister Carol Fatass's but judging by the abundance of facial hair, they must have been related. Clearly, Sister Mary Joseph was well aware of her mustache because she often stroked it while grading papers. Looking up from a workbook, I'd see her hold a paper in one hand while stroking her deformity with the other.

A mean old bitch who loved to hear herself shout, Sister took great pleasure whacking our knuckles with her thick, wooden ruler and did so at the slightest provocation. She yelled if we couldn't recite the Apostle's Creed quickly enough or name the Ten Commandments in proper order fast enough. Although Latin was no longer used during Mass, Sister demanded we learn the name of each and every part of the celebration in the ancient language. Frequently, I woke up in the middle of the night, reciting "Gloria, Sanctus, Agnes Dei" and so on.

Sister Mary Joseph kept a rigid schedule and there were no deviations. When it was time to go to lunch, she opened the classroom door and called us by row to quietly walk into the cloak room to retrieve our lunches. We lined up in silence, single file at the door.

While waiting in line, I noticed the name plate on the classroom door. I'd never really paid attention to it until then and it caught my eye. "Sister Mary Joseph Cox." While the old bat was still in the cloak room, preventing any malarkey from sneaking into her well-ordered classroom, I slipped out of line. With both hands, I covered the words Mary and Joseph so the name plate read "Sister Cox." My classmates covered their mouths, trying not to laugh, when suddenly they looked like they were at gun point. I felt a familiar bony finger poke into my back. I removed my hands from the name plate and turned to find Sister Carol Fatass smiling at me. It wasn't a friendly smile. It was more like one a hungry cat gives a cornered mouse.

"Shouldn't you be in line, young lady?"

What? That's it? This old bitch had already beaten me in front of the entire school, breaking three bones and leaving bruises that lasted until they turned all colors of the rainbow before finally fading away. She caught me messing with a name plate to make it say something dirty and all she's gonna do is send me back in line? The old crow must be losing her touch or perhaps she needs new glasses. Maybe she doesn't know about cocks. *Bingo!* We have a winner.

Coming in from the playground that afternoon, we followed our standard routine. Each row of students took turns in the bathroom before silently returning to their seats. Sister Mary Joseph erased the blackboards. She picked up a piece of chalk and without a word, wrote in giant letters: "F   U   C   K." *Oh, my God in Heaven, she's lost her mind.*

"Who can tell the class what this means?" she asked our completely stunned classroom.

As if any of us were gonna raise our hands to answer that! No one said a word. Everyone wore the same look of fear mixed with nervous laughter. Without warning, a laugh choked out of my throat. I lowered my head behind the kid in front of me to keep out of Sister's view. I wanted no part of that show.

"I heard some of you monsters used this word on the playground today. What does it mean?" she yelled louder, causing her chubby face to turn an unhealthy shade of bluish-red. *Uh oh, this is gonna be bad.*

Completely discolored, Sister stood at the front of the classroom, glaring and daring us to say the word but no one moved. After several uncomfortable minutes, during which I prayed she'd have a stroke and end our misery, she finally screamed "FUCK!" The unnatural color deepened.

"For Unlawful Carnal Knowledge!" she barked through clenched teeth. "Fucking without being married! Now you know what fuck means, use it properly!"

Sister left "F U C K" on the chalkboard for the rest of the day while she taught math and spelling. Completely distracting doesn't adequately explain what it was like to see that word written on my Catholic School blackboard. If only Sister Fatass would walk in and see this!

In total contrast to my usual prayers regarding Sister Fatass, which typically involved explosive diarrhea and hairy facial worts, instead I prayed she'd walk through our classroom door. Slightly worried that imploring the Virgin Mary to get Sister Mary Joseph in deep shit might be a sin, I decided it was a chance I was willing to take. Unfortunately, Sister Fatass never made it to our end of paradise that particular afternoon and the faculty never knew about her x-rated chalkboard.

After supper that night, I told Peter what happened while Dad slept in front of the evening news with Walter Cronkite. Scott was out in the car talking on his CB radio, and Mom was on a rare evening phone call with a lady from Parish Council, so I wasn't worried about being overheard.

"She's a nut case for sure," Peter admitted, after I told him what Sister did.

"Do you think I should tell Mom and Dad?"

"Are you crazy? They won't believe you and you'll get spanked for saying 'fuck.' Do nothing," was his advice.

"But she's a crackpot and should get in trouble for what she did!"

"You're pissing up a rope if you think you can get her in trouble. Jesus' Band of Mustached Knuckle Crackers stick together and you'll never win. Just bide your time, Pat. You've only got one more year in that dump," said my wise older brother.

"That bites. I hate nuns," I said, wishing the Pope would excommunicate every nun other than Sister Mary Margaret, wherever she was.

"Join the club. Let's steal cookies while Mom's on the phone!"

I helped Peter steal peanut butter cookies from the Tupperware container on top of the fridge, but my heart wasn't in it. All I could think about was the unfairness of Catholic School. On one hand, our seemingly saintly teachers insisted we learn about Jesus and His love for us, but on the other, they beat us and bullied us into submission. Why does God allow nuns to be so cruel?

I contemplated the cruelty of nuns while walking through Nativity's basement on my way from lunch to recess. Someone called my name from the janitor's hallway. Mr. Chatman, the head janitor, walked toward me with a bag in his hand.

"Hi, honey. Will you please take this to Sister Mary Joseph? She asked to borrow it for class," he said, handing me the bag.

"Sure, no sweat. Tell Mrs. Chatman I said hi."

"Will do, honey. Be good."

The Chatman's were kind southerners with heavy accents. Casual acquaintances of my parents, they were the nicest, most generous people in the world. What I loved most about Mrs. Chatman was she loved to swear and didn't give a good goddamn who was listening. To my Mom's great dismay, she chain-smoked and drank beer in the middle of the day.

Needless to say, my parents didn't have a lot in common with the Chatman's but my friendship with their son brought the two couples together. I looked out for their adopted son Hughie, who was my age and rode my bus. Mildly retarded and socially awkward, Hughie was an easy target for the school bus bullies. Fortunately for Hughie, my reputation for having kicked Stevie Hayes' ass a few years earlier guaranteed his safety.

In return for my bodyguard services, Mrs. Chatman gave us free haircuts. Taking turns in an old barber chair on their back porch, Mom and I sat while she and Mrs. Chatman gossiped. Whenever one of them came up for air, I cracked jokes from MAD Magazine or The Muppet Show. After each delivery, Mrs. Chatman called me "a little pint of piss" and offered me a sip of beer. I knew it upset my Mom but whenever she suggested Mrs. Chatman refrain from sharing her beer, the woman would say, "Maybe you need to loosen the straps on your Jesus knickers, Betty. Life is fun, why don't you try joining in?" I didn't really understand what it meant but it sure did put the kibosh on Mom's nagging.

Looking at the bag in my hand, I wondered what the hell the Chatman's had that Sister Mary Joseph needed. My bowels threatened to let go when I looked inside and saw a leather whip, neatly coiled. *Oh shit. What the fuck is that crazy woman gonna do with a whip?* I thought about tossing it down the chute to the furnace but since my public beating I'd grown a little reckless. I had a false sense of bravado and figured I could take on a pig-faced nun with a whip. Hell, I was a cross between Pinky Tuscadero from Happy Days and Jo from The Facts of Life. Bring it on, you flying penguin.

When I handed her the whip, Sister Mary Joseph cackled like an old hag stooped over a bubbling cauldron of dried bat wings and dead man's toe. She clapped her hands and shouted for everyone to line up. Opening the heavy door to the hall, Sister ordered us to face the wall, hands over our heads. An alarm went off in my head! I've been in this stance before in this very school and had my ass publicly beaten. I wasn't happy to find myself being told to assume the same position a second time.

Everyone lined up and looked at the crazy old bat over their shoulders. Snapping the whip, Sister cracked it very loudly against the tile floor. Most of us jumped a couple of inches. *This nun is fucking crazy!* Sister cackled again and walked back and forth behind us, cracking the whip on the floor. She talked but whatever spewed forth from her crazed lips didn't register in my brain. All I heard was a resounding chorus of, "*I gotta get the hell outta here, 'cuz this bitch is dangerous*" repeating in my head.

Apparently, I wasn't the only one getting nervous because amidst the shouts from my brain to run for cover, I heard crying and snickering from the other end of the line. Scared to death, Sarah Evans wet her pants and John Lynch snorted with laughter. Sister Nutcase cracked the whip across both Sarah and John's backs, causing them to cry out in pain. The rest of us screamed, frozen with panic. Doors to the other two classrooms opened and teachers flew into the hallway, prepared to hand out some serious discipline to whoever was causing the ruckus.

Taking in the spectacle of Sister Nutcase cracking her whip and children screaming in panic, the teachers simply stood, stuck to the floor, mouths hanging open. Sister continued to cackle and crack the whip. Coming to her senses, Miss Butt spun around and picked up the black receiver hanging on the wall inside her classroom. It connected directly to the office. Unable to hear what she said, I watched her make whip cracking gestures with her free hand. Without taking the time to put the receiver back on its hook, Miss Butt dashed into the hall and shooed my classmates into her room. The other teacher stood in her doorway, mouth agape, not moving.

"Move your ass and get those kids into your room!" shouted Miss Butt.

I can't believe she said 'ass'! I can't believe she's trying to help us. This was the nasty woman partly responsible for my oh-so very public beating last year. As the two teachers herded my classmates to safety, Sister Mary Joseph continued to cackle and whip crack. From my vantage point behind Miss Butt's ample rear-end, I saw Sister Carol Fatass run up the stairs. She smoothed her skirt and walked calmly toward the craziness.

"Sister Mary Joseph, put that whip down right this minute."

"Or else?" asked the crazy nun.

"Do as I say! You are making a terrible mistake," warned the mustached wonder.

"The only mistake I ever made was working for you in this stupid school! I hate teaching, I hate these kids and I hate you! Jesus Whore!" screeched Sister Nutcase as she cracked the whip and walked toward our principal. "Jesus Whore! Jesus Whore!"

The smile on Sister Nutcase's face reminded me of something from the imagination of Stephen King.

Holy shit. I couldn't believe Sister Mary Joseph continued to call Sister Fatass a Jesus Whore. I didn't have any idea what it meant but I knew it was bad. Sister Fatass stopped moving but didn't back away. She didn't look particularly frightened, so they must have practiced the scenario in nun school, the same way we practiced fire drills.

Partially hidden by Miss Butt's generous caboose, I watched Mr. Chatman sneak up behind Sister Mary Joseph. Our Principal must have seen him too but she didn't give his position away. Instead, she repeatedly told her crazy colleague to put down the whip. As the crazy old bitch raised her arm to crack the whip once again, Mr. Chatman yanked it out of her hand. The tail end whipped around and smacked Sister Mary Joseph in the boobs.

Turning toward Mr. Chatman, she screamed, "You son of a bitch! You whipped my bosoms!" Plural.

With an impressive round-house punch, Sister Mary Joseph connected with Mr. Chatman's unsuspecting jaw. There was a loud crack, after which she jumped up and down, yelling about a broken hand. Mr. Chatman recovered quickly and spun the crazed nun around. Pulling her flabby, white arms behind her back, Mr. Chatman tied them in place with the whip. The fat, ugly nun continued to shout about her bosoms and broken hand while Mr. Chatman and Sister Fatass led her downstairs and out of our lives.

I never saw Sister Mary Joseph again. The rumor was she went to a psycho ward and somehow managed to get her hands on a janitor's uniform. Masquerading as a male cleaning person, she escaped the mental hospital and was on the loose. That pig-nosed, big-bosomed nun with a broken hand haunted my nightmares for years. Jesus Whore.

11 MEAN GIRLS

I coveted my last year at Nativity, knowing my sentence in Hell was finally coming to an end. Outgrowing my little school and weary of being forced to practice Sacraments I didn't completely understand, I was relieved we weren't facing another in sixth grade. Preparing for Confession had been physically and emotionally damaging, and I'd uncovered gaping holes in my religion's logic no one was willing to address. Asking questions that seemed quite reasonable, resulted in public beatings and broken bones. My suffering and humiliation served as a warning, preventing other kids from asking questions that might get them into trouble. My classmates prayed as instructed and believed in whatever they were told. It was similar to the way terrorists are trained.

After mustached Sister Mary Joseph's mental breakdown last year, during which she brandished a whip and called our Principal a Jesus Whore, our class shrunk to nine girls and three boys. Many parents were smarter than mine and took their kids out of Nativity in favor of a public middle school. My best friend, Barbara Ann, was one of the lucky ones with smart parents. She left our small Catholic prison for public school freedom, and we lost touch.

Since there were so few of us, our teacher gave us a lot of individual attention. Mrs. Fitzcracker was the sort of person who made me want to do my best. Wanting to please her and earn much needed positive recognition, I worked harder at my studies than ever before. The harder I worked the more compliments I received. Using my homework and essays as examples, Mrs. Fitzcracker earned me the moniker of Teacher's Pet. It's lonely at the top.

A girl with whom I'd grown close since she moved to our town in second grade wasn't happy about my newfound stardom. Suzanne was accustomed to being in the spotlight due to her unusual, exotic look and she had difficulty adjusting to the loss of attention. To show me what she thought of my lofty position, Suzanne decided to hate me and became best friends with Nicole, who was dumber than a box of rocks with all the smart ones taken out.

Nicole's parents were extremely wealthy and lived in an enormous, well-appointed home with an in-ground swimming pool. Nicole gave my former friend expensive gifts during their weekend sleepovers and I couldn't compete. All I had to offer was a modest farmhouse in the middle of nowhere, fields of cattle and three weird brothers.

Suzanne and Nicole turned into classic mean girls and their sole purpose in life was to make mine a living hell. They mocked me when I answered questions in class, teased me for wearing the same unfashionable pants every day and complained about my body odor. I knew I needed deodorant but my Mom said I wasn't old enough. Whenever possible, I snuck into her bedroom to use Dad's Old Spice deodorant before school, but the opportunities to do so were rare. Most days I smelled like a farm hand.

It was the 1977/78 school year and the movies Grease and Star Wars were both released. My parents wouldn't let me see either because they thought the movies were "raunchy". *What the hell?* If they got off the goddamned farm once in awhile to somewhere other than church, they might have a clue about what's going on in the world around them.

Some of this was my brother, Peter's, fault because when he was too young to get into an R rated movie, he convinced my parents to take him to see Animal House. Tits, ass, drinking, swearing and even a fuck scene thrown in for good measure. I think my parents must have thought they were going to see something like Mutual of Omaha's Wild Kingdom with Marlin Perkins, but instead they got a shitfaced John Belushi trying to get laid.

How did I stand a chance of breaking out of the nerd herd if I couldn't talk about two of the greatest movies ever made? Nicole and Suzanne went to see Grease with their cool Moms, and because they liked it so much, their Moms let them stay for a second showing. My Mom was probably giving me a crappy home perm or crocheting granny squares.

After choreographing a dance routine, the Mean Girls got permission to perform it for our class. They dressed like Sandra Dee, complete with poodle skirts, bobby socks and pony tails. Obviously, Mrs. Fitzcracker hadn't seen Grease either because she gave them permission to dance to "Greased Lightening," which they had on cassette tape.

When our clueless teacher heard lyrics about chicks creaming, she let out a loud gasp and jumped out from behind her huge metal desk, nearly knocking the tape player on the floor. Visibly shaken, Mrs. Fitzcracker stopped the music. When Nicole asked her to turn it back on Mrs. Fitzcracker mumbled something about "disgusting filth" and led us to the chapel to pray.

Although I was abundantly happy the Mean Girls didn't get to finish their stupid routine, and even happier Mrs. Fitzcracker was upset with them, I wanted more. As we knelt on the floor of the chapel crowded together in prayer, I farted loudly and blamed it on Nicole. Everyone moved away from her because it stunk to High Heaven. With a look of supreme disgust, Mrs. Fitzcracker sent Nicole to the hall to find her manners. I never smiled so much while praying.

Wanting to get back at Nicole for ostracizing me and stealing my friend, I nicked her math book from the counter in the back of the classroom and stashed it in my desk. When Mrs. Fitzcracker sent those of us who were excellent readers into the hall to read quietly while she worked with the less intelligent, more popular kids, I added Nicole's math book to my stack of belongings. No one noticed.

In the hall with the other nerds, I decided to toss Nicole's book down the chute to the furnace. The other girls were horrified and scared we'd get caught. Although they didn't want to be there when I sent Nicole's book to a fiery end, I threatened to beat them worse than I'd beaten fat-assed Stevie Hayes if they didn't accompany me. The timid girls responded as I hoped, and we snuck through the double doors at the end of the hall to a small alcove that housed the magical chute to the furnace. More than a little scared, I pulled the handle that opened the square, metal door on the wall labeled "Danger. Fire" and threw Nicole's book down the chute. Smiling victoriously, I slammed the door and waited impatiently for our next math class.

Unfortunately, we were a very small Catholic school that put more stock into teaching religion and character building than math or science. Three days later, when Mrs. Fitzcracker decided it might be wise to spend a few moments on math, poor little rich bitch Nicole couldn't find her book. I relished the thought of her being in deep trouble. It came as a complete and utter shock when Sarah raised her hand.

"Mrs. Fitzcracker?" she said, to get our teacher's attention. "Patti Anne took Nicole's book and threw it down the chute to the furnace."

She's dead meat.

Mrs. Fitzcracker looked at me in disbelief and demanded to know the truth. I hesitated for only a second before blurting out, "Sarah's the one who did it! She forced me to steal Nicole's book and made me watch while she threw it into the furnace."

Being the Teacher's Pet paid off. Mrs. Fitzcracker bought every word and Sarah was sent to the Principal's office to be paddled for disrespecting school property. She had her lily white ass beaten and had to call her parents to confess her evil sin. I guess Sister whacked my classmate hard enough to make her believe she actually did it, because Sarah never mentioned the subject again.

Sarah's parents had to replace Nicole's book and make a separate offering during Mass. I sat in my pew and watched their shame without an ounce of guilt. I was angry Nicole didn't get in trouble for losing her book and wanted to find another way to humiliate that blond-haired, fat-assed Mean Girl. Who knew the Boy Scouts would come in so handy?

Every Monday night, I went to Nativity with my Mom and Dad to pick up Peter from his weekly Boy Scout meeting. I was hot for Jacob, one of the boys in my brother's troop who had already escaped the religious tentacles of Nativity, and was in seventh grade at the public school. Slightly taller than me, with sandy brown hair and light brown eyes, he was the cutest boy I'd ever met. In my efforts to flirt, I'd chase him around the meeting room, kick his shins and tell him I smoked cigarettes. I was very sophisticated.

One Monday night, while my parents gossiped with friends, I managed to chase Jacob from the basement where meetings were held, to the third floor. Except for the light streaming in the windows from the street lamps, the third floor was dark. We slowed down and Jacob took my hand. His palm was sweaty and I was afraid he was going to kiss me. I wanted him to, but I'd eaten tuna noodle casserole for supper and was afraid I had fish breath.

As I debated running back to the meeting room, Jacob pressed me up against the cold tile wall and put his lips on mine. He had a hairy upper lip I didn't care for, because it brought images of Sisters Fatass and Mary Joseph to mind. Who wants to think about hairy-lipped nuns when kissing? Apparently Jacob ate something as malodorous as Mom's tuna casserole because his breath smelled like cow ass. Our kiss was quick and I didn't really kiss back because it happened so fast. When Jacob pulled away, I was unsure how to act or what to say so I suggested he help me with a nasty prank. Being a good, Catholic Boy Scout he was happy to oblige.

We snuck into my sixth grade classroom and found Nicole's desk. It was the metal kind with a lid that opened and a wooden chair attached at the bottom. I took a permanent black magic marker from Mrs. Fitzcracker's top drawer and wrote "FUCK" in large letters all over the inside of Nicole's desk. Deciding that wasn't severe enough, I wrote "I HATE JESUS" on her wooden seat. *Brilliant!*

I put the marker back in Mrs. Fitzcracker's top drawer, exactly as I found it, and ran with Jacob to the basement as if the devil himself were on our heels. We'd probably been gone fifteen minutes or so, but no one seemed to notice and the fear we'd been caught kissing or writing obscenities began to subside.

Sauntering into our classroom Tuesday morning, I found the principal and Mrs. Fitzcracker staring at "I hate Jesus" scribbled on Nicole's chair. I was full of eager anticipation and anxious for Sister to crack Nicole's ass even wider than the Good Lord had made it. The Mean Girl stood beside her desk, crying.

She cried harder when Mrs. Fitzcracker opened the desk to reveal the many repetitions of "fuck" written inside. Both women cupped a hand over their mouths and gasped. My classmates strained to see between the women whose ample backsides blocked the view. Sister Fatass was the first to recover and ordered everyone out of the room, in single file, to stand against the wall. Waiting silently in the hall with my classmates while listening to Nicole insist she didn't do it, I was comfortably content. My classmates, on the other hand, looked quite nervous. Within minutes, Sister Fatass dragged a screaming Nicole down the hall, much like Lucifer drags a stolen soul to Hell. Mrs. Fitzcracker led the rest of us to the Chapel to pray.

All evening, I was comforted by the image of Sister dragging uppity, nasty Nicole down the hall on her way to meet the legendary, unforgiving paddle. Stepping eagerly into the classroom the next morning, I expected to find a subdued, reticent Nicole. I was utterly confused and disappointed to find she was back to her usual, holier-than-thou self. I overheard Nicole brag that her generous parents surprised Sister Fatass with a very large, personal check when they came to pick their accused vandal from the Principal's office the day before.

"My parents and I donated enough to replace every single desk in the entire school," bragged the rich bitch. "Not only that, we've hired an artist to make a bronze bust of Sister Fatass!"

She explained the bust would be displayed in the school foyer, as a tribute to our esteemed and accomplished Christian Crusader for Education. Sister Fatass was so appreciative, she told Mr. and Mrs. Whittaker their daughter suffered enough humiliation and a paddling was out of the question.

What the hell is going on? Why didn't Sister beat Nicole's ass the moment she dragged her away? The only possible answer was Sister took into account the Whittaker's substantial wealth, as they were the primary funders of all improvements to our school since time immemorial. The nun's greed for additional cash convinced her to postpone Nicole's beating until she knew what the Whittakers would cough up in exchange for leniency. Talk about a Jesus Whore.

My blood boiled just thinking about the Whittakers greasing Sister Hairy Lip's palm to ensure their daughter escaped punishment. Sister Mary Margaret wouldn't have sold her soul the way Sister Fatass did. If my parents were prosperous bankers who leveraged their wealth to influence others rather than poor farmers who obeyed the bidding of their religious leaders, I could have escaped my public beating and broken bones. Since that wasn't the case, I decided to take matters into my own hands and deliver some much needed come-uppance.

As promised, the Whittakers delivered a piece of art to Nativity. On the day of the unveiling ceremony, the faculty and student body gathered inside and around the foyer. Standing in the middle was a large object draped with red velvet. Seated in chairs nearby, were Mr. and Mrs. Whittaker and Nicole, dressed for an evening at the opera.

Mrs. Whittaker wore a fur stole around her shoulders and what appeared to be a very expensive pearl necklace. Mr. Whittaker's tux was perfectly pressed and the handkerchief in his pocket matched the color of Mrs. Whittaker's turquoise evening gown. Nicole wore a blue, satin dress with pleats. She had matching shoes and gloves and looked like a miniature version of her mother. She even wore the same look of entitlement upon her face. Sister Fatass sat next to the Whittakers, unshaven, looking like a lumber jack in a habit. Several parents who tried to keep up with the Whittakers were in attendance, also rather elegantly dressed for a morning gathering at a small Catholic school. I, on the other hand, wore the same pants and shirt I'd worn for the past three days.

"Ladies and Gentlemen, boys and girls, welcome. Today, we are gathered to witness the exciting unveiling of an artistic masterpiece, so generously commissioned and donated by the philanthropic Whittaker Family," announced Miss Butt. Trembling with excitement, her turkey neck wobbled back and forth like a hypnotist's pendulum. "I'd like to introduce you to our kind benefactors, John and Emily Whittaker," she said, gesturing to the rich folk seated to her right.

"The Whittakers recognize Nativity of the Blessed Virgin Mary is very blessed indeed. A truly brilliant and unselfish leader in education has been bestowed upon this school and we are grateful for her ecumenical guidance," she sang. "Without it, our students and faculty would be like lost sheep in search of their protective shepherd."

"Bullshit," I coughed. Mrs. Fitzcracker shot me a questioning look, but I coughed again and she was satisfied she hadn't actually heard me swear.

"Mr. and Mrs. Whittaker, Nicole, your family has been instrumental in improving our school's ability to provide a quality, Catholic education for our children. Without your generous financial support, we would still be without full-length mirrors in the girl's lavatories, a popcorn maker for the faculty, many wonderful statues of the Virgin Mary, beautiful office furniture for our Principal, a healthy bank account and of course, what we are about to unveil today."

As if that crap provides a better education. We haven't gotten new library books since Kindergarten. How about donating the math and science textbooks this dump can't afford? Common sense is no match for cold hard cash.

"Without further ado I give you, "Tribute to Sister Fatass; A Saint in the Making", thundered Miss Butt, as she swept the red velvet from the masterpiece it had been hiding. There were murmurs of approval throughout the crowd as they applauded politely.

Unable to believe my eyes, I read the plaque beneath the bronze bust carving of Sister Hairy Lip that read:

"Tribute to Sister Fatass: A Saint in the Making

It is with great respect and appreciation for

her endless efforts to improve the quality of education

that we dedicate this small token to Sister Carol

on June 3rd, 1978

John, Emily and Nicole Whittaker, benefactors"

Who do they think they're kidding? That monster deserves this dedication about as much as Jack the Ripper deserved the Nobel Peace Prize.

Lying awake night after night, I was consumed by the desire to make

Sister Fatass pay for beating me publically without cause and caring more about money and fame than the well-being of our school. She's a nun, for Christ's sake! How can she whore herself to the Whittakers in exchange for a ridiculous bronze statue? The more I thought about that farcical statue, the more I realized it was the answer to my prayers.

Armed with two black, permanent markers, I went with my parents to Nativity one Monday night to pick up Peter from Boy Scouts. Nervous and excited, I waited for Mom and Dad to start jawing with other parents. With them lost in conversation, I snuck from the basement to the foyer, one floor above. It was dark except for the dim illumination from the street lights filtering through the ancient maples lining the property.

Knowing I didn't have much time, I uncapped a marker and approached the ostentatious bust of Sister Hairy Lip. With a shaking hand and the sound of my heart thundering in my chest, I drew a large mustache on Sister's face, slightly tapered at the edges, to make the bust more lifelike. I took a few steps backward to admire my work and stifled a giggle. It looked good, but needed to be darker to ensure people noticed it from a distance and so it would be nearly impossible to remove. I spent a few moments drawing over the lines under her schnoze to darken them.

I stepped back to take another look. Hmm, something's missing. *Aha!* I returned to the pedestal on which the bust sat and wrote "Jesus Whore" on the forehead.

Satisfied with the results, I turned to run downstairs before anyone noticed my absence but the door to Sister Fatass's office beckoned me. It was a blank canvas begging to be drawn upon.

With only a moment's hesitation, I scribbled all over Sister's light maple wooden door. In letters of varying sizes, I wrote "Jesus Whore" again and again until it was mostly covered. A snort of laughter scared the crap out me and I dropped the marker only to realize I'd been the one from whom the noise had come. I was briefly concerned about my sanity. *I'm no doubt going crazy after seven years in this nut house.*

I wasn't satisfied with my work because it wasn't nasty enough and needed more punch. It had to be something that would kick Sister Hairy Lip in the gut as payback for the misery she'd dished out during my tenure.

In the middle of my masterpiece was an empty space I'd left blank and planned to fill with a drawing of an erect penis. I wasn't sure I could draw one and I knew it didn't really make sense, but Sister would be highly offended by the image of a big dick on her door and that was good enough for me. I wonder if she'd know what it is. I changed my mind and wrote, "Watch your back. Love, Sister Mary Joseph."

Despite repeated changing of the locks on the doors to school, Sister Hairy Lip's door was defiled again and again over the next several years and the bust was removed. Through church gossip, I learned she became nervous and paranoid, jumping in fear when anyone walked up behind her. Perhaps the threatening notes she received from Sister Mary Joseph, formed by letters cut out of newspapers and magazines glued onto notebook paper were beginning to rattle her nerves. Maybe the nasty messages written on her car windshield were becoming too much for the old bat to handle.

Whatever the reason for her increased nervous behavior, it never bothered me and I never felt obligated to mention it during Confession. Jesus Whores sometimes get what they deserve. .

12 A CATHOLIC VACATION

Michelle and I told everyone at school we were cousins, but in truth, her Dad and mine were only childhood friends. Her parents were old fashioned, boring farmers like mine and we commiserated about the dreary, unfair life of a farmer's daughter. Michelle understood what it was like to live in the middle of nowhere and have unexciting, staunchly Catholic parents who never went on vacation to Disney or the Grand Canyon. My parents' idea of a vacation was an annual five-day stint in Quebec, staying with Dad's drunk, Irish cousins. Who buys that T-shirt?

Friends only at school, we'd never even been to each other's houses so it was completely unexpected when she invited me to their cottage on Lake Pleasant for two weeks. I thought I'd won the lottery. *Two weeks off the farm and on the water? Sign me up.* I imagined lounging on a raft in a string bikini with hot boys drooling all around me. *Oh yeah. I don't own a string bikini because I'm a chubby farm kid and the only boy who drools around me is my dog, Rex.*

The first glimpse of what lay in store came when Michelle's parents, whom I called aunt and uncle, announced we had to pray five Rosaries on the way to the lake. Allow me to clarify. Not five Hail Mary's but five complete Rosaries. The Rosary has fifty-three Hail Mary's, in addition to Our Father's and other prayers. *Do these people honestly expect us to recite five entire Rosaries? Are they nuts?*

As I questioned my decision to vacation with these weirdos, Michelle's parents told us to ride in the back of their cab-covered pickup truck. *Perfect, they won't be able hear us back there.*

"Michelle," I said, "we'll turn our backs to the window between the cab and the bed. Your parents won't know if we're praying or swearing. Problem solved!"

"Um, Theresa Marie is sitting with us," she informed me, rather sadly. *Aw crap, that kid's mouth is even bigger than my ass.* We prayed for hours on end.

The first few days at the lake were consumed with cleaning. *Huh? Cleaning?* The cottage hadn't been used since they closed it up the previous fall, so I had the privilege of sweeping out seven months of dust and cob webs, while Aunt Lillian prayed out loud all day long. Michelle had to help my uncle put in the floating dock and repair window screens.

The cottage had only one bathroom, and I was warned about using it before we'd even left Michelle's driveway. "Pat, don't use a lot of toilet paper because the toilet won't flush," warned my aunt. "If you can't clean yourself with just a couple squares of paper, you need to wash off in the lake."

Stop the presses! Was this woman telling me if I took a massive dump requiring a lot of toilet paper, I was supposed to trot down to the lake to finish cleaning the shit out of my crack? In the same water I planned to be splashing and diving for the next two weeks? I decided if I caught anyone washing their shitty ass in the lake, I'd shove a sliver-laden canoe paddle up it.

Meal time at the lake became something to dread and when you consider how much I liked to eat, that's really saying something. Holding hands with those next to us, we each had to say an impromptu prayer, out loud and proud. After several minutes of hand holding and listening to my hungry belly grumble, we raised our hands skyward and shouted out a thundering "Amen!" *I'm stuck in a nut house.*

With several days of cleaning and repairing behind us, Michelle and I were allowed to take out the ancient, banged up rowboat. "You girls take Theresa Marie with you, and no monkey business," warned my aunt in between Hail Mary's.

I knew if that little brat came with us, I'd end up drowning her. *I just spent three days cleaning your freaking house and now you're gonna make me take that little shit-stain with me on the water? Have we arrived in Hell?* As we were about to push off the dock, I said, "Hey kid, go grab some pretzels or something in case we get hungry." The minute Theresa Marie was out of sight, I rowed as fast as possible, leaving her stranded in The House of Perpetual Prayer.

Michelle and I rowed the perimeter of the lake, taking turns with the oars. When not discussing boys, we sang the theme song to *The Dukes of Hazzard*, love songs by Kenny Rogers and a few of John Denver's more upbeat tunes. Warm sun on my shoulders, a light breeze in the air and a few precious hours without prayer made me very happy. Although I didn't like cleaning in prayer for three days straight, the freedom we had at that moment surrounded by the beauty of the quiet mountain lake made it all worthwhile.

Rounding a bend, we almost ran into another boat with three passengers. They were boys. Shirtless, tanned boys. *Oh my.*

Michelle's parents were even more protective than mine and the only boys she'd been exposed to were Jesus and His merry gang of do-gooders. At least I could brag about having kissed someone of the opposite sex. My pretend cousin didn't need to know it was just a quick peck from a Boy Scout with ass breath. I told her Jacob and I made out all the time and I let him feel me up. Michelle was very impressed and considered me as experienced and worldly as Valerie Bertinelli in *One Day At A Time.*

As we approached the rowboat of half naked boys, Michelle started to giggle. I knew she was nervous but she acted mildly retarded and I didn't want her to embarrass me. Hatching a half-baked scheme to get their attention, I quickly said, "Let's swamp the rowboat and pretend we're drowning. When the guys jump in to rescue us, pretend you're unconscious so they'll give us mouth-to-mouth." Michelle shook her head violently from side to side, seemingly unhappy with my brilliant idea. "Listen to me!" I said urgently. "As soon as they put their mouths over ours, we start making out." *What would she do without me?*

Michelle didn't like my ingenious idea but I didn't give her much choice. Standing up and leaning to one side, I tipped the canoe and over we went. I gurgled and bobbed, arms out of the water and over my head, while Michelle floated on her stomach like a dead person. The boys looked at us like we were stupid until one of them decided we might actually need help. He unhooked the oar from its holder and passed it over my head for me to grab. Unfortunately, his aim sucked and he nailed me in the eye. At that point, I really was in distress. I couldn't see and the pain was like none I'd ever experienced. Michelle continued to play dead, oblivious to my injury. *If I could see out of this goddamned eye, I'd drown her!*

The boy who hadn't maimed me jumped in and swam to Michelle. When he discovered she was fine, I thought he might drown her anyway. "What the fuck is wrong with you?" he asked, doing a piss-poor job disguising his irritation.

"It wasn't my idea," Michelle said, almost too softly to be heard.

"Will somebody please help me? I'm blind for Christ's sake!" Together, the boys heaved my fat ass into our rowboat and did the same for Michelle. Watching them row away, shaking their heads in disgust, I knew we'd blown the only chance we'd have to get kissed on this shitty religious holiday. I almost didn't care if I ever got kissed again, because I was sure I'd lose my eye. Who wants to kiss a girl with only one eye? *I'll probably wind up being a nun because I'll be too ugly for anything else. At this rate, I'll probably grow a mustache by morning.*

Rowing back home, Michelle tried to concoct a story to tell her parents about how I'd been injured. We couldn't tell them we were trying to get rescued by strange boys when I took an oar in the eye, they'd kill us. I didn't care what the hell we told them, as long as they could repair my eye.

Inspecting my maimed peeper, Uncle Chuck said, "Holy shit!" *What? This coming from Mr. Prayer Hound? It must be bad.* "How did this happen?" he wanted to know.

Michelle mumbled some bullshit about a loon that landed on her head and she whacked at it with an oar, but hit me by mistake. Oddly enough, her parents didn't buy it. *What a moron.* I told the prayer-crazy whack jobs exactly what happened and said it was my idea. I didn't care what they did to me, I just wanted something to stop the pain.

After what seemed like hours of answering the same stupid questions over and over, I convinced my uncle I needed medical treatment. We rode the entire ninety minutes to the emergency room in awkward silence but at least we weren't praying.

Announcing I had a nasty scratch on my cornea, the doctor said I had to wear an eye patch and apply some sort of ointment for a week. When he mentioned the word "patch" I pictured the black, pirate kind with an elastic band to go around my head. *Cool, that's not so bad.* Instead, he applied a large white square of gauze secured with medical tape. *Sexy.*

Back at the cottage, my aunt and uncle informed me I'd be punished for being promiscuous. *Promiscuous? Does that mean horny?* The entire family participated in an hour long prayer session, asking God's forgiveness for my evil sins. During the second hour, we prayed God would protect Michelle and prevent her from being influenced by my disgusting, boy-crazy behavior. *I'll never complain about my parents again.*

The day kept getting better. Following the prayer marathon, Uncle

Chuck said, "To help you realize the gravity of your sins, your aunt and I have decided to restrict you to the spare bedroom for the rest of vacation." *Anything is better than participating in your ridiculous Jesus freak show. He probably wishes He'd never created you.*

I was sentenced to spend the remainder of the two weeks alone in a bedroom, curtains drawn. My companions were limited. There was a single bed, an ancient dresser with one drawer missing, a Bible, several daddy-long-leg spiders and a window facing the now-forbidden lake. Allowed to leave for bathroom breaks only, I dined alone on the meals delivered by my aunt.

Watching from my window as the moon shone on the still and quiet lake, I felt like a prisoner held captive in a castle tower by the enemy. *I need to escape.* Looking down, I decided I could probably jump without breaking any bones, but then what? We were hundreds of miles from home and I didn't know how far it was to the nearest town. *I'll figure it out later.*

Barely able to squeeze my generously-sized backside through the window frame, I said a silent prayer that God liked me better than the crazies I was leaving behind and jumped. Hitting the ground hard and grunting in pain, I realized I'd never make it as a ninja. Scared my less-than graceful jump and resulting groans may have wakened my aunt and uncle, I raced down the driveway toward the desolate, mountain lake road. *I hope there aren't any hungry coyotes or bears wandering around in search of a two-legged meal.*

Realizing I lacked any sort of plan and afraid of being eaten by some sort of nocturnal beast, I decided to ask for help. The lakefront was full of cabins and cottages, surely I could find someone willing to help me escape the House of Crazies. I decided not to approach any cabins in the vicinity of my aunt and uncle's cottage, in case the Sickness of Perpetual Prayer was contagious. I needed to find normal people.

I found a rustic but homey cabin, lights on, about a mile from Michelle's cottage. A few bikes left in the front yard among some faded Adirondack chairs and a chaise lounge suggested normal people lived there. The dark woods to my right provided all the encouragement I needed to head for the cabin and knock loudly on the door. My heart sank as my brain registered the "Jesus Lives Here" sign, hanging crookedly above the door. *If whoever answers the door looks religious, I'll pretend I'm selling Girl Scout cookies.*

The man who opened the door, revealing a comfy, nicely furnished home, looked normal enough. His wife sat in a recliner watching TV and eating popcorn. *That's a good sign. The Jesus Freaks don't have a TV.*

"May I help you?" asked the man I hoped would be my savior.

"Yes, please!" *Now what?* "Um, I'm staying with my aunt and uncle in a cottage down the road. They've gone crazy and tried holding me captive." I was afraid they'd think I was a bit crazy because I was nearly shouting, and despite efforts to keep calm, I spoke too quickly. "Can I please use your phone to call my parents?"

From inside I heard the woman say, "Let her in, Dick. She sounds scared to death."

Thank God.

Good 'ole Dick motioned me in and closed the door behind me. *Uh oh.* There was a life-sized painting of Jesus on the wall. "Actually, you know what? It's okay. I don't wanna bother you," I said, reaching for the door.

"Nonsense," said Bob, turning the bolt. "We'd be terrible people to let you wander around in the dark all alone. Don't worry about bothering us, we're just watching Jesus of Nazareth. It's our favorite movie because it's six full hours of Christ!"

What's next? Locusts?

"Now tell us, honey, in what way did your aunt and uncle go crazy? Are they drunks?" asked Bob's wife, taking in my auburn hair, fair skin and freckles. "Are they Irish?"

"No, they don't drink. They're, well, they're very strict and, well, they...," I stammered, unsure what to say. "They beat me," I said, unaware the words were forming in my mouth until I heard them hit my ears.

"They did? How awful!" sympathized Mrs. Dick. "You poor dear. Good thing Dick's a policeman. He'll handle this, won't you, honey?"

Holy Shit. I can't win. "Oh, thanks, but I don't wanna *do* anything about it. I just want to call my parents. May I please use your phone?" I asked, looking around for anything that would serve as a telephone. I'd have settled for some string and a tin can.

"Oh, we don't have a phone," said Dick. "We find it disrupts prayer far too often."

You gotta be kidding me? A cop without a phone? Even Barney Fife had a fucking phone. "Okay, well, thanks anyway. I'll just be going," I said, turning toward the bolted door.

"I'm afraid we can't let you do that," announced 'ole Dick, hands on hips. "I can't let an unsupervised minor wander around in the dark. You'd just be asking for trouble. I'll take you home," he said, grabbing a set of keys from a rack on the wall shaped like Noah's Ark.

"You will?" I asked, incredulously. "Are you serious?"

"Of course. I'd want a trustworthy person to make sure my daughter got home safely. I'll be home soon, honey," said Dick, unlocking the door.

Soon? I don't think so, Dick. I live hours from here. "Well, goodbye. Nice meeting you," I said, realizing I never caught her name. She waved absently, entranced by the Jesus movie.

Dick opened the passenger door to the Blazer parked in the drive and I hopped in, allowing him to close the door. He walked around the front of the truck and climbed in. "Okay, let's get you home," he said, bringing the engine to life.

"This is so nice of you. I really do appreciate it," I said, honestly.

"Oh, it's nothing. Now, which cottage is yours?" he asked, flicking on the high beams.

"What? I'm not going back there! I thought you were taking me home!" I said, knowing I sounded nasty but unable to mask my anger. "There's no way in hell I'm going back to that nut house!"

"You will refrain from using profanity in my presence, Miss!"

"Oh, my God! You've gotta be shittin' me! Let me out of this kook mobile! What the hell is wrong with this lake? You're all freaking crazy!"

"That's enough!" shouted Dick, bringing the Blazer to a halt. "Not only do you have a filthy mouth, you've taken our Lord's name in vain! If this is how you've behaved, it's no wonder your aunt and uncle became physical! You need a good beating!"

Folding my arms across my chest, I stared out the windshield silently cursing Dick.

"If you don't tell me which is theirs, I'll drag you to the front door of every cottage until someone recognizes you. Don't think I won't, demon!" said Dick, spittle flying.

Did he just call me 'demon'? This dude's even crazier than Michelle's parents. Unable to come up with a better solution, I directed him to the House of Perpetual Prayer and braced myself for the tirade I knew waited there.

As Dick opened his door I told him, "You don't need to walk with me. I can take it from here. Thanks for nothing!" I said, slamming the passenger side door. I instantly regretted my words.

"Oh, I'm coming with you, Missy. Your aunt and uncle are about to get an ear full," said Dick, hitching up his pants and rearranging whatever was causing discomfort between his bowlegs.

"Don't bother. I'm in deep enough shit without your help!" I snapped, disgusted by the guy's crotch grabbing.

Ignoring my request, Dick got out of the truck and walked me to the doorway to Hell. Not bothering to knock, I opened the door and walked in knowing the next several days would be horrendous. Expecting to find my aunt and uncle fervently praying the Rosary, my heart threatened to seize as my eyes took in the unholy scene unfolding in the kitchen.

Uncle Chuck was dressed in priestly garb and his eyes were masked with something reminiscent of what Zorro wore. My naked aunt was bent over the kitchen table, her sickeningly white skin stark against the dark wood. "Repent, sinner!" barked my uncle, shoving a wooden crucifix into my aunt's exposed behind.

"What in tarnation?" Dick's yelp of disgusted disbelief yanked me out of my sex-induced stupor. I'd completely forgotten he was there because my aunt and uncle's disturbing behavior had nearly put me in a coma.

Aunt Lillian dropped to the floor and crouched behind her priest, I mean husband. I thought I heard her make a guttural, whining sound but I didn't trust anything my senses were telling my brain. Uncle Chuck ripped of his mask and hollered, "How dare you sneak up on us!"

"You sick bastard!" howled Dick. "How dare you impersonate a holy man of the cloth while engaging in such...filth! No wonder this girl is trashy! I should arrest you here and now!"

Seeing my aunt and uncle in a new light, I realized I had the upper hand. They were visibly shaken, disgraced because their repulsive sexual behavior had been exposed. "Unless you remove any restrictions on my behavior and let me say and do whatever I want until we go home, I'll tell everyone what I just saw!"

Aunt Lillian grabbed a blanket off the back of the davenport, covered her repulsive flesh and ran to her bedroom. Uncle Chuck was a changed man. Reduced to tears, he begged my forgiveness and promised to do anything I asked in exchange for my vow of silence. Turning to Dick, who still shook with rage, I said, "I guess your work here is done, Dick."

"You people are on the fast track to Hell!" assessed ole Dick, making the sign of the cross as he walked out the door, not bothering to close it behind him.

"I'm hungry, Uncle Chuck. I'd like a big, fat juicy steak. Rare," I said, wearing a vindictive smile. The next several days were wonderful. I ate when I was hungry, lay in the sun and played in the lake without one word of interruption from Michelle's parents. The House of Perpetual Prayer morphed into one in which the adults worked overtime to make me happy and keep me comfortable to buy my silence.

"I can't believe how lucky you are!" exclaimed Michelle. "I don't know what you did to my parents, but I wish they'd act like this all the time."

"I can help you with that," I said. Michelle looked at me quizzically. "The next time your parents jump on the Jesus Train or act overly protective, all you need to do is say one magical phrase."

"Yeah, what's that?"

"A crucifix is a pain in the butt," I said, laughing at my endless wit.

"That doesn't make any sense," said Michelle, shaking her head. "That won't work. You know how my parents feel about the crucifix."

"You bet your ass I do!" I howled, tears running down my face.

13 GOODBYE NATIVITY OF THE BLESSED VIRGIN MARY

After seven years of a mostly hellacious experience, except for Sister Mary Margaret and Miss Redman, I graduated from Nativity and was on my way to public Middle School. Gone were the tedious days of Catholic indoctrination. No more would I be forced to accept religious beliefs that didn't make sense. Free to wear jeans and sneakers instead of skirts and dress shoes, I could wear my John Schneider T-shirt and chew gum in class. The most exciting and appealing aspect of public school was the lack of brutal, mustached nuns.

Entering the three-story, red brick building on my first day of seventh grade, I realized I was up the proverbial creek and there wasn't a flipping paddle in sight. Nativity had a total of seven classrooms in the entire school and my new one appeared to have at least twenty in the main hall. I panicked.

With schedule and locker assignment in hand, I set off in search of what would serve as my home base for the next year. Several minutes later, a bell sounded and the halls emptied. *Am I the only moron who can't find their freakin' locker?* I was still searching for it when another bell rang, signaling the end of homeroom. About ten minutes into first period, I found the goddamned thing and gave it a good, hard kick for being so elusive. Unfortunately, it took me another ten minutes to figure out the goddamned combination. I still have nightmares about roaming those halls, searching for a non-existent locker.

I was happily reunited with Barbara Ann and thrilled to discover we were in the same English class. To start the year, we began reading Johnny Tremain, a novel set in Boston during the time of the American Revolution. To alleviate the boredom of reading a novel out loud with a class of thirty students, some of whom couldn't read at the fourth grade level, Barbara Ann and I wrote our own chapters of the book.

In our collaborations, Johnny was almost always whacking his meat or sticking things up his ass. After getting busted by Mrs. Brickster for disrupting her class too often with loud outbursts of laughter, some of our classmates wanted to know what we were doing. We were an instant success and within days, everyone wanted to read our chapters of Johnny Tremain. Our work was in such high demand, Barbara Ann and I snuck into the teacher's copy room. We couldn't produce them fast enough the old fashioned, hand-written way.

We'd make lousy Navy Seals, because within a few seconds, the Vice Principal walked in behind us. "May I help you with something?" asked Mr. Highland.

"Umm...no thanks. We're fine," I said, turning away, hoping he'd wander off and mind his own business.

"What exactly are you doing in here?" He was persistent.

"Making copies," Barbara Ann said, pointing out the obvious.

"Well, I can see that. What are you making copies of?"

Man, this guy is nosey. Obviously, being a Vice Principal is one of the easiest jobs on the planet, because you have a lot of time to loiter around the copy room asking obnoxious questions. "Um, it's something for Mrs. Brickster's class," I stammered. It was almost true.

"So, you're telling me Mrs. Brickster asked you two to make copies for her?"

"Yep," I lied, wearing a sweet, angelic smile. I guess what Miss Butt said about sinning getting easier when you don't go to Confession was true, because I'd managed to avoid entering a Confessional for a couple of months and found it very easy to lie to Mr. Highland's face.

"I see. So, you won't mind if I take a look at what you're copying then, right?" he asked, eyebrows sky high.

Oh shit. Go find something to do! "You can't look at it because it's a secret project no one can see until it's finished," I lied again, without a hint of Catholic Guilt.

"Well, if it's such a big secret and no one can see it, then why are you making..." he leaned over to look at the display window on the copier, "fifty copies?"

Damn fine question, Baldy. Please go find something else to do.

"It's a long story, Mr. Highland, and we're gonna be late to math if we don't hurry," replied Barbara Ann, which I thought was very well played.

"I can write you a late pass. Answer the question." Barbara Ann and I stood with our backs to the copier, trying to block Mr. Highland's view. Neither of us said a word. "Step aside please, ladies." We were glued to the floor and didn't move. "I repeat. Step aside!" he barked.

We looked at each other and stepped out of Mr. Highland's way. Pressing the stop button, he picked up a few of the pages sitting on the dispensing tray and began to read. I was sweating. Apparently, Mr. Highland got the gist after a paragraph or two, because he didn't read for more than a few seconds. Collecting the rest of the papers in the copier, he told us to follow him to his office.

Mr. Highland gestured us into his palatial office and invited us to sit in the two, stuffed chairs facing his desk, which was so large it could have doubled as a barge. I did a quick scan of all four walls. No paddle.

That's a relief.

"I'm very disturbed by what I read on these pages, very disturbed. Explain yourselves," he said, arms on desk and hands folded.

"My brother, Scott, gave them to me yesterday and told me if I didn't make fifty copies, he'd drown my dog."

Who said that? Another lie had flown out of my mouth before I had a chance to see it coming. Barbara Ann whipped her head around to look at me, which wasn't helping Mr. Highland buy into my bullshit. I cut my eyes at her until she looked down at her lap.

"So, the words on these pages were written by Scott? They aren't yours?" he asked, rather suspiciously.

"Right." I thought he might actually buy the bird-brained story.

"I remember Scott only too well. He was a trouble maker with a mouth like a truck driver. It doesn't surprise me one bit he'd be in possession of this type of filth," said Mr. Highland, speaking more to himself than us.

No shit. He's actually buying this crap. What a dufus this guy must be!

"You go home and tell Scott I'm on to his game. Tell him if he touches one hair on your dog's head – or your own for that matter – I'll call the police. Is that clear?"

"Yes, Mr. Highland, it is. Thank you for helping me," I said, in the most deflated and brow-beaten tone I could muster.

"You girls may go now. I'm sorry you were put in this situation. If this trash is any indication, Scott needs to be put away for some serious mental help. Only a very sick and twisted individual could come up with this sort of heinous material."

Everyone's a critic.

Later that afternoon I became a woman, at least in the biological sense. I got my period. You know, that thing my mother never talked about? The thing I had to read about in Are You There God, It's Me, Margaret? The only sex talk I had with my Mom was on the way home from Seymour Library on an exceptionally hot and humid day. I checked out a couple Judy Blume books and apparently, that was my Mom's cue to begin a dialogue about sex or at least elude to the fact there might be something about sex we should probably consider discussing.

"I see you have some Judy Blume books there," she observed as we drove past Larry's Garage, a car repair joint about half a mile from the farm.

"Yep."

"Well, do you have any questions about anything? Because if you do, you know you can ask me, right?" she said in a softer tone than usual.

I have all kinds of questions! What does a full grown dick look like? With hair? What are guys balls for? When will my boobs show up? What's a blow job? "I don't have any questions," I lied.

My Mom had already demonstrated how willing she was to talk about topics she found uncomfortable when she told me to use Vaseline because my vagina was sore from my brother's sexual abuse. I was pretty sure asking her about dicks, balls and blow jobs wouldn't be any more successful.

I did what most kids did for sexual education. I listened to the talk at the back of the school bus and learned a wealth of knowledge on number 66. None of it was accurate, but it gave me loads of great stuff to talk about with my friends. I felt like Dr. Ruth Westheimer as I explained in order to give a blow job, you lick the pecker like it's a lollipop and blow on it until your spit dries.

After reading all the Judy Blume books our library had, I thought I was prepared for the arrival of my period. I was wrong. Sitting in Science class wearing white jeans, I noticed my underwear felt pretty moist. I didn't panic right away. A few minutes later, I felt an uncomfortable amount of moisture drip out, and that's when I panicked. *Oh shit. Should I get up and go to the bathroom? What if there's blood leaking through? I should have remained a boy!*

The bell rang almost forty minutes later and I pretended to have difficulty closing my three-ring binder. As soon as the room emptied out I stood and looked at the seat of my chair. Seeing a river of blood accumulated in its grooves, I immediately sat back down. Looking behind my chair and down at the tile floor, I was mortified by the droplets of blood dripping from my seat to the floor below, resembling water dripping from a melting icicle.

"Is something wrong?" asked Mrs. Kimble, who was so thin you could count her ribs through her blouse. "Don't you have somewhere to go?"

"Um…" I tried not to cry. The next class would be coming in any minute and then what? I couldn't stand up and let them see my bloody jeans but I couldn't just sit there all day either. *I can't tell this woman I just got my period! She'll probably yell "Gross!" and run out into the hallway shouting "Patti Anne just bled all over my classroom!"* I sat there like an idiot, not talking, not moving, just dripping.

"Young Lady!" she said, as she walked toward my desk. Her gaze moved from my face to the floor behind my chair. "What on earth? Gadzuks! What have you done? You dirty little monster! Get out of my classroom right now!"

Why is this crazy woman yelling at me and calling me dirty? Does she think I purposely conjured a blood fountain so I could embarrass the shit out of myself? What a fucking moron!

"Get OUT!" she screamed again.

Grabbing my binder, I jumped up and ran past her desk on my way to the door and, out of desperation, snatched the sweater hanging on her chair. Too busy glaring at the mess I'd made, she failed to notice I'd stolen her one-of-a-kind, hand knitted sweater. As soon as I got to the hall, I wrapped it snugly around my waist, covering my crimson-stained pants and wished it could cloak my embarrassment as easily. Choking back tears, I headed for the nurse's office.

Walking through the open door, I saw an eighth grade social studies teacher talking with Miss Bates, the school nurse. Mr. John Loden was from Great Britain and his accent sent shivers down my spine. I wanted him to tutor me privately. Standing in the doorway, I watched him talk and laugh with Miss Bates. She was a bimbo with a face that could make a freight train take a dirt road, but she had enormous knockers. It was obvious Mr. Loden wasn't looking her in the eye while they spoke. His neck and head were actually bent so as to get closer to those monsters. Miss Bates acted like she didn't notice and laughed louder as she stuck her boobs out farther. It made me and my 32 AAs wanna puke.

They finally noticed me. "Yes? Can I help you?" asked Miss Monster Boobs.

"Um...no. Not really." *Brilliant.*

Mr. Loden and Miss Bates looked at me standing in the doorway wearing an ugly, old lady sweater around my waist. They looked at each other for a moment and then back at me. "Where are you supposed to be?" asked Mr. Loden.

"Math."

"Well then, you'd better go. The bell has sounded and class has commenced," said Mr. Loden in a way no one else could.

"I – I can't," I stammered.

"Why?" he asked.

"I can't tell you." *Why hasn't one of you dumb shits figured this out? A teenage girl, almost in tears, wearing a bulky sweater around her waist is standing at the door to the nurse's office and she's unable to tell you what's wrong. Hello? Did either of you go through puberty?*

Finally, Boobie said, "Ohhhhh," like only a dumb blond can, "I think I get it." Looking at Mr. Loden, she actually said these words out loud. "I bet she's men-stu-rating!" Spoken as three, separate and distinct words, Boobie sounded as if she'd just discovered a cure for cancer.

My face and ears burned with embarrassment. I wanted to crawl in a very large hole and die quickly. Looking at me like I had leprosy, Mr. Loden was obviously anxious to get away but I blocked the door. *He probably doesn't wanna get too close 'cuz I might drip on his penny loafers.* I was pissed at them for making the ordeal harder than it had to be, so I didn't budge from the door. *Let Mr. Loden stand there feeling uncomfortable. Let's see how he likes it.*

"Well, then. Do you prefer a tampon or a maxi pad?" asked Blondie.

This isn't the cafeteria, you moron! I'm not ordering lunch.

"I must trot off. Um...well then," said a very uncomfortable Mr. Loden.

"Gee, it was really great sharing this moment with you, Mr. Loden," I said, "I'll never forget it."

"Lovely." It was Mr. Loden's turn to blush. He disappeared and left me with the large breasted, brainless wonder.

"Do you want me to show you how to insert a tampon?" she asked, sounding quite hopeful.

"Um, no thanks. Can I call my Mom to come get me? I can't walk around in these jeans all day."

Mom didn't answer so I called my Godmother. She answered on the second ring. "Hi, Aunt Elizabeth, it's Patti Anne. Will you please pick me up at school and take me home?"

"Ach, what'd ye do?"

"I'm not in trouble. I'm – I'm sick," I stammered.

"Well, I don't want yer germs! Where's that arse weed of a mother of yers?"

"I don't know. She didn't answer the phone. Please, Aunt Elizabeth? I just need to go home."

"Ach, all right. Let me find a hat and I'll be off."

The old Buick haphazardly made the turn into the half moon drive in front of school. Thankfully, there weren't any school buses around because Aunt Elizabeth came barreling in the exit. Slamming on the breaks, she skidded the old tank to a halt. Elizabeth knew only two speeds while driving; heavy on the gas pedal or standing on the break. It often made for a very nauseating ride to which I'd never grown accustomed.

Sliding into the passenger seat, I said, "Thanks so much, Aunt Elizabeth. I couldn't wait to get the hell outta there!"

"Aye, and now we're grown, are we? Swearin' like ye know how. Ye don't look sick to these peepers," she said, slamming on the gas pedal. We drove on the grass as she took the curved drive at break-neck speed. I grabbed the Jesus handle above my door and held on tightly.

"I'm not technically sick," I said. Before I could continue, my Godmother slammed on the breaks, making me hit my head on the dash. "Ouch! For Christ's sake, Elizabeth!" I bellowed.

Holding my forehead in my hands, I felt my demonstrative, quick-to-anger aunt slap the back of my head. "Ouch! What was that for?"

"First ye lie to me, tellin' me that yer sick when yer not! Then ye take Our Lord's name in vain! To top that, yer callin' by me first name? Shit flies high when it's hit with a stick!"

My Godmother's face was red and I didn't think it was from her flask. She accused me of being uppity and pretentious because I didn't call her "Aunt." *Sorry, but you almost broke my head open on your freaking dashboard.*

"I'm sorry, Aunt Elizabeth, I wasn't trying to be uppity or rude. I'm not technically sick but I, um, I got my, well, my period. Okay? I got my period in school and bled all over my chair! And rather than help me, my teacher yelled and called me dirty!" The color of my face matched my aunt's, freckles and all.

"Away on tha!" she said, waving her hand in disbelief.

"It's true! Mrs. Kimble called me dirty and yelled at me as if I could magically stop the blood from pouring out!"

Aunt Elizabeth was my Godmother and dutifully fulfilled her God-given responsibility to slap, criticize and correct me as she saw fit but she was fiercely protective. Without warning, she threw the old car in reverse and weaved between the mowed lawn and the paved circle drive, not bothering to use her rearview or side mirrors. She didn't brake until the back end was firmly on the sidewalk.

"Stay here, love. I won't be a minute," she said, pulling one of her favorite, garishly decorated hats over her unruly red hair. Walking through the front door, Elizabeth yanked her dress out of her bum and disappeared from sight.

Images of my well-intentioned aunt forcing her way into the Principal's office and demanding justice flooded my mind. My gut told me whoever was on the receiving end of her tirade was going to wish they'd called in sick. *At least she's not drunk.*

Fifteen minutes later, wearing the look of vindication, my Godmother marched out of school and to the car. Removing her remarkable hat, she slipped behind the wheel and placed the hideous thing carefully on the back seat. She reached into her purse, which was large enough to carry an eight pound corned beef, and pulled out a flask. *Here we go.* Tipping her head back against the head rest, my aunt took the first of many swigs.

"Just a wee bit of reward for me hard work," she explained, as I looked at my watch and then at her. "It's never too early to pat yerself on the back."

"What happened in there?"

"Ach, I had words with that numpty, Mrs. Kimble, because the Principal was nowhere to be found. She could chew an apple through a tennis racket! Never saw sech a set of choppers a person in all me puff," said Elizabeth, shaking her head at the image of my teacher's enormous, crooked teeth.

I should tell her Mrs. Kimble's married to a dentist, that would really give her something to rage about. "What did you say if you don't mind me asking?" I said, as politely as possible. *I've gotta hear this.*

"Well, with a face like a bulldog chewing on a wasp, I didn't wanna get too close to her, but I did anyway because she needed a powerful ear-full. Told her I'd bust her on the gob the next time she's rude or unkind to me wee doll," explained Elizabeth, patting her flask. Whenever she used that term of affection, it instantly warmed my heart. After another generous mouthful, she continued. "I'd a left it right there, too, but she had to start."

"Uh oh, what'd she do?"

"Tha no good hoor called me a drunk, she did. A drunk! Those front teeth a hers won't be givin' her no more trouble. I did her the kind favor of knockin' 'em outta her dial! She's so ugly now, not even the tide will take her out," Elizabeth said, with a big nod.

"Oh, my God, Aunt Elizabeth! You mean you knocked her teeth out?" *Holy shit, I'm gonna be kicked out of school.*

"Aye, hope the eejit likes soft food," she said, taking another pull from her almost-empty flask, "because she won't be eatin' nothin' requiring teeth! Now, what say we take ye to my house, run a hot bath and make a cuppa tea? You're a woman now, so there's a lot to be tellin' ye."

Oh shit, I can hardly wait. This ought to be good.

14 SHARP LESSONS

As far back as I could remember the Sharp Family was part of the Nativity Church fabric. The boys served on the altar, although they were much older than my brothers, and Mrs. Sharp led the Folk Group at ten o'clock Mass. Her husband did scripture readings and served as a Eucharistic Minister, handing out the holy wafer during Communion. My earliest church memories include the Sharp's, especially their son Stephen.

He was ten years my senior and although I was only thirteen when I realized I loved him, I didn't mind the age difference. In fact I liked it because it felt inappropriate and most likely, something the Church would frown upon. I knew that someday I would marry the boy.

Stephen was a volunteer firefighter, which I found ridiculously sexy. To make a buck, he managed the local roller skating rink, which provided the perfect venue for him to take my virginity. A naive farm kid without exposure to anything outside my little town, I had no way of knowing a volunteer firefighter who managed a skating rink was probably a total loser.

Stephen's Dad died rather tragically, leaving Mrs. Sharp to raise ten children. She began giving piano and voice lessons to help make ends meet. I didn't want to play piano, but convinced my parents otherwise because I needed an excuse to get inside the Sharp's house. Although he was twenty-three years old, Stephen still lived with his mom and siblings. That should have been a clue. I prayed for his decrepit mother to fall asleep during a lesson, so I could sneak upstairs to find Stephen's room. When I did, I planned to force myself on him.

After enduring four of five months of scales and such, during which I failed to develop any musical ability, Mrs. Sharp slipped off into a tea-induced coma and began to snore. Removing my fingers from the keyboard, I waited a few moments to make sure she didn't stir. Swinging my legs over the bench, careful not to let it creak and wake my instructor, I tiptoed to the staircase with my heart pounding loudly.

At the first landing, I listened carefully for movement above and below. Except for the sounds of three or four of Stephen's brothers playing basketball in the driveway, I heard nothing. The house seemed quiet, as if listening to my unwelcomed and unapproved wanderings through the family's private living spaces. I climbed to the next landing and walked by a bathroom and a couple bedrooms, doors ajar and thankfully empty. *If I run into one of Stephen's brothers or sisters, I'll tell them I'm looking for the bathroom...even though there's one in plain sight of the old Steinway.*

I heard music, muffled and low, which sounded a bit like the Bee Gee's. *Bingo. Stephen loves those douche bags.* I continued down the hall until I found the source of the offensive noise. The door was closed but there was no doubt, Barry Gibb was singing his heart out on the other side. Taking a deep breath and not bothering to knock, I turned the door knob and opened the door.

Holy Mother of God! Stephen's pants were around his ankles and he was yanking on his dick while looking lovingly at a poster of Dorothy Hamill. As he jerked off, he sang ,"How Deep Is Your Love."

Wow! This is definitely not what I expected!

Stephen stopped in mid-stroke, screamed like a frightened girl and hobbled with his pants still around his ankles to his bathroom and slammed the door.

"What the hell are you doing in here?" he demanded to know.

"I could ask you the same thing but it's pretty clear. Dorothy Hamill? You're hot for Dorothy Hamill?" I asked, through my laughter.

"Get out! Get out!" he screamed.

"You don't have to be so touchy, ya know. Get it?" *I'm a regular fucking Richard Pryor.*

I was in the throes of hysterical fits of laughter and fell to the floor, holding my gut. It was all very funny until I realized Mrs. Sharp was standing in the door to Stephen's bedroom. The look on her face told me she didn't share my tremendous sense of humor. *She's never been a funny woman.*

"I'd really like to hear your explanation for being in my son's bedroom," she said.

"You would?" I asked, stalling. She didn't answer but continued to glare at me, threatening to drill holes through my soul with her Catholic dagger eyes.

"Mommy, she walked in while I was undressing! Get her out of here!"

Did he just say 'Mommy'? I may have to rethink this marriage.

"Is that so? Aren't you a dirty little bird? Get downstairs this very minute, wait for me on the piano bench and don't you dare move another muscle," Mrs. Sharp hissed through clenched teeth.

I stood, hung my head and walked downstairs. I knew I was in deep shit but I couldn't stop giggling. *Stephen whacks off to Dorothy Hamill while singing Bee Gee's songs! At the ripe old age of twenty-three, he still says 'Mommy'. It's all too much.* When Mrs. Sharp joined me at the piano, I was still snorting with laughter but she was all business.

"This is no laughing matter, young lady. I can't tell you how disappointed I am in your behavior! I've known you since the day you were born, and I know for a fact your devoted parents raised you better than this!" she said, sending a spray of spittle through her dentures. "Your poor father will be crushed when he hears about your behavior."

What? You're telling on me? "What are you gonna tell my parents?"

"It's not so funny now is it, little miss comedian? I'm going to tell them the truth," she said, digging in her sweater for a hankie with which to wipe her perpetually drippy nose.

She doesn't know the truth. There's no way Stephen told 'Mommy' about me walking in as he spanked his monkey. "I'm sorry, Mrs. Sharp. I went up there to go to the bathroom, that's all."

"That's a bunch of Malarkey! You know full well there's a bathroom right there!" she said, pointing at the black and white tiled john less than twelve feet away.

"I was afraid to use this one because, well, because I had to poop. I can't poop when I know there's someone right outside the door," I lied, trying to look embarrassed.

"If that's true, which I highly doubt, then why did you pass the upstairs bathroom and open the door to Stephen's room? Explain that, missy."

Damn, you're smarter than I thought. "Well, I wanted to make sure I was alone up there. I heard music playing and like I said, I can't poop if someone's nearby," I lied, expecting that pesky Catholic Guilt to make an appearance but it stayed wherever it was hiding.

"I don't believe you and I'm calling your parents to tell them this arrangement isn't working out. I won't teach students I can't trust!"

Shit. "Um, Mrs. Sharp, my parents aren't home. They dropped me off for my lesson and were going to run errands. I'll just wait outside for them to come. I really am sorry," I said, standing to make my exit. *This lying business gets easier all the time.*

"Don't think you can pull the wool over my eyes that easily," said Mrs. Sharp as her nose threatened to let loose once again. "Two can play this game. I'll walk you to your Aunt Elizabeth's house. I know that crazy old... well, I know your aunt will give you what you deserve!"

Aw fuck. Dealing with this crap isn't worth catching Stephen with his pecker in his hand. Not by a long shot.

We walked the block and a half in silence, for which I was grateful. Elizabeth was outside, wearing an enormous gardening hat to which she'd glued small birds and tiny terra cotta pots. She was working on her Nativity scene, which was a permanent fixture in her front yard. My aunt liked to rearrange the Holy Family, Magi and barn animals while she talked to them.

"They get bored if they stay in the same position for too long," she'd explained more than once. I thought it was rather sweet, although it made my mother's blood pressure soar whenever I broached the subject. It's one of the reasons I found it so endearing.

"How's the big size of ye?" inquired Elizabeth, which was one of her favorite ways of asking how things were going.

"Just fine, thanks. Aunt Elizabeth, do you know my piano teacher, Mrs. Sharp?" I asked, knowing full well they were acquainted.

"Former piano teacher," reminded an angry Mrs. Sharp. "Hello, Elizabeth, how are you?"

My Godmother sensed trouble and eyed us both suspiciously. "Why are ye darkening my door this afternoon?"

"Well, I'm very disappointed to have to be the one to tell you this, Elizabeth, but your niece behaved most improperly while in my home," she said, in a way that suggested I may have farted on the Bible or strangled innocent baby ducks.

Elizabeth looked at me quizzically and then back at my former piano teacher. She said nothing and waited for Mrs. Sharp to continue. "I'm sure you'd like to know what she did," Mrs. Sharp said, rather abruptly.

"I've a feeling yer gonna tell me either way, so ye best get on with it," my Godmother said, hands squarely on her hips.

"During Patti Anne's lesson, I dozed for a moment, just a moment mind you, and the minute my lids closed she was upstairs searching the bedrooms for naked boys. She had absolutely no business up there, but up she went!" explained Mrs. Sharp, wiping her nose before it dripped onto the front of her shawl.

I couldn't look my Godmother in the eye, although I felt her hard stare upon me.

"She walked right into Stephen's room while he was getting dressed. He is distraught with embarrassment at having been seen in his underpants!"

Underpants? No one says underpants. I opened my mouth to speak but Elizabeth beat me to it.

"So my Godchild is boy crazy, is that what yer sayin'?"

"I'd say that's a fair assessment."

"And she went upstairs knowing yer son was wearin' nothin' but his britches and that's why she opened his door?" asked Elizabeth, looking slightly annoyed.

"Yes. Absolutely!"

"That's not true! I had no way of knowing that Stephen," I began, but my aunt cut me off.

"Hold yer wheest, I'm talkin'!" my Godmother snapped, telling me to be quiet. "We're talkin' about a curious thirteen year old child, here. Isn't yer son a grown man and a little old to be livin' with his Mum?"

"My son's age has nothing to do with the fact that your dirty-minded niece tried to see his private!" shouted my former piano teacher.

"I didn't have to try, Mrs. Sparks! When I opened his door, his 'private' was firmly in hand and he was stoking it back and forth while singing a Bee Gee's song to a poster of Dorothy Hamill!" *Oh shit, I can't believe I just told her that.*

"Ha! Yer makin' that up, ye are," laughed my aunt, slapping her thigh.

"It's the truth. I swear to God, Aunt Elizabeth."

"Ye caught him pullin' the pin then, did ye, my love? Serves ye right, Sparks," sneered my aunt at the drippy nosed woman standing before her. "The higher up a tree the monkey climbs, the farther up its arse ye see," observed my wise Godmother.

Never heard it referred to as 'pulling the pin'. Where does she get this stuff?

"Why can't you speak English? What did you say to me?" Mrs. Sparks clearly didn't get the reaction she'd expected from my Godmother.

"I said, yer actin' all high and mighty 'bout my niece bein' interested in boys, but your son is committin' a mortal sin by beatin' his banger!" Elizabeth explained. "On yer bike!" That was Elizabeth's colorful way of telling people to get lost.

"Well, I'll be! No wonder the child is such a pervert having you as a Godmother!"

As my former piano teacher stormed off, unhappy with the outcome of the discussion, I looked back at my aunt who was once again muttering to her statues as she lovingly rearranged them. "Best go call yer Mum.

Tell her yer doin' work for me and I'll take ye home later," muttered my Godmother, continuing her handiwork.

"Okay, I'll be right back. Thanks, Aunt Elizabeth," I said, skipping into the house to call home.

"Don't thank me yet. Yer goin' to Confession."

Aw crap.

15 JUVENILE DELINQUENTS

I spent a lot of time with two of my younger cousins, who were on my Mom's side of the family. Their parents worked full time and they couldn't be trusted at home, so my Mom offered to watch them for the summer. I never understood why but my cousins actually liked coming to the farm, in spite of the fact that we lived in the middle of nowhere and there was nothing to do.

Unless it was raining, we were expected to play outside but there would be hell to pay if we weren't back by noon to set the table for lunch. After we'd eaten and the dishes were done, we were sent back outside. Among the places forbidden to us were the canal, train tracks, gravel pit and cemetery. Needless to say, we spent a lot of time in the cemetery.

Behind our barn was a wide, well-worn path called "the lane." Flanked on each side by trees and bushes, it had well-worn grooves from Dad's John Deere. About halfway down a little creek ran under the lane. My parents called it a "crick", which meant I did too, until someone with a little more education informed me of the proper pronunciation. I was in high school.

Every spring, we'd scoop pollywogs out of the crick with Mom's metal colander and put them into mason jars filled with crick water. Taking the jars home, we put them in a window to watch the little buggers grow legs. The same person who informed me about cricks explained pollywogs are known as tadpoles by people who don't live in the woods. We had the best of intentions and planned to return them to the crick once they were small frogs, but because we never changed their water or gave them anything to eat, we ended up killing hundreds of poor pollywogs. My face is on wanted posters in pollywog post offices all across New York State.

Farther down the lane, the trees became older and more impressively massive. I spent so much of my childhood there, I knew every inch. The lane curved gently and ended at the bottom edge of Mount Olivet Cemetery, which belonged to Nativity of the Blessed Virgin Mary. My grandparents, Uncle Patrick and my brother Tim were buried there, along with a few thousand others. Sprawled on a hill dotted with enormous pines, the shadow play of the sun through the boughs made the cemetery a place of beauty and peace. The sound of the breeze rustling through the pines was musical and made me feel peaceful and safe, in spite of the dead bodies under my feet. My cousins, on the other hand, thought it was spooky because they focused too much on decaying flesh and not enough on green grass and ancient trees.

For the first few weeks of summer, we were happy to wander the cemetery, reading the carvings on gravestones from the late 1800's. Some of them were cracked and tilted, others covered with moss and lichens. When we weren't deciphering their worn and faded engravings, we played hide and seek, interrupted by the occasional visitor. Some left a pot of flowers on a grave and others sat and prayed. My cousins and I did our best to stay out of sight until they left and the cemetery was ours once again. We'd resume our game but the cemetery's closely cut lawns covered such a wide expanse, whoever was hiding often became bored before being found. We'd give up and look for something else to do, like defecating on a headstone.

I never pooped at school or at a friend's house because it was too embarrassing to do so anywhere but home. I imagined pooping an enormous monster that wouldn't go down the hole and backing up the john until it overflowed onto the floor. How do you explain that to a friend's mom? If I had to poop, I waited until I got home. I'd wait for several days, if necessary. Until that day.

It was only a fifteen minute walk from the cemetery down the lane to my house, but I decided to poop in the cemetery, instead. I announced to my impressionable cousins I was going to drop a log on someone's grave. Looking at me like I had three heads, their miniscule brains processed my words until an image formed, then they cheered me on. I didn't require a lot of encouragement to act like a complete ass and their support sealed the deal.

I walked behind a very large gravestone at least five feet tall and three feet wide. Dropping my shorts, I backed up to the cold, black marble. I walked sideways while letting it slide out and wiped with a couple of tissues that were in my pocket from God knows when. They must have gone through the washer and dryer a couple times because they fell apart and didn't do a very good job. I turned to look at my masterpiece and snorted with laughter as my cousins ran around from the other side. Eyes as big as baking potatoes, they gawked at my repulsive creation.

"That thing came outta you?" asked Sam.

"Duh, ya think I was hiding it in my pocket?"

"Holy Shit!" Bobby exclaimed, not without a hint of admiration.

"Well, it is indeed. We're in a Catholic cemetery after all, so I guess it is a holy shit!" I thought I was a regular Johnny fucking Carson.

"I can't believe a girl can shit like that," said Sam, letting out a low whistle.

"Quit looking at it. Let's go before somebody sees us." I was worried a car would drive in and be able to place us at the scene of the crime.

About halfway through supper that night, the conversation took an uncomfortable turn. "You'll never believe what I saw on a grave today," announced George, as he struggled to cut through one of Mom's well-burned pork chops. He cut grass in the cemetery as one of his summer jobs.

My Dad perked up and made a noise that generally signified "do tell." I wanted to shove George's pork chop down his throat to keep him from talking. "Hey George," I interrupted, "want more creamed corn?"

"Your brother was talking, Pat. Wait your turn." I hated being called Pat.

"Someone crapped on a grave," George said casually, as though it happened regularly.

I thought Mom might choke on her dried out pork chop. She coughed so hard, I gave serious consideration to trying my hand at the Heimlich. My Dad was so startled by what George said, he didn't even look at Mom as she hacked and choked on pig.

"No way! What did it look like?" Peter was fascinated.

"What did you say?" asked Dad, now giving George his full attention.

"I'm not kidding, Dad. Some sicko took a dump on a dead person's grave."

Well, when you put it like that, it doesn't sound nearly as funny as it did a few hours ago. I was stuck to my chair and unable to move.

"That's hysterical!" At least I had Peter's support.

"You gotta be kidding me. Who does that? No one does that. Are you sure it wasn't from an animal?" asked our incredulous father.

"Do animals wipe their butts with Kleenex? There was a wad of Kleenex smeared with crap right next to the turd, Dad. I'm pretty sure a coyote wasn't responsible."

"Huh. Who does that?" asked Dad yet again. *Gee Dad, I don't know.*

"I wanna to see it! How do you crap on a gravestone?" Peter was almost clapping his hands with joy. *I had no idea my brother was so interested in turds.*

"What's for dessert?" I asked, trying to change the subject. Mom was breathing normally again, although her face was red from coughing.

"You don't need any dessert," she replied, without looking at me.

My Mom just told me I was fat in her usual, backhanded sort of way. I wanted her to start choking again but instead, Scott sang.

"Fatty Patty, two by four

Couldn't fit through the bathroom door

So she did it on the floor

Licked it up and did some more."

"Scott, that's enough. Peter, no one is going to look at that mess. Now George, who could have done such a thing? Did you see anyone up there today?"

"I didn't see anyone except Pat and the boys." *Oh uh.*

All four of them turned their heads in unison to look at me. I felt my cheeks get hot and beads of sweat formed on my upper lip.

"Why are you looking at me?" I asked, knowing full well why.

"Were you in cemetery today?" asked Mom in a voice suggesting she was close to erupting.

Duh. George just told you he saw me. "Yes."

"You know you're not supposed to be in the cemetery! It's off limits!" she reminded me for the hundredth time.

"Why? There's nothing to do around here! What's the big deal about the cemetery? All we do is play hide and seek and pray at Tim's grave." *Bullshit*. I'd never prayed at Tim's grave in my life. I'd never even met the kid.

"Do you know anything about the poop?" Dad asked, wearing an expression that said he hoped I'd had nothing to do with it.

"No." I hoped they believed me.

"I certainly hope not or you're gonna get the fanny warming of your life." I hated when Dad used that phrase.

"I said I didn't do it!" I snapped, much snottier than I knew was allowed.

"Don't raise your voice to me. Go to your room and don't come out until morning," Dad said, in a way that left no room for discussion.

There was no point in arguing or complaining and at least being sent to my room ended the line of questioning about the turd. I heard my family clear the table and do the dishes. They were talking but I couldn't understand much until I heard the phone being dialed. We had a big, black rotary phone attached to the kitchen wall, probably a leftover from the Eisenhower days. There was no way to dial that old relic quietly.

"Hello? Kathy? It's Betty." *Oh shit. She's calling my aunt.*

"Listen, did the boys mention anything about the cemetery today? Oh they are? I forgot there was a game tonight. Okay, well, we can talk tomorrow. See you then."

Fuck. I was afraid those little jerk offs were going to spill the beans. I couldn't begin to imagine the trouble I'd be in. I'd have to go to Confession and tell our priest that I shit on a holy piece of marble just for the fun of it. He'd probably blab it to the nuns because he'd be so disgusted, and they'd go to church and tell everyone what a sicko I was for pooping on a grave. I'd be excommunicated and my parents would ground me until high school. I'd probably never get kissed by a boy again. What boy wants to kiss a girl who craps in a cemetery? I was doomed.

There was no way to warn my cousins they were about to be questioned regarding my grave-top masterpiece. I'd never called their house before so if I called now it would be too suspicious. I had to wait until morning and hope those little bastards could keep their big mouths shut. *Knowing those two morons, I'm probably screwed.*

Morning came and I left my room to eat what would probably be my last meal before my parents killed me. I chose Peanut Butter Cap'n Crunch. *Who cares if it cuts the roof of my mouth? I'm gonna be dead by supper time anyway.* I poured a second bowl and by the time I finished it, I had hunks of skin hanging from the roof of my mouth. *Why the fuck can't that gay Quaker Oats dude figure out how to make this shit so it doesn't rip your mouth to shreds?*

I heard Aunt Kathy drive in and I begged God for help. *I promise never to take a shit on another gravestone if Bobby and Sam can just keep my secret. I promise to never again wipe boogers inside missellettes at church or lick the filling out of Oreos and put them back in the package.*

I was still making promises when Aunt Kathy walked in with my cousins. They looked as clueless as ever and Mom went in for the kill.

"Boys, do you know anything about poop on a gravestone?"

"Excuse me?" said Aunt Kathy, no doubt deciding Mom had finally gone off her nut.

"George found a turd on a grave in the cemetery yesterday and he saw Pat and the boys playing up there. Boys, look me in the eye. Do you know anything about it?"

I'm fucked. These two are wearing the guiltiest looks on their pathetic little faces I've ever seen. They looked at each other and then at me.

These two dumbasses lie to their parents all the time without the slightest problem, why do they have to choke when my fat ass is on the line?

"Answer me!" barked my Mom, causing the boys to jump.

"Take a deep breath, Betty, before you blow a gasket." Aunt Kathy could tell my Mom to shut up without saying those words and I loved her for it. "Sam. Bobby. Do you have anything to tell Aunt Betty?" Aunt Kathy was probably reconsidering her choice of summer babysitter.

"Well, we saw Father John up there. Maybe he did it," offered Sam, with a slight shrug of his shoulders.

"Do you actually expect me to believe that Father would crap on a gravestone? Do I look like I was born yesterday, Mister!" Mom looked like she might have a stroke and if she did, I wasn't going to interfere with God's divine plan by performing CPR. Neither of my cousins spoke and Mom glared at me. Aunt Kathy to the rescue.

"Betty, it looks like the kids don't know anything about what happened. Why don't you just forget about it and let them play in the cemetery? It's close to the house, George works up there almost every day and the kids can keep an eye out for the Mystery Pooper."

Mom begrudgingly gave in and said okay. We jumped up, high-fived and ran out the back door towards the lane.

"So, how are we gonna top yesterday's shit?" Bobby asked. I'd already forgotten all about my promises to God and was back in sinner mode.

"We're gonna knock over gravestones!" I declared. It sounded like a great idea.

"Maybe we'll see dead bodies!" Sam pointed out. I hadn't thought about dead bodies. Hell, I hadn't thought about anything, I just shouted the first bad idea that popped into my head.

Walking down the lane to the cemetery, we could hear the rumble of thunder in the distance and the wind picked up. We wandered over to the far corner of the cemetery where the oldest and most dilapidated stones stood, guarding their long forgotten owners. Many of them were crooked and cracked and looked like a stiff wind could knock them over.

"Watch this," I said, walking towards an old marble cross leaning to one side. I shoved it backwards with both hands and it fell to the ground with a thud.

"Fuckin' A!" bellowed Bobby, which I interpreted as both approval and encouragement. I walked to another headstone about three feet tall with rounded corners. The letters had been worn almost completely away and I couldn't make out the name or the date, not that I cared. Whoever was buried beneath my feet had been there so long nobody cared about them or their headstone anymore. I pushed hard and with a little elbow grease it went down with a much louder thud than the cross.

I looked around expecting to see my adoring fans cheering me on, but instead they were busy knocking over stones of their own. The thunder crashed louder and the sky darkened, intermittently lighting up with flashes of lightening. I continued to knock over graves without a single ounce of guilt or shame. My cousins didn't seem to be having any problems with their consciences either.

The thunder and wind were so loud we never heard the car drive up behind us. Hearing what sounded like the hum of an engine, I turned and saw an old Cadillac on the gravel road behind us.

"Run!" I shouted.

My cousins turned and saw the car. The three of us headed down the hill toward the railroad tracks, running in the opposite direction of home as the rain began to pelt us. We kept running, which wasn't easy with the wind gusting and blowing against us. The rain came down hard and cold, stinging my face and blinding my eyes. Finally slowing down and gasping for air, we looked behind us. No one had followed.

"This way," I said, motioning them off the tracks and into the brush. Soaked through to the skin and out of breath, we looked at each other and panted while we wiped the rain from our faces. I was scared.

"Do you think they saw us?" asked Sam, almost in tears.

"Of course they saw us, you idiot! They drove up right behind us!" *What if the driver recognized me and tells Mom and Dad what we were doing?* Unable to shake the nagging feeling the car looked vaguely familiar, I told myself I was being paranoid but the notion wouldn't go away.

"We've gotta go home or Mom's gonna kill us," I said, stating the obvious.

"We can't go back through the cemetery." *No shit, Bobby. You must be a member of Mensa.*

"We'll go through the gravel pit and cut through the fields to the lane. Come on, Mom's gonna be pissed," I said, turning them around towards the cemetery.

We stayed off the tracks, kept low and watched for signs of anyone looking for us. Only the severely retarded would be out in a storm like this. These two goobers sure do fit that description. We made it past the cemetery and to the gravel pit without incident. As we approached the forbidden hole, I realized we were breaking another well-established family rule. The three of us knew the gravel pit was strictly off-limits but I couldn't think of a better way to get home without the risk of being seen from the cemetery.

The only way past the pit was to climb down into it and out the other side. Within seconds, each of us wound up on our backsides and slid most of the way to the bottom, making troughs through the red clay. It had been raining hard for several minutes, transforming the clay into paste that smeared all over our clothes. We walked across the floor of the pit and found climbing out wasn't nearly as easy as sliding down. On all fours, we used our hands to claw our way up. Our skin was stained red by the time we reached the top and our fingernails were caked with the evidence of unheeded rules.

Leaving the forbidden pit behind, we crossed a hay field into the lane. As we approached the house, Mom came to the back door.

"Where have you been? You had me worried sick!" she shouted.

We walked to the back door but my Mom immediately shut it, leaving us out in the storm. *What is wrong with this crazy woman?*

"You are filthy!" she said, talking through the screen door. "You're not coming in here like that! Go down cellar and get out of those disgusting clothes."

'Down cellar' is what my family called the basement and apparently, the only people who called it that were the ones who also said crick and pollywog.

"Wait just one minute. What's all over your clothes?"

Uh oh, we're screwed.

"That's clay. You've been in the gravel pit haven't you?"

"No." All three of us shook our heads hard enough to make them fall off our necks.

"Don't lie to me! What has gotten in to you? I let you go in the cemetery but that wasn't enough, was it? You had to break yet another rule and go into the gravel pit!"

"We had to," I said, feeling my cousins look at me. Even I didn't know where this was going.

"You had to?" Mom asked, hand on hip and eyebrows raised.

"Yeah, Mom, really. We were in the cemetery and saw a cougar. We ran to get away but it chased us into the gravel pit." *A cougar? Maybe an elephant would have been more believable.*

My cousins were shaking their heads and saying "cougar" over and over as if they were trying to convince themselves. I told them to shut up.

"Do you honestly expect me to believe you saw a cougar? I didn't fall off the turnip truck yesterday, you know! How stupid do you think I am?" I didn't think she really wanted me to answer, but I was hoping she was dumb enough to buy my story and forget to tell Dad about it when he got home from Kodak.

"The three of you go down cellar and get out of those clothes. I'll throw you some towels to wrap up in and then you get up here and get in the shower. Your arms and legs are stained from the clay. You've really done it this time," she said, slamming the door.

We slowly walked around the house and down the little hill to our walk-out cellar. "We're in deep shit," observed Sam. *I'm surrounded by geniuses.*

We opened the old wooden door to the dirty, dark, cobwebbed cellar. My cousins didn't want to go in, nobody ever did, because it looked like the sort of place you'd run into Freddy Krueger. Even my brave dog, Rex, wouldn't go down there unless I went with him.

Mom had thrown down three, thread-bare towels and they were lying on the dusty, concrete floor in a heap. I grabbed them and gave one to each of my cousins. "Okay, I'll turn away and face the wall. You guys strip down, throw your clothes in the washer and go upstairs to shower. When you're gone, I'll get undressed and come up."

They actually did as they were told without arguing, so I knew they were worried. When they were gone, I stripped out of my clay covered, rain

"You're gonna be very sorry. Elizabeth told me she saw you breaking headstones in the cemetery! What has gotten into you? Do you have any idea what kind of trouble you're in? When your father hears about this you'll be lucky if he doesn't skin you alive!"

"That's not true. I wasn't breaking anything. All I did was knock a couple of them over and they were falling down anyway!" I offered, in my defense.

"Away on a tha! I watched ye cafflers knock down more than a dozen. Outta bust ye in the dial," said Elizabeth, as she curled up her man-sized fist.

"Well, I really don't see what the big deal is. They were practically on the ground anyway," I said softly, putting distance between me and my Godmother's powerful swing.

"The burden ye place on me very soul. As yer Godmother, 'tis up to me to make sure yer arse makes it to Heaven's Door." Out came the flask from Elizabeth's enormous purse and she took a generous pull before putting it back.

"Just cuz yer mum's one brick short of a load, don't give ye an excuse for being an arse weed," said my Godmother.

"What are you talking about, Elizabeth? You're probably drunk already. You're no help to me, so why don't you just go home?" Elizabeth had always managed to rub my Mom the wrong way.

"I'm not goin' nowhere without me Godchild. She needs to be taught a lesson, she does, and since yer thick as champ the job is left to me!"

Crushing my forearm in a vice-like grip, Elizabeth pulled me toward her and out the door, amidst shouts from my mother warning Elizabeth to stay out of it. Mom yelled threats about what would happen to me if I went with Elizabeth, but I figured my chances with a half-drunk Irish woman were better than those with my enraged mother.

Handing me her car keys, Elizabeth told me to drive. Although I didn't have a permit, much less a license, I'd driven the tractors and pickup truck around the farm so I thought I could probably handle it. That damn Cadillac was almost as big as my Dad's John Deere 3010. As I started the engine and began to creep down the driveway, Mom ran out of the house waving her arms and shouting. I concentrated on the driveway and pretended I didn't see her.

"Pish. Betty's as dried up as a nun's tit, she is," Elizabeth said, thumbing her nose at my incensed mother. "Now then, what in God's name were ye thinkin', messin' with gravestones? Are ye tryin' to catch the express train to Hell? No matter, yer gonna make it right. We're goin' to church," she said, digging for her flask.

Oh shit. She's gonna make me go to Confession. Over the past year or so, I'd started lying about my sins during Confession. I knowingly lied in church and God hadn't sent down a single lightning bolt, which I interpreted as His approval. I didn't buy the Church's load of crap about Jesus requiring me to confess my sins to a priest in order to be forgiven and welcomed into Heaven. I figured my sins were between me and God, so when I went to Confession, I confessed things like fighting with my parents and coveting my friend's clothes. I never confessed anything of substance and I didn't feel the slightest twinge of guilt.

"Aunt Elizabeth," I said, struggling to keep the tank between the lines on the road, "You do realize I'm wearing Dad's barn coveralls, right? They're covered with crap and not appropriate for church, ya know."

"Matters not. Yer goin' to Confession and I don't care if yer wearin' barn clothes or no clothes!"

I managed to drive to church without hitting anyone and I only ran one red light. I had a bitch of a time trying to park the damn thing and finally, Elizabeth told me to leave it where it was. The caddy was crooked and taking up parts of three parking spaces, but considering what could have gone wrong, it turned out pretty well.

"Get inside, Patti Anne. Ye have some confessin' to do or yer gonna end up as useful as a back pocket on shirt. Now away and pull yer wire," said Elizabeth, waving me towards the vestibule.

We sat in a pew near the Confessionals and I waited for someone to walk out so I could go in and put this mess behind me. Entering the dark, cherry wood Confessional, I hoped Father Lyntz was on the other side of the screen. In the years since my First Reconciliation, he fell asleep more frequently and had probably only heard about thirty percent of my sins.

Luck was not on my side and rather than finding Father Lyntz waiting for me, it was a priest assigned to our parish only a few months earlier. Father Robert was middle aged and gave the distinct impression he disliked teenagers. Whenever I saw him around kids, the look on his face suggested he was smelling shit.

I kneeled in front of the screen and began the ridiculous dance known as Confession. "Bless me Father for I have sinned. It's been one week since my last Confession and I have been fighting with my parents and not being completely honest with my Godmother."

It seemed good enough to satisfy the requirement but before Father Robert could pass judgment on my minor infractions, the door to the Confessional burst open. Elizabeth traipsed in and closed the door behind her. *Oh shit, she's finally lost the last few marbles she had.* "Aunt Elizabeth!"

"Shut yer dial!" she said, pressing her face to the screen. "Whoa, ye've got a face like a busted cabbage, you do. Pardon me interruption of yer blatherin' but I wanna make bloody sure this numpty gives ye the whole truth," explained my deranged Godmother, as she peered through the Confessional screen at a very surprised Father Robert.

"Aunt Elizabeth! This is private. You can't be in here."

She slapped me hard across the face, almost knocking me off the red velvet kneeler. As I recovered, I noticed the look on Father Robert's face said he was afraid of this crazy old Irish woman. To be honest, I was a little afraid of her, too.

"Ma'am...this young lady is attempting to repair her relationship with Christ through the Sacrament of Penance and it's meant to be performed in private. Now, if you'll please leave us to it." Father gestured to the door.

"Well I can tell ye was weared on the hind tit," observed Elizabeth, shaking her head. I was fairly confident Father Robert had never been spoken to in that manner. Before he could react, Elizabeth pushed aside the intricately carved wooden screen that was separating us. "I don't suppose this arse weed told ye she's been knockin' over gravestones, has she?" Elizabeth's strong hands were poised on her hips.

Father Robert looked at her like she was speaking a different language. After taking a nip from her flask, my Godmother continued her tirade. "The head on thon one was unreal, hi! Ye need to give her the beans, Father. She's rotten to the core, messin' with gravestones like a hooligan."

"Translation please?" asked Father, looking at me wearing a shit-smelling facial expression.

"My aunt said I've been acting in distasteful ways and you need to put your foot down because I'm rotten to the core for knocking over tombstones like a criminal." I said with my eyes on the kneeler.

"Some touch. Ye do know how to tell the truth after all. Now tha's sound," Elizabeth said in an approving tone.

"Is this true, young lady? Have you molested the sacred resting places of our dearly departed brothers and sisters?"

Geez dude. You don't have to use the word 'molested' just because you're a priest. "I guess so."

"Ye guess so, do ye?" Elizabeth slapped me hard across the face a second time.

"Yes! Yes, I knocked over gravestones!" I yelled loudly enough to capture the attention of everyone in church who wasn't already eavesdropping on the spectacle playing out in my Confessional.

"Please ma'am, take your leave. I will handle it from here. You can trust I have things under control."

"Right," Elizabeth said as she turned to go. "Useless sooskin couldn't pour shit from a shoe if the instructions were on the heel." I fought back a grin. Now was not the time to let this man see I appreciated my aunt's talent for speaking her mind so creatively.

"You have confessed a very grave sin."

Get it? Grave? I decided against pointing out his very funny pun.

"What concerns me even greater than your delinquent behavior is your lack of contrition. Only the penitent sinner can be absolved of their sins. Without contrition, there is no forgiveness and there is no grace," Father explained, hands folded solemnly on his lap.

"I am sorry. I wish I'd never done it." I was sincere.

"Are you truly sorry for what you've done or are you sorry you were caught? They are quite different, you know. I cannot absolve the sins of anyone without believing their hearts are pure and contrite."

"I am contrite. I'm very sorry." How many times do I need to say it? I'm sorry! It was a stupid thing to do and I wish we'd never gone near the cemetery, but I can't change what I did.

"This is a difficult decision, but I must tell you I don't believe you. I am confident your sorrow about these events stems from your unhappiness at being apprehended. I do not believe you are truly sorry and therefore you will not be forgiven of your sins."

"What do you mean?" I asked incredulously. *I've been absolved of far worse than this, I assure you. Father Lyntz absolved me of killing Uncle Patrick and masturbating, surely you can absolve minor vandalism!*

"I mean exactly what I said. Your sins will not be forgiven. You have severed yourself from God," Father Robert said sternly.

"That's ridiculous. I said I'm sorry and I am!"

"It's too late. Your sins remain in your heart and prevent you from being in a state of grace."

"That's a bunch of crap!" I said, as Father Robert gasped. "I don't think God expects anyone to confess their sins to a priest anyway, so I really don't care what you think. My sins are between me and God," I was speaking far too boldly and loudly for a Confessional, but nothing that had transpired within those four walls had been private, so I wasn't worried about being overheard again.

Storming out of the Confessional, I found every pair of eyes focused on me. "I'm guilty! I knocked over some gravestones in the cemetery, okay?" I practically shouted.

Most people had the decency to look away, but some of the old biddies glared at me while clicking their tongues and shaking their heads. Ignoring their judging expressions, I looked for Elizabeth and found her passed out in a pew, flask on her lap. "Aunt Elizabeth," I whispered, touching her shoulder.

"Git yer stinkin' paws off me good dress!" she bellowed. She didn't have a clue who I was or where we were.

"You're dreaming. Come on, it's time to go," I explained.

Given my aunt's state of intoxication, the driving responsibilities rested firmly on my shoulders once again. Thankfully, Elizabeth lived only two blocks from church. I drove her home, helped her to the davenport and covered her with a handmade afghan. Dialing home and waiting for someone to answer, I considered stealing my Godmother's car and running away. George's voice on the other end interrupted my daydream.

"Hi. I'm at Elizabeth's and she's too drunk to drive. Will you please come get me?" I waited on the front porch until George pulled in. "I guess I'm in deep shit when I get home, right?" I asked.

"For sure. I tried to calm Mom down, but you know how she is. When we get there tell her you're going to babysit and work at the farm stand until you earn enough to pay for the headstones to be repaired. You went to Confession, right?"

"Yeah, Aunt Elizabeth made me go, but Father Robert said since I wasn't really sorry for what I did he wouldn't give me absolution. He's a dickhead!"

"Yeah, he is, but you don't need to tell Mom and Dad that part. Just tell them you went to Confession and you'll pay to get the stones repaired. She'll calm down in a few days but until she does, you better not pull any more stunts like you did today," warned my oldest brother.

I knew he was right and I was thankful to have him as an ally. I knew he thought I was a moron, but he didn't say it. "Thanks George," I said appreciatively.

"No sweat, kid."

When we pulled into the drive, Mom was out of the house faster than I expected. She was yanking open the passenger door before George put the car in park.

"Mom, I'm really sorry for what I did. It was stupid and I'll work until I've earned enough to pay for all of the gravestones to be repaired." I spit it out so fast, I wasn't sure she understood me.

"Oh…" Clearly, it wasn't what she was expecting to hear and I had taken the wind from her sails.

"I went to Confession and have a lot of penance to do, so I'm going to my room to pray," I said, turning to walk away. I didn't give my Mom a chance to respond. I walked into the house with my head down like a beaten dog, but when I closed my bedroom door I did a touchdown dance.

I was truly sorry for what I did to the graves of innocent people and I knew it was wrong. It would take forever to earn enough to repair all the headstones we trashed, but I was happy I'd silenced my mother because I'd never managed to do it before.

As far back as I could remember, the only person I knew could consistently stifle my Mom was my Godmother. Hell, she could probably silence E.F. Hutton.

16 BEER AND BOOZE

In 1983, my parents thought I'd found the Lord, but I knew it was just my vagina talking. I discovered the best way to persuade my parents to let me hang out with boys was to capitalize on their devotion to Our Lord and Savior. Our church's Youth Group was the perfect disguise for my raging teenage hormones. My parents were so pleased their teenage daughter wanted to follow in the footsteps of Jesus they never considered I could have an ulterior motive.

Youth Group met weekly in the basement of my former school, Nativity, which threatened to put a damper on my sex drive. I'd spent seven long years in that prison and its walls contained memories better forgotten. During our meetings, we often broke into small groups of two or three to study a scripture which we later shared with the group as a whole. Normally, about thirty teenagers showed up each week and the two adults who led the meetings were overwhelmed, so it was easy to slip away unnoticed.

Todd was one year my senior although I towered about four inches above him. He was a tight soccer player with hard gluts and completely uninterested in me until I told him I had weed. I became hotter than Bo fucking Derrick.

Every week, we'd sneak off to smoke a joint in Bolger Hall, the very place I'd received my public beating. We sat on stage getting stoned just a few feet from where Sister Fatass assaulted me with her legendary paddle. While we got high, I tried to be sexy and look absolutely delicious so Todd couldn't resist the urge to crawl all over me.

We managed a few awkward kisses but I was so much bigger than Todd, it was uncomfortable. I was taller, thicker and more muscular than itty bitty Toddy Woddy. I felt like the Jolly Green Giant groping a Care Bear.

After a few weeks of sneaking away from Bible study, Todd caught a really bad case of Catholic Guilt. He was overcome with feelings of irresponsibility and regret for choosing weed over Our Lord. Thankfully, his condition wasn't contagious.

"I'm going to Confession and I suggest you do the same," said a very unsexy and serious Todd.

"I suggest you kiss my holy bong!" I retorted.

Todd's change in attitude made him utterly unattractive and I didn't like the way kissing him made me feel like a great big man, so I turned my attention elsewhere. I wished I hadn't shared any weed with him because, aside from getting high, which I could have done alone, there was no payoff. I believed if I shared pot with a boy, he better make it worthwhile and cop a feel. I wanted to run this body like a business, but no one was interested in shopping.

Keep it in the family, isn't that what they say? I started chasing Todd's older brother, Chuck. Their younger sister, Keira, was a good friend of mine and I spent quite a bit of time at their house. I figured since I was sleeping overnight anyway, I might as well work the brother scene. I'd like to point out while I certainly was an asshole, I really loved Keira and didn't befriend her just to get closer to her brothers. *What kind of slut do take me for?*

On a chilly Friday night in western New York, the autumn sky was painted shades of red and gold and the night held promise. After much begging and doing extra chores, my parents gave me permission to attend the varsity football game and dance that followed. I planned to search the stands for Chuck and figure out how to get him to ask me out. Assuring my parents I had a ride home, I promised to be home by ten o'clock.

"You're sure you have a ride?" Mom asked for the tenth time.

"Yes, I'm sure. Amy's parents said they'd drop me off."

"You better be home before ten. Not a moment later," she warned.

"Amy's parents know. I'll be home by ten."

"And you better not leave this stadium until the dance. You don't have permission to go anywhere except the game and the dance. Is that clear?"

"Yes, Mom, I know. You've told me about a million times," I said as I rolled my eyes.

"Don't get fresh with me or you can get right back in this car and spend the evening ironing sheets."

"Okay, Mom. I get it. I'll see you later."

She finally drove off as Amy came up behind me. "'Bout time you got here. Me and John are walking to the liquor store to get some booze. Chuck's coming too. Wanna join?"

Is that a trick question? Amy and her boyfriend paired off, leaving me and Chuck to follow suit. I hoped. The liquor store was a short walk from the stadium, past Ginther Elementary and through an apartment complex. Huddling outside the liquor store on the sidewalk of a strip mall, we watched an old guy approach us. He looked dirty and his hands were shaking.

"You guys wait here," instructed Chuck. He walked over to the old guy and although I couldn't hear what was being said, I saw Chuck hand him a few bills. The stranger walked into the store and Chuck rejoined our group, huddling close to stay warm. For the price of a forty-ounce can of malt liquor, the desperate old man bought us a bottle of peppermint schnapps. Chuck hid the bottle in his knee length parka and the four of us backtracked towards the stadium.

"Want a butt?" Chuck asked, as he handed me his pack of Marlboro Lights.

"Sure." *I hope I can figure out how to light the damn thing.*

"Come on, Patti Anne, you don't smoke. Don't be stupid," ragged Amy.

"You should talk, Amy. Since when do you drink?" I asked.

"Touche! Here, baby, lemme light it for you."

Oh God, Chuck called me baby and now he's got my cigarette in his mouth. Once lit, he placed the cancer stick suggestively between my lips. I felt a shiver go through my body and it wasn't from the dropping mercury.

"You cold?" he asked. *So he's not brilliant but who wants to snuggle up with a rocket scientist anyway?* "Get closer." Chuck opened his parka and motioned me inside of it. We walked like we were doing a three-legged race while I tried to smoke as if I knew exactly what I was doing.

"This is probably the best place, guys. Let's stay here," said John, when we arrived at the playground on the backside of Ginther. We were hidden from both the stadium and street traffic and the glare from the street lights didn't extend to the playground. They only cast faint shadows so we felt safe to indulge in our booze and each other.

"Bottoms up!" exclaimed Amy, as Chuck handed her the bottle. She took a swig, coughed and handed the booze to me. I'd never had so much as a drop of champagne, but I put the bottle to my lips and took a big gulp. *Holy shit!* It burned like hell going down and I coughed.

Within a few seconds, I felt warmth spread across my chest.

"Whoa," I said, amazed at the feeling.

The other three mimicked me and laughed. We passed the bottle and after a few swigs, I no longer shivered from the cold. After a few more, Chuck had his tongue down my throat. I was happily buzzed and being wrapped inside Chuck's parka, drinking schnapps, was the greatest feeling I'd ever experienced.

Amy and John wandered off to a private corner of the playground, leaving me and Chuck to finish off the bottle. We drank and made out, although I had trouble concentrating on the rhythm of his tongue. His mouth tasted like a minty ash tray, but I didn't care because I was happy to have a boy all over me.

Happy that is, until Chuck shoved my hand down his pants and somehow expected me to know what the fuck to do with one of those things. I'd never even seen a teenage dick up close, much less touched one. I had no idea what to do but I'd heard about hand jobs. I did my best, but his jeans were tight and I was drunk and inexperienced. It wasn't pleasant and got worse when I heard three words I'll never be able to erase from my memory.

"Get the balls! Get the balls!" he moaned as he shoved my arm further down his pants.

Get the balls?! And do what with them? Oh God, I never should've left Nativity. I should've skipped this and waited for Stephen to grow up and leave his Mommy. It's his fault my hand is down some guy's pants and I'll never forgive him for putting me through this!

We somehow managed to untangle ourselves when Amy and John walked over and said it was getting late. As we walked to the dance, our foursome continued to sneak sips of Schnapps from the almost empty bottle. I staggered but Chuck had me wrapped up with him inside his parka. I was happily content, assuming since I'd "gotten the balls", Chuck and I were going out.

Before we got to the high school, John tossed what little bit of schnapps was left in somebody's back seat. As we got to the cafeteria door to buy our tickets, my new boyfriend said he had to take a wicked piss and was out of sight before I could get money out of my pocket. I managed to pull out a couple singles and was handed a ticket in return. Without warning, Amy puked all over our assistant principal who was manning the cash box. She proceeded to cry, telling him she'd been drinking and went on to name exactly who she'd been drinking with. *What the fuck is wrong with you, Amy?*

I snuck into the crowd, drunk and scared, looking for Chuck. After wandering the dance floor for a few minutes, I found him in a lip-lock with one of the biggest sleeze bags in school. I boldly walked to them and tapped Chuck on the back.

"What are you doing?" I asked, fairly confused because I had my hand down his pants only fifteen minutes ago.

"Get lost," he said.

I was drunk and started to cry. I wanted to go home but the person who was supposed to take me had recently barfed on our assistant principal and a faculty member was probably driving her home right that very minute. I found a pay phone and called home. I could barely put my words together but after playing twenty questions, Mom said she'd come get me. When I finally poured myself into the family station wagon, I prayed for death.

Drunk and vaguely aware of my mother's jarring voice, I wanted the disjointed feeling of inexperienced inebriation to end. Oddly enough, intoxication ceased to be fun when Amy puked all over our assistant principal and ratted me out. To make matters worse, it was pretty obvious Chuck was gonna let someone else "get the balls". I pieced together the obvious and realized we probably weren't going out.

As bad as I felt, the worst was yet to come. The following Monday, I was summoned to the office and informed of a three-day suspension for drinking on school property. Describing a letter addressed to my parents regarding my debauchery, the principal directed to me get their signatures and return the letter the next morning.

Did I mention my parents were very strict Catholics? After I killed Uncle Patrick, they stopped drinking and looked down on anyone who gave into the weakness of the Drink. To make matters worse, my geeky brothers failed to do their jobs by paving the way. They failed to wreck cars, get drunk and do other stupid stuff normal boys are notorious for doing.

My brothers' failure to properly break in my parents caused me unnecessary hardship. Mom and Dad weren't prepared to receive a letter from school and I blamed my brothers. Regrettably, my relationship with my parents wasn't such that I was able to initiate a conversation about the mess I was in. I didn't know how to talk to them or ask for help and I was scared to death.

I called Amy and begged her Dad to come to my house to tell my parents what "we" had done. Hoping if another parent broke it to them, saying things like "kids will be kids" and "no one got hurt", it would be easier for me. Mr. Pepper was kind enough to tackle a burden that didn't belong to him.

My timing sucked. The minute I hung up with Mr. Pepper, who promised to be over in less than ten minutes, my Godmother drove in. *Ah hell, I don't want her here for this!*

Based on the way she walked, my aunt wasn't there for a social call. She had something on her mind. *Why did they saddle me with this woman as a Godmother? Holy crap! What if she already knows what happened?*

Without knocking, Elizabeth threw open the door and bellowed, "Where is she, then?"

Yep, she knows.

"What in the blue blazes?" said Mom, wiping her hands on a dish towel and heading into the family room. "What's going on, Elizabeth?" Mom asked, while I contemplated an early death.

"Where's me godchild? She's got some answerin' to do!" Elizabeth slurred.

Uh oh, she's drunk and mad. Not a good combination.

I knew I couldn't avoid the tongue lashing and face slapping that was heading my way, so I walked into the family room to get it over with. I'd learned the hard way that letting my Godmother stew too long was dangerous.

"Hi, Aunt Elizabeth."

"Don't you hi me, yer in deep. Just what in the bloody hell were you doin' hangin' around with that Pepper girl? She's a no-good strumpet, she is!"

Excuse me? Could it be she doesn't know about the schnapps?

"As usual, you're drunk and not making any sense. What are you talking about?" said my Mom, rolling her eyes.

"Unless ye want a knuckle supper, feck away!" barked Elizabeth, waving her large man paw at my Mom. "This is between me and me Godchild!"

"In case you didn't notice, that godchild of yours happens to be my daughter!"

Glancing behind my aunt, I saw Mr. Pepper at the back door and waved him in. *Please help me!* He let himself in just as my poetic aunt gave her assessment of the situation.

"Well, then, yer doin' a lousy job as a Mum if yer lettin' her tramp around with that Pepper girl. She's a lousy hoor, she is."

"Excuse me? Are you talking about my daughter?" asked my friend's Dad. He looked extremely confused.

Take me now, God. I'm ready to die.

"Aye. Ye let that girl tramp around all hours of the night with that boyfriend of hers, who's already got one girl knocked up. Mark me words, Pepper, yer girl is next. Best be getting' out yer knittin' needles and whip up some booties, 'cuz yer soon gonna be a granddaddy!"

"Now, just one minute! You don't even know my daughter and you have no right to say such things!"

"Elizabeth, please! I'm sorry, Bill," Mom said to Amy's Dad, "don't listen to anything that comes out of her mouth. She's plastered. Can I do something for you?"

"Well, I came to talk to you and Mac about some trouble the girls got into Friday night, but maybe this isn't a good time," stammered Mr. Pepper, eyeballing my aunt as she drank from a flask.

"Ach, this is a great time. Spill the beans. What'd yer little tramp get me wee doll into, then?" asked Elizabeth, tugging off a large hat to reveal an unruly mass of red hair.

There's no way this can end in anything but disaster.

"Well, it seems the girls and two friends got hold of some liquor and did a little drinking before the dance Friday night," Amy's Dad said, very calmly and quietly.

Little? We nearly polished off the whole damn bottle, but hey, I like your version better.

"Aw, naw," said my aunt, in a way that made my skin crawl. "Who told ye this?"

"Amy got sick at the dance and told the assistant principal what they'd been doing. The kids each have a three day suspension."

"And why are you telling us this?" asked my Mom.

"Cuz he's lookin' to lose some teeth, that's why!" snapped my Godmother.

"I'm here because your daughter begged me to tell you," said Mr. Pepper, backing away from my aunt and closer to the back door. "She said she couldn't talk to you about it. I'm beginning to understand why."

"What's that supposed to mean?" asked my Mom, glaring at Mr. Pepper.

"Are ye startin', then? I'll knock ye right through that door!" shouted Elizabeth.

"Good luck, kid," said Mr. Pepper as he turned and walked away. I couldn't blame him for leaving. I wished I could go with him.

"Is this true? Were you drinking?" asked my Mom.

"Yes."

"Now ye've gone and wrecked me nerves!" Elizabeth slurred, reaching for her flask. "Ye sure have made a holy show of things, so ye have."

"Elizabeth, will you please let me deal with this? Just go home and put yourself to bed!" shouted my Mom.

"Ach, ye've made a bags of things as it is, Betty. Patti Anne is me godchild and I'll see to it she gets to Heaven's door. Be of use for once and go learn how to make a cuppa tea!"

My Mom and Godmother pissed back and forth for several minutes. It was pointless to interrupt and I was happy to let them wear each other out because it might mean they'd have less energy to put into my punishment. I sat down and waited for them to finish. Dad walked in from the barn.

Ah crap. Can this get any worse?

"What's going on in here? I could hear you two shouting from the barn."

"Ach, Mac. Our girl has turned to the bottle, she has. I'm blamin' it on Betty."

"What are you talking about?" asked Dad.

"Bill Pepper was just here to tell us that Pat and Amy were caught drinking at school Friday night. She didn't have the courage to tell us herself and asked him to do it for her!" Mom was shouting at my Dad and he was glaring at me.

"Is that true? You were drinking and you asked someone else to tell us?" asked my Dad, looking disappointed.

"Yes."

"What were you thinking?" shouted my mother. "Do you know how embarrassed I was to have to be told by another parent? You should have told us yourself!"

"Hold yer wheest, Betty! Why do ye think the poor girl didn't tell ye? Ye're not easy to talk to and ye never listen. Now, Patti Anne, ye know yer goin' to Confession , right?"

"Just hold on a minute, Elizabeth," interrupted my Dad, "I appreciate your concern but Betty and I will handle this. She's our daughter and we'll decide what her punishment will be."

"So yer tellin' me to feck off, then?" asked my Godmother.

"That's exactly what he's saying! You blame her drinking on me? You're the one with a flask permanently attached to your face! You're a bad influence on her! Go home!" barked my Mom.

"Mom! That's not true. It's not Aunt Elizabeth's fault!"

Whack! My Dad spanked me on the butt with his huge farmer hand. He hadn't spanked me since I was a young child and I'd forgotten how powerful his hands were. I held back tears of pain and embarrassment.

"Don't you ever speak to your Mother like that again. You will speak to her with respect. Is that clear?" asked my Dad.

"Yes. I'm sorry, Mom." I said but I didn't really mean it. It wasn't my aunt's fault.

"The only thing stoppin' me from bustin' yer dial is the love for me Godchild. Ye make me sick as a plane to Lourdes," Elizabeth hissed at my Mom. She grabbed her hat and pulled it over her shockingly red mane. Standing directly in front of me she warned, "We're not done here. I'll be over to pick ye up after school on Tuesday. Yer goin' to Confession."

When Elizabeth was gone, my Dad motioned for me to sit. "I'm really disappointed in you. I thought you were smarter than this. I don't blame Elizabeth for your decisions, the blame rests squarely on your shoulders. You're grounded until your Mom and I tell you otherwise. Now go to your room and don't come out until you're told."

Grounded for three months, I did chores whenever I wasn't in school or doing homework. My parents barely acknowledged my presence, except to bark out orders about what needed to be cleaned, stacked or washed. I spent Halloween scrubbing the bathtub with a toothbrush while my friends ran around town having a great time. I missed the rest of the football games and dances of the season. No sleepovers, no boys and no more "getting the balls".

17 GIFT FROM A DEAD LADY

Mom was at a hospital fundraiser, Dad was working in the barn and I was alone in the house when the phone rang. A man on the other end asked if I'd seen a woman who'd taken a taxi to our house earlier that morning.

"Dude, you should lay off the drugs. Do you know where we live? I've never even seen a taxi in town, let alone on our road."

He insisted the cab company gave our address as her drop off location. I told him he had a severe drug problem and hung up.

An hour or two later, a strange car pulled into the drive. The man behind the wheel turned out to be the crack head who'd called earlier, although he didn't look the way I thought a druggie should. With a worried expression, he introduced the lady with him as his sister. Their mother was the woman who supposedly took a cab to our house and, according to her children she was a few tacos short of a fiesta platter. They were worried she'd been confused, wandered off and might be in need of help. Giving us his phone number, the man asked us to call if she showed up.

"Well, I guess we better take a look around. Let's start with the barn and the milk house. Guess we should check the shed, too," Dad said, after they drove away.

"We should split up," I suggested. "I'll check the canal."

Never in my life had I stood on the bank of that goddamned canal, but I told Dad that's what I was going to do. I expected him to forbid me to go near it, as he had all my life, but he didn't even flinch. He's worried. I walked down our driveway to the road, looked both ways, and crossed to the canal bank.

I was sixteen years old and on the bank of the Erie Canal for the very first time. What a letdown. *What the hell is the big deal?* It was a big ditch of dirty brown water with huge boulders along the bank. *Why would my parents think I'd ever even consider getting in this water? They know I have a paralyzing fear of snakes!* That shit looked like snake heaven. I decided to take a quick peek in each direction and the get fuck away before a nasty cotton mouth jumped out and put me in an early grave.

As I looked upstream (hell, I don't know if it was up or down. It was left.) I saw what looked like clothes on the bank. I walked closer. *Yeah, those are clothes. Neatly folded and stacked on top of shoes. Oh shit.* I looked over the bank and saw the second dead person I'd ever seen, but this one wasn't all fancied up and in a coffin like my grandmother had been. This one had a nasty, bloody head wound and was floating face down, naked and bloated. I screamed.

Dad heard me and was by my side within moments. Putting his huge, farmer hands on my shoulders, he turned me away from the canal and sent me back to the house to get help. After calling 9-1-1, a phone call I don't remember making, I went back to the canal and looked at the dead, naked woman. *Why would you strip before committing suicide? Or did your skinny dipping plan go horribly wrong?*

As if from a great distance, I heard doors opening and people talking. An ambulance had arrived. I never heard it coming and was surprised to see it.

Stephen stood in front of me, but he wasn't my smiling, happy Stephen.

He wasn't Dorothy Hamill's Stephen either. Instead, he was Professional Emergency Man and spoke sternly as if he were my father.

"Go back to the house and stay there."

I looked at him in disbelief.

"Go on! Get outta here!"

I started to cry and walked up the long drive to the house. I cried more because Stephen didn't ask me if I was okay than I did for the poor dead woman.

The rest of the afternoon and early evening were a fog. I wasn't hungry and wasn't paying attention to what was on the boob tube. As I sat on the davenport, thinking about the afternoon's events, I heard a light knock on the screen door. My Dad let Stephen in and thanked him for his help with the dead lady. Before Stephen could answer, my Dad said goodnight and wandered off to bed.

My former crush sat next to me on the davenport while my heart pounded. It was the closest Stephen had been to me since I walked in his bedroom three years ago and caught him whacking off to a Dorothy Hamill poster. Although I made out with every boy I could, Stephen's mere presence made me decide I still loved him. If only I could get rid of Mom.

She made small talk about the dead lady and the skating rink but I didn't listen. He was sitting so close our legs were touching. Recognizing the heat of passion stirring in my nether region, I was surprised my parents hadn't sensed the change in air pressure it must have caused. I fully expected my Dad to appear with a butcher knife and chase Stephen away.

"I've had enough for one day and I'm going to bed. Goodnight you two," announced Mom as she disappeared from the family room.

What just happened? My parents are leaving me alone with the man I

wanna bang like a screen door in a hurricane? Am I being framed?
Dead women should show up more often if this is what happens.

Stephen stood, leaned over and took my hands in his. They were nice
and soft, not hard and rough like farmer hands. He pulled me to my
feet and hugged me tightly. "I came back to see if you're okay," he
whispered in my ear.

Standing so close our bodies pressed together, I felt his warm breath on
my neck. The sound of his voice in my ear made me shiver. Stephen
put his hands on my face, causing temporary paralysis. I was unable to
move or speak. *This is what I've been dreaming of, or at least the*
prelude to what I've been dreaming of.

"Are you alright? I'm sorry I yelled at you but I didn't want you to see
anymore than you already had. I was worried about you."

I smiled and shrugged my shoulders. He smiled back and planted a
gentle, soft lingering kiss on my unsuspecting lips. So surprised to find
myself in that position, I didn't kiss back. *I didn't kiss back!* Before I
could register what happened, Stephen took a step backwards.

"I better go before I do anything stupid."

"I like you when you're stupid," I replied. I'm such a smooth talker, I
shock myself.

Taking a step forward, I wrapped my arms around Stephen and kissed
him the way I'd always wanted to. He responded the way I'd hoped and
we kissed passionately, as if we'd never be given the opportunity to do
so again.

For reasons I can't explain, images of Stephen "pulling the pin" to a
Dorothy Hamill poster while singing a Bee Gee's song flooded my head.
I couldn't make them go away and started to giggle.

"Why are you laughing?" asked Stephen, pulling away from me slightly.

Pull yourself together! "I'm sorry, I couldn't help it. It's over, it won't happen again."

"What made you laugh?" Stephen asked, looking a bit worried.

"It's nothing. Forget it." I tried to continue with our kissing but instead, I snorted and cackled. I let go of him and doubled over, unable to contain myself. Tears ran down my face.

"What is so funny?" he sounded mad, which made me laugh even harder.

In spite of the extreme hilarity that threatened to choke me with laughter, I managed to shriek, "How deep is your love?" I fell to the floor, unable to stand as I chortled and sniggered at my true love's expense. I wasn't trying to be mean but it was so damn funny I couldn't pull myself together.

"My Mommy was right! You are a dirty bird!" snapped Stephen.

I was still laughing as his headlights disappeared down the driveway.

18 THE WEDDING

While attending college at the University of Buffalo, my brother Scott matured and changed for the better. He was no longer the nasty, evil brother from my youth. He was happier and kinder than ever before and I attributed his new, likable personality to the wonderful girl with whom he'd fallen in love. She certainly brought out the best in him.

Berta was a local girl from a wonderful family, proud of its Polish heritage. Our two families met and Berta's parents introduced us to delicious Polish specialties like pierogie and makowiec, a poppy seed cake. Pierogie to me were what crack is to an addict. I couldn't get my fill of those damn things.

Everyone was thrilled when Scott and Berta announced their engagement. Everyone that is, except Aunt Elizabeth.

"The stinkin' Poles are our enemies, Mac! How can ye let the boy marry one of their kind?"

"Elizabeth, she's a nice girl. Who cares if she's Polish?" laughed my Dad.

"Aye, who cares indeed! What if she was black? Would ye be so happy then? What about it, Betty? What if this girl was Puerto Rican?" My aunt's hands were firmly planted on her hips and she was all business.

"That would be an entirely different story," replied my Mom. "Berta is

white and we don't care if she's Polish. Thank God she's not a nigger,"
she said, wiping her brow. Apparently, just the thought of a black
daughter-in-law caused her to sweat.

"Have ye forgotten, then, the damn Poles invaded Ireland! Ye shouldn't
even be talkin' to those bloody dossers! Mark my words, they're
nothin' but trouble, they are," warned Elizabeth.

In spite of my Godmother's warnings, the wedding plans were
underway and I couldn't have been more excited. Berta asked me to be
one of her maids of honor and the best part of that was I'd been paired
with Berta's oldest brother, David. He was the best looking man in
North America, aside from John Schneider, and I was madly in love. This
wasn't like being in love with Stephen. This was real love, I was sure of
it.

I thought I looked fairly nice in the pink and burgundy, off the shoulder,
hoop skirt dress that Berta's parents had tailor-made for the girls of the
wedding party. My biggest concern was my bust. I must have been
absent the day they handed them out. The other girls in the wedding
party all sported double D's but I could barely fill my modest A cups. If I
was going to get David's attention, I needed some tits and I needed
them fast because we were scheduled to be at the church in less than
an hour.

My strapless bra did little to help matters. Rather than pushing up and
boosting what little breast meat I had, it flattened my little baby
boobies, causing the bodice to hang like an empty sock. *Socks! That's
it!*

I rummaged through the dresser of the guest room in Berta's parents
house, where I'd spent the night, desperately looking for socks. I found
a couple pairs, probably belonging to her Dad, and shoved them into my
empty bodice.

Looking in the mirror, I saw a girl with lopsided bumpy boobs, but at
least she had boobs. I knew I had to do better though, because what

twenty-three-year old man is attracted to a sixteen-year-old girl with lopsided lumpy hooters? *Hopefully, David.*

Deciding against the socks, I headed downstairs to find a better ingredient for my fake tit kit. Sitting on the kitchen table were stacks of plates and bowls for the endless parade of hungry people expected over the weekend. The bowls caught my eye and without giving it more than a moment's consideration, I grabbed two of them and high-tailed it back up to the guest room.

Cupping my less-than-adequate boobs within each bowl, I rearranged the bodice and inspected my reflection in the mirror. *Presto! I have yabos!* My figure was much more acceptable until I turned to assess the side view and one of the bowls slipped into the gathered waist of the dress. *Great, now my belly button has a tit!*

Desperate to arrive at church with an ample and eye-catching bosom, I removed both bowls and headed downstairs in search of duct tape. *It might hurt, but it'll be worth it. I hope.*

"Mrs. Sadowski, can I please borrow some duct tape?" I asked Berta's mom.

"What in the world do you need duct tape for?" she asked, rummaging through a kitchen drawer.

Trust me, you don't want to know. "Um, there's a tear in my backpack and I want to tape it before anything falls out."

She sent me to find her husband, Charles, who handed me a roll of tape and offered to help fix whatever needed to be repaired. I declined his generous offer.

Back in the guest room, I tore off several pieces of tape in preparation for my breast augmentation. Positioning a bowl over one boob, I taped several pieces around the bottom half. I decided not to tape the top half of the bowl because I was afraid it would show. I fashioned a matching fake boob on the other side and rearranged the bodice of the dress.

With a couple bowls, some duct tape and a little creativity I created an amazing rack that rivaled that of Dolly Parton. I walked around the room, twirled and waved my arms to make sure they'd stay in place. *Just wait till David gets a look at these babies. I won't be able to keep him off me!*

The needs of the cattle back home prevented my parents from staying in Buffalo the night of the rehearsal dinner. They left me at the Sadowski's house and drove home to do chores, planning to drive back the next morning for the wedding. If I was lucky, I wouldn't see them until I walked down the aisle. By then, there'd be nothing they could do to stop me and my D cups from wowing every pair of eyes in the church.

I heard the bridesmaids and Berta's family gathering in the front hall. Wrapping in my parka to hide my newfound wowsers, I headed down to join them. Mrs. Sadowski, assigned everyone to cars and I almost wet myself when she told me to ride with David. We were going to be alone in his car and my imagination delivered images of him pulling into an empty parking lot and having his way with me. *Maybe he'll skip the church altogether and check us into a motel.*

David drove some sort of four door sedan. I didn't know a Chevy from a corvette and all I cared about was getting David's attention, and perhaps his hands, on my sweater meat. Once in the passenger seat, I slipped off the parka, which I really didn't need. Although it was mid-October, the temps were in the sixties and the sun was shining brightly.

"How far is it to the church?" I asked, as he pulled away from the curb in front of his childhood home, which had a flock of plastic pink flamingoes in the yard.

"Oh, probably about twenty minutes," he replied, glancing in my direction. He did a double take and I was pleased to see his eyes were focused on my girls.

I leaned forward slightly as I asked, "Do you mind if I turn on the radio?"

"Um, what?" he asked, still staring at my impressive rack.

"You're about to rear-end your parents' car, you know," I cautioned.

Forcing his eyes off my chest and back to the road, he stepped on the brake until we were at a safe distance once again. After a couple of seconds, he glanced back again, his eyes trying to take in the magnificence that was my chest. The eighth wonder of the world.

"Is something wrong?" I asked, amused by his sudden interest in my anatomy.

"Huh?" he asked, without making eye contact. "What? Oh, sorry," he said, looking away.

We rode mostly in silence, with David spending more time staring at the twins than at the road in front of us. I was dizzy with the attention and intended to do whatever was necessary to keep him focused on me. On them.

David parked the car and like a perfect gentleman, opened my door and offered his hand. I happily put my hand in his, surprised to find it clammy. I made sure he got a full frontal view as I rearranged the hoops of my skirt.

"Do I look okay?" I asked.

"You look smashing," David responded, in a fake British accent. I giggled.

After dropping me off in the church's back vestibule, my new heartthrob left to join the other groomsmen on the altar. As I waited with the rest of the bridesmaids, I came under attack rather quickly.

"What the hell happened to you?" asked the maid of honor.

"Holy shit! You didn't have those things last night!" chimed in Berta's friend Lisa, as she reached out to grab a handful.

I slapped her hand away before she could cup my tit, I mean bowl.

"Mitts off. Grab your own goods and leave mine alone," I said, turning my back to them. It was difficult to ignore their slew of disparaging remarks, but I tried to remind myself they were simply jealous of my knock-out knockers. I couldn't really blame them. They were stunning.

I walked, as instructed by Mrs. Sadowski, slowly down the aisle behind my little cousin Marie. She was the flower girl and looked simply precious in a dress identical to mine. In fact, until I'd given myself a boob job, her bust had been identical to mine, too. She was in preschool.

"It's not a race," Berta's mom instructed during last night's rehearsal. "Walk gracefully, not like a pack of elephants." Looking ahead, I tried to ignore the elbowing and staring from both sides of the aisle. There could be no doubt, my new tatas were very noticeable.

As I passed my Godmother's pew, I heard her gasp aloud. "Ach, will ye look at the jugs on that one! Oh Lord, is that me wee doll?"

Against my better judgment, I glanced at Elizabeth and wasn't at all surprised to see her struggling to shove the man at the end of her pew out of the way. *She's gonna try to yank 'em out!* In direct violation of Mrs. Sadowski's orders, I picked up the pace, almost stepping on the hem of Marie's dress. Once safely on the altar, I refused to make eye contact with my aunt but I could hear her muttering throughout the Mass.

"Bad enough I've gotta share the company of a lousy bunch of Poles...just look at those ridiculous sweater cows...sech a disgrace, but I warned 'em those Polaks would be bloody trouble...just look what they done to her."

I pretended I couldn't hear her and tried to relax in spite of the fact that every eye in the church was fixed on my rack, even the priest seemed mesmerized by them. Maybe I over did it.

Berta and Scott said their "I do's", giving Aunt Elizabeth something else to complain about, and then the wedding party headed down the aisle to begin the celebration. David offered me his arm and I was so distracted by his handsome face, I didn't realize my Godmother was blocking the aisle until I bumped into the bridesmaid ahead of me.

"Just who do ye think yer foolin'? Those big 'ole fun bags aren't real!" she bellowed, as she reached around Lisa to yank at the bodice of my dress.

I heard a scream and realized it came from me. In her attempt to grab my chest, my Godmother whacked Lisa in the face, which seemed to irritate her date. He must have thought he had something to prove because he stood between them, shoulders back, chest out.

"Yer face is so sour ye could make yer own yogurt. On yer bike!" said Elizabeth, giving his chest a little shove.

"You crazy old bat! If you even think about laying a finger on me or Lisa again, you'll live to regret it."

Uh oh. Elizabeth never backs down from a challenge.

"Are ye startin' then, 'cuz I'll knack yer ballix in!" replied my aunt.

Before he could translate my aunt's Irish slang, she clobbered him with an uppercut to the chin. He went down, dragging Lisa to the floor with him. The hoops beneath the bridesmaid's skirt shifted and caused the lower half of her dress to reach skyward, giving everyone in attendance a clear shot of what she'd neglected to wear underneath.

Feeling guilty for my contribution to the mayhem, I leaned over to yank her hoops down, ending the beaver shot she was dishing out to the entire congregation. As I bent over, the tape on my upper ribcage let go, probably because I was sweating like a construction worker, and a bowl escaped.

Smash! My fake melon hit the tile floor of the church and crashed into a thousand, tiny pieces. Everything went silent. Embarrassed to the point of being unable to breathe, I straightened as everyone looked back and forth between my monster hooter, my non-existent hooter and the smashed ceramic bowl on the floor.

"Ach, have a jook at that! Ye done invented a brand new over the shoulder boulder holder!" laughed Aunt Elizabeth, digging through her suitcase-sized purse for a flask. After knocking back a generous mouthful, she offered this advice: "Yer no floozie and I've taught ye better than to determine yer self worth by the size of yer cup, wee doll. If ye have to wear bowls in yer bra to impress a man, he ain't worth impressin'."

She stepped over Lisa, shaking her head and continued to hand out her sage advice, "Ye can't make chicken soup outta chicken shit. Wear some drawers, ye dirty trollip!"

Shortly after Scott and Berta's wedding, which was the talk of the town for weeks on end, they bought their first house and threw a huge Christmas party for family and friends. Scott and I had become much closer since he'd become engaged to Berta. I discovered my brother had a great sense of humor and he'd even let me sneak a beer every now and then. Scott had become the cool older brother every kid wants.

A new and improved Scott did a bang-up job of getting into the holiday spirit and was quite drunk a couple hours into the party. "I need to talk to you about something. Follow me," Scott said quietly.

My stomach dropped. I knew where this could be heading and I didn't want to be there but I didn't know how to get out of it. Before leaving the kitchen to follow him, I grabbed Berta's Kahlua and cream, tipped it back and drained it. Aunt Elizabeth couldn't have done better.

"What the hell?" asked my sister-in-law. I shrugged and walked away.

Following Scott upstairs to one of the guest bedrooms, I wished I was more like my Godmother. She simply would have told my brother, "On yer bike", and ignored him. Instead, I walked into the bedroom behind him and stepped aside as he closed the door behind us.

"Sit down," he pointed to the bed.

I sat down and began to sweat but I didn't know whether to attribute it to liquor or fear. I fully expected to puke all over the afghan covering the bed, which I suspected had been knitted by Gram because we had one just like it at home.

"I don't know if you remember this, but...," Scott said as he sat next to me. His level of intoxication couldn't mask his embarrassment.

"I remember," I said, looking straight ahead to avoid eye contact.

Holy shit. Why is he doing this? I wanted to run to my parents' car that was parked out front and drive away. Too bad I didn't have a license. Not that a lack of one had stopped me from driving Elizabeth's enormous Cadillac. Twice.

"Well, I just want to apologize. I was a stupid, horny little kid and I'm sorry."

"It's okay. It was a long time ago," I replied. It had to be very difficult and uncomfortable for my brother to discuss the subject and I gave him credit for trying to make amends. He sounded genuinely sorry, but I just wanted get away from him and the discussion before I was forced to remember too much.

"So, we're good? You're not mad at me?"

"No, I'm not mad. It's over." I meant it. I wasn't mad at him for something he did as a kid, twelve years earlier. He hugged me and told me he loved me. No one in my family had ever told me that.

What a fucking Kodak moment. Norman Rockwell should have painted the scene because it would have been a masterpiece.

Thankfully, the bedroom door burst open providing a much needed interruption. It was Aunt Elizabeth and she wore the biggest hat I'd ever seen in my life. I held back a giggle.

"What in the hell's goin' on in here?" my aunt asked from the hall. Her hat would never have cleared the door frame.

"Oh, nothing. We were just talking," replied Scott.

I gave my aunt a look that said, "Get me the hell outta here!"

"Well, whatever ye were talking about, it's obviously upset me wee doll. She looks full as a gypsie's bra, she does! Have ye been drinkin'?" asked my Godmother who apparently thought I looked drunk.

We need to work on our non-verbal communication. "Of course I haven't!"

"Well, then what have ye been talkin' about that's made ye so upset?" From my ever-protective Godmother's perspective, only she had the right to make me miserable.

I looked at Scott and gestured to him. He could tell her whatever he wanted, it was his problem. I confess that watching him squirm was quite enjoyable.

"It doesn't matter. Let's go downstairs," he answered, trying to get past her and her gigantic hat.

"Now just one bloody minute, Mr. Homeowner. Ye haven't answered me question and yer not leavin' this room until ye do!"

"It's really none of your business, Elizabeth. It's between me and my sister," Scott said.

That's a mistake you might not live to regret.

No sooner had the words come out of his mouth than my aunt's fist connected with it. She pulled her fist back and wiped it on her skirt.

"Anything ye have to say to me wee doll is my business, it is. Ye best be keepin' that in mind or I'll loosen some more of yer choppers. Come on, love," she said, waving me past my brother who stood bent over with blood trickling into his hand.

"Thanks for the talk, Scott. Let's do it again sometime," I said, slapping him on the back.

19 A PRIEST? OH BROTHER

I knew, in fact, it was my vagina speaking rather than Our Lord and Savior, when I fell in love with a priest. Technically, he was still a deacon but well on this way to becoming a man of the cloth. He'd been married to a well-to-do lady from high society and they had one handsome bouncing baby boy. At some point during the marriage, he heard the Lord calling him to become a priest. Following the annulment of their marriage, he began walking the lonely path to priesthood. I was determined to drag him back to a life of lustful lovemaking.

I was sixteen when Christopher came to Nativity. He had a charming English accent and during his very first sermon, he divulged the sordid details of his past. It was brilliant! Tell the congregation everything up front before they have a chance to speculate and gossip. He immediately won everyone over and I was entirely smitten, consumed by the sudden, urgent desire to become an altar whore, I mean server.

Our church had recently begun to allow girls to serve and the timing couldn't have been more perfect. Sometimes I served two Masses a day, but found it very enjoyable as long as Christopher presided over the liturgy. The scenery was second to none.

Christopher's ordination was imminent and much to the excitement of the congregation, it was to be performed at our church by the Bishop. Naturally, I was selected to serve. Surely, before he accepts his Holy

Orders, Christopher will see me on the altar and realize he loves me. I imagined him taking me lovingly in his arms, kissing me passionately in front of God, the Virgin Mary and everyone in attendance. The Bishop would join us in Holy Matrimony and we'd live together as man and wife. Unfortunately, Christopher actually heard the Lord calling rather than my hungry loins, because he became a priest rather than my lover.

I wasn't giving up that easily. Between altar serving, cleaning the rectory and Youth Group retreats, I managed to spend several hours a week with my holy crush. He must have been able to read my inexperienced attempts at seduction, but he never let on. Christopher stayed honest, true and trustworthy and it irritated the hell out of me. I wanted to taste the holy tube steak, but I couldn't find a chink in his armor.

Upon learning my holy man was leading a youth retreat at a nearby college, I immediately signed up. My parents were so pleased with my never-ending dedication to serve Our Lord, they happily paid for me to go and, even better, they asked Christopher if I could ride with him.

My British escort picked me in a beat up, two-door piece of shit one would expect a priest to drive. They take a vow of poverty for Christ's sake, literally for His sake. Climbing in, wearing a skirt sans panties, I tried to give him a beaver shot several times, but he refused to notice.

After some mindless discussion about prayer and the Bible and blah blah blah, I asked if he'd ever seen the movie The Thorn Birds. One of my favorites, it's the story of a priest falling in love with a girl who becomes a woman and they make passionate, desperate love. I hoped discussion of the movie might get his mind moving down the path of romance and crazy, dirty sex. I couldn't have been more obvious if I'd painted a picture of a penis slamming into a vagina.

Oh, he got my drift alright. Christopher pulled the car over, put it in park and turned to face me. Leaning in and puckering, I was convinced he was going to ravage me right there in his winter beater. Instead, he spoke to me like a father speaks to a naughty child.

"Don't ever mention that movie in my presence, Patti Anne. Do I make myself quite clear?" he said, in his distinguished accent.

I held back tears and shook my head. Throwing the dilapidated old buggy in drive and pulling onto the road, Christopher resumed driving. Once I regained control of my voice and tear ducts, I put my hand in his holy crotch and asked, "Does this mean you won't fuck me?"

Christopher damn near drove us over the guard rail and into the dirty, brown waters of the Genesee River.

20 LETTING GO

Graduation Day grew ever closer. Accepted and enrolled at Geneseo State University, I couldn't wait to fly the coop. I ached to be off the farm and do whatever I pleased, whenever I pleased. Counting the days until I was away from my parents' prying eyes and endless religious pressure, I treasured the thought of life without Mass, Communion and especially Confession.

It was most peculiar to realize in a matter of days, I'd answer to no one. The freedom for which I'd waited eighteen years was staring me in the face but rather than elation, I felt apprehension. I was becoming more nervous about moving to a strange place in which I had no connections. Mom must have sensed I was clinging to my friends more than usual.

"Hopefully, your roommate will be nice. You know how girls can be," she said, out of the blue.

"I'm not worried about it," I lied.

"Well, I would be. When I went to college, I lived at home so I could stay close to my friends. Too bad you didn't want to go to college in town because you could have lived here, saved a lot of money and kept your friends," Mom reminded me. I'd heard this song and dance since my freshman year of high school.

"You forget, my friends are smarter than yours were and they got into much more academically challenging universities. The only kids going to college here are the ones who couldn't get into a real college," I said. I knew it was mean and untrue, but I wanted to hurt her feelings the way she was trying to hurt mine. *I wouldn't live at home if you paid me.*

Graduation Day arrived with Mom outlining the agenda she expected me to follow. She told me what time I'd be dropped off at school, where to meet after the ceremony, what I should wear and some other things I didn't listen to because I couldn't believe the crap she was spewing. This was my Graduation.

"Mom, Barbara Ann is picking me up for Graduation and I wasn't planning to come right home away. We're going to a bunch of parties."

"Oh no, you're not! Your brother and his girlfriend are coming over for hots and hamburgs and we're eating dinner together. You will be here, or else."

"Mom, it's my Graduation! I'm going out with my friends. I'm never gonna see some of these people ever again."

"You live under my roof and you'll do as I say. You're not gonna be out ramming around town with those wild friends of yours. You're gonna be with your family, where you belong," she snapped. "Besides, I made angel food cake and have fresh berries. Meet us outside the girl's locker room right after Graduation."

She knew I hated angel food cake and never ate any kind of berry but I didn't bother to answer. Angry beyond words, I was afraid to open my mouth because I might tell her to kiss my fat, white, dimpled ass. As the thought crossed my mind, so did a wonderfully evil idea. Forming in my mind was the perfect way to show Mom what I thought of her plans for my Graduation night. A maniacal smile, similar to that of the Grinch as he hatched his plan to dress as Saint Nick and steal Christmas from the Who's, spread across my face.

The ringing of the big, black rotary phone on the kitchen wall interrupted my thoughts.

"Yo," I said, my latest way to answer the telephone.

"What's that supposed to mean?" asked a woman in a familiar, heavy Irish brogue.

"Oh, hi, Aunt Elizabeth. Do you know what today is?"

"Aye. That's why yer ear is pressed to this here contraption. What time do I get to see my wee doll graduate tonight?" I loved when she used that term of affection.

"It starts at 7pm. You shouldn't have any trouble spotting me in the crowd. I'll be the one in the white cap and gown." I never ceased to amuse myself.

"Ye better study hard at Geneseo 'cuz ye won't make it as a funny person."

"They're called comedians, Aunt Elizabeth," I said, rolling my eyes.

"Well, ye won't be one a those neither! I'll see you tonight. Make sure yer arse weed of a mother saves me a seat."

"Will do. See you later," I said. "Hey, Mom, Aunt Elizabeth said to save her a seat."

"She can find her own damn seat. What does she think I am? Her butler?"

"Geez, Mom. Don't be so pissy."

"If you had to deal with someone telling you what to do your whole life and nothing you did was ever good enough for them, you'd be pissy too."

Um, I do. I just looked at her, raised my eyebrows and tilted my head, hoping she'd realize she just described herself.

While waiting in the holding room for the ceremony to begin, I felt a heavy tap on the shoulder. Turning around, I was struck in the eye by the brim of a very large hat.

"Ouch!" I said.

"Oh, sorry, love. Are ye alright, then?" asked my Godmother, rearranging the humongous hat on her head.

"Yeah, I'm fine. It just surprised me mostly," I said, rubbing my eye.

"Well, I just came to tell ye how very proud I am. If ye hadn't killed yer Godfather, I'm sure he'd be standing next to me sayin' the same thing."

"Aunt Elizabeth..." I was so tired of being told I'd killed the man when I was no more than three months old. He was a no good drunk who died of heart attack, not because a tiny infant committed murder.

"Ach, hush, it doesn't matter now. Ye've turned into a fine young woman, ye have," said my aunt, trying to hug me but her hat made it nearly impossible. "I've gotta go now before yer arse weed of a Mum gives away me seat. I just had to see me wee doll one last time before she graduates."

I waved as she walked away and thought about how much I loved the crazy, old bat. She was a hard woman to please at times but she was always there. *What am I gonna do without her at Geneseo?* I choked back the tears and decided to think about it later.

As I stood among my classmates dressed in caps and gowns, I heard my name called. The eruption of a few cheers from the crowd and my classmates made me smile. Walking proudly across the floor to the podium where Mr. McCullum stood, I shook his hand and accepted my diploma.

Watch this! Turning away from the audience seated in front of the stage, I hiked up my white gown, as well as the mini skirt underneath. Without fear of punishment or judgment, I boldly dropped my drawers and showed my lily-white ass to the entire community.

Barbara Ann had painted a great big "M" on each cheek and my asshole served as the letter "O" in the word "Mom". The roar from the crowd was all the thanks and approval I needed.

Over the din of the crowed, I heard Elizabeth. "She's as bent as a nine-bob note, she is!"

Glancing back at Mr. McCullum, I imagined how my colorful Godmother would describe the look on his face following my display of non-decorum. I suspected she'd say something like, "He had a face on him like a well slapped arse."

21 JESUS WHO?

Although I still dreamed of Christopher's hard altar candle, I realized he was serious about his Holy Orders and would never indulge my fantasies. It was pointless to torture myself by standing next to my Holy Man on the altar and waiting for him to invite me back to the rectory to help him out of his chasuble and stole. Although I knew it was probably a sin, I thought he looked perfectly edible wearing a dress, even more so than in the black slacks and shirt he wore off the altar. The sexual frustration was overwhelming so I quit serving.

"Patti Anne," Christopher said, as I returned my surplice and cassock, "why in Heaven's name aren't you serving any longer?"

"I just don't wanna do it anymore."

"But, my dear, you're an exemplary server and your presence on the altar means so very much to me. Promise you'll reconsider."

"Christopher, I can't," I said. I refused to address him as 'Father'.

"Enlighten me, why do you feel thusly?" he pressed.

Because, I want to fuck your brains out. "Christopher, you don't want to know, trust me. Just leave it alone."

"Oh, my dear, you're troubled." He put his arm around my shoulder and pulled me close enough so I could smell his signature fragrance of soap mixed with Bible. "How can I help you? You must know you're special to me and I'd do anything to help you."

Apparently, he's forgotten about the time I grabbed his crotch. "Well, there is something you could do…"

"Just name it," Christopher said, leaning in to make sure he heard whatever it was I was about to request.

Spinning on my heel, I threw my arms around him and planted my lips on his. He hadn't the time to register what happened before I forced my tongue into his mouth in search of its occupant. Christopher must have suffered a mild stroke because he was slow to react. Slow enough, in fact, I had time to lower one hand and cup his Holy Sack. I gave three loving caresses, one for the Father, the Son and The Holy Spirit.

Pushing me violently from him, Christopher's breath was ragged and his chest heaved. *I have that affect on men.* "Patti Anne, how could you?" he asked, sounding confused rather than disgusted.

Well, that's a good sign. "Christopher, can you honestly say you didn't notice how attracted I am to you? That's why I decided to quit serving. Being so close to you and unable to touch you sucks big time."

"I'm married to The Lord and all of me belongs to him. I think we should both go to Confession," he suggested.

"Confess this!" I said, lifting my shirt and bra to expose myself. Christopher turned and walked away. *Maybe I need a boob job.*

Christopher, Youth Group and Church tossed aside, I turned instead to Mother Nature for comfort and inspiration. Barbara Ann and I spent our last summer together getting stoned in the sun. From what I remember, it was a great time and we packed in as much fun as possible before adulthood forced us in different directions.

My endlessly artistic friend fashioned a pipe out of clay. Shaped like a dick, the ingenious creation was small enough to hide in a pocket and a great conversation starter with members of the opposite sex. The only drawback was, its small size required frequent reloading. Looking to create something bigger and better, we found an enormous cardboard roll that once held some sort of cloth or paper. About five feet long, it had an opening big enough to accommodate our faces.

We called her The Proud Mary and after only one hit, you were done. Unfortunately, its considerable size made it impossible to take to the beach in the back seat of Barbara Anne's Valiant and we couldn't carry it through the cemetery either. It was reserved for those times when her parents and sisters weren't in the house and those times were treasured.

After a brief encounter with Proud Mary, we usually headed to Tony's for a large pepperoni pizza and a couple Cokes. Tony's was a local dump that served damn fine pizza and the guys at the counter were usually so stoned, they never charged us more than five bucks. After filling our bellies, we'd climb into the Valiant. Radio cranking and windows down, we'd race off to the sandy shores of Lake Ontario looking for hot guys. Actually, any guys with a pulse were acceptable.

Charlotte had a well-known dive called the Penny Arcade we'd heard about for years because of the bands that played there, but we were too young to get in. Feeling invincible, Barbara Ann and I walked boldly to the front door. Never having set foot in a real bar, we weren't sure how to act. It was too early in the afternoon for a bouncer so we walked in like we owned the joint and ordered a couple beers.

"You got any ID?" asked the bartender.

"Yeah, we but do but we're strippers and unfortunately we left our wallets at the club last night. We can't get them back until it reopens later tonight." My skills at lying hadn't really improved since grade school.

"Strippers, huh?" asked the bartender, checking us out from head to toe.

We shook our heads wondering if the dumbass was really gonna buy that story. We looked more like nuns than strippers.

"Well, I wouldn't want to prevent two working girls from having a good time on their day off now, would I?" He winked, put two beers on the bar and laughed as he walked away. *So, he doesn't believe us, but who cares? At least he gave us beers.*

We drink beer and did shots of tequila for the next several hours and as we drank, the bartender became more and more attractive. I mean, he was some kind of hot. I wanted to help him take inventory in the stock room or replace the little cakey thing in the urinal. Anything to get close enough to touch him.

While I made small talk with the barkeep, Barbara Ann flirted with some guy shooting pool. Within minutes, she and her new friend left for the parking lot to smoke a joint and do whatever else came naturally. My heartthrob bartender was getting hotter by the minute and I couldn't take it any longer. Given the amount of alcohol I'd consumed, I wasn't exactly subtle.

"I love sucking dick," I announced. They sing a song about me called Smooth Operator.

"My name's Rick. Glad to meet you," he said, shaking my hand.

Rick took me behind the bar, which smelled like sour beer mixed with old urine, and led me through a hallway and into a hot and humid stockroom. As the radio played an old classic by the Eagles, we started making out. With one hand, Rick swept everything off the table standing in the middle of the room. Gently, he pushed me backwards and onto the table. As I lay on my back, he crawled on top of me, unbuttoning my pants.

Quite unexpectedly, the table collapsed and we crashed to the floor. I didn't have a clue what was happening but there was a lot of noise, the sense of falling and then I puked on some guy's back. *Oh yeah, that's my bartender.* Oddly enough, he no longer looked like he wanted to get in my pants now that he was covered in barfed up beer and tequila. *Well, excuse me. It's your fault for over serving me.*

I managed to stagger my fat ass out the door of the store room and headed back to the bar, but it wasn't where I'd left it. My sense of direction was broken and I found myself in the kitchen. *Perfect, I'm starving.* I opened the fridge and helped myself to a couple slices of American cheese and a pickle. I walked out without being seen by the cooks or dishwasher. Perhaps they saw me but I was too drunk to notice. I wasn't in top form.

Where the fuck did the bar go? I pushed on a door and was assaulted by bright white lights. *What the hell is going on?* I turned back the way I came, but the door was locked from the inside and I was alone in a deserted parking lot. I may have barfed again but since there wasn't anyone there to hear it, it didn't make any noise.

I staggered around the corner of the building trying to find the swinging doors. A van pulled up, windows down and I heard a familiar voice call my name. *Huh?* I looked closer and realized it was my beloved crush, Stephen. He'd come to my rescue again. I climbed into the van and he started to play the unwelcome role of parent.

"What are you doing out here? Who are you with?"

I answered by covering his mouth with mine. I must have stunk to high heaven, but if I did he didn't show it. Throwing the bus in park, he led me by the hand to the back of his love shack on wheels. He was obviously a pervert because there was a mattress covered with a puppy blanket and fringed throw pillows on the floor. I didn't care. I'd been dreaming of being naked with this man for as long as I could remember thinking about being naked with anyone. Except maybe John Schneider.

I told Stephen I loved him and always had.

"I've waited for this moment for a long time, you know. It killed me to kick you out of my house all those years ago," he said, between kisses.

"You know I'm eighteen, right? Jail bait no more."

"Don't think for a minute that I'm not aware of that, Dearest Patricia."

"Take me." I was drunk but I knew what I was doing.

"I don't want it to happen here, like this." he said.

Umm...but you have a mattress with blankets and pillows in the back of your van. You must have wanted it to happen with someone. "I can't wait another minute. I need you."

I woke up in Barbara Ann's car, sitting in her parent's driveway. My mouth was as dry as a nun's crack and tasted like someone had taken a dump in it. Barely able to focus my eyes because of the hammering in my head, I thought of Stephen and his van and abruptly sat up, smacking my head on the ceiling. More puking. Barbara Ann's Mom came out of the house and chased me out of the car with a broom. She was just a little upset that I barfed in the front seat of their vintage Valiant. *Touchy.*

Two weeks later, I left the farm for Geneseo, New York. Elizabeth stopped by to say goodbye before my parents drove me to college.

"Ach, I'm sicker than a plane to Lourdes. I'll miss me wee doll more than ye know," she said, tears running down her flushed, freckled face.

I really didn't want to cry. I'd waited eighteen years to get away from the farm and experience more than cows and chores and church but now that it was time to go, I realized how much I loved my home and family.

I wrapped my arms around my Godmother, nestling my face in her neck. Her familiar smell of soap and corned beef, mixed with whiskey, made me homesick even though she was right in front of me. Unable to stop myself, I cried like a small child.

Elizabeth stroked my hair and rocked, muttering things I didn't understand but found soothing anyway. I think she was speaking in her native tongue, something she did on occasion in her sleep.

"Never forget who ye are, love. Don't try to be somethin' yer not. It always backfires, it does. Be a good girl, study hard and for the love of Pete, don't start smokin' cigarettes! Call yer Godmum once in a while, 'cuz I sure will be blue without ye here."

I couldn't stop crying and I didn't want to let go but I knew my parents were watching and waiting their turn to say goodbye. It was time to let go.

"Goodbye, Aunt Elizabeth. I'll miss you more than you know. I love you," I whispered and then kissed her cheek. I walked outside to the family station wagon to cry alone until my parents followed.

The day I thought would be so exciting and wonderful sucked. My heart ached and all I wanted to do was crawl into the little bed I'd slept in for eighteen years and go to sleep. But I couldn't. It was time to go.

My Godmother stayed in the house and out of sight until we drove away. *I hope she'll be okay without me.*

Once we'd found my room and unpacked my boxes of clothes and stereo from the car, there wasn't much left to be said. I dreaded saying goodbye to my parents and wished I could just go to the bathroom and find them gone when I came out.

"Well, I guess this is it. Study hard and don't go boy crazy," said my Dad, who was already tearing up.

"I'll do my best, Dad."

"Do you have everything you need? Do you want us to take you to the store for anything before we go?" Mom asked, looking like she might actually cry too.

"No, thanks. I think I have everything I need. I'll call you in a few days."
I just wanted them to go so I could cry before my two roommates
showed up.

"Kicking us out? We get the message. Okay, well, have fun and work
hard," my Mom said as she hugged me goodbye. "Be sure to call us."

Dad stood off to the side, looking desperately lost and sad. "I can't
believe you're old enough to leave home. Now it's just me and Mum,"
he said, with a sad smile.

"Don't forget George, Dad. He might be almost thirty years old, but he's
still living at home. You and Mom aren't alone yet," I said, trying to
make light of the awkward moment.

"Be careful and make sure you lock your door at night," said Dad,
hugging me.

"Okay, bye! I'll call you soon," I said, closing my door.

I waited about ten seconds before throwing myself on my bed and
burying my head under the pillow. I sobbed until there were no more
tears.

22 SINNING IS FUN

I recovered from my initial bout of homesickness after a day or two and began to enjoy my newfound freedom by sinning. I was so happy to be out from under the proverbial Thumb of Catholicism, I sinned as much as possible. Big sins, little sins, any and every sin I could think of. I cheated on tests, stole beer, had unprotected sex with strangers and started fights between suite mates just to watch them go at it.

On more than one occasion, I snuck into the dumpier bars in town and flirted with the local red necks, letting them buy me a few beers. When the field hands got a little too friendly, I'd tearfully tell a bouncer they were harassing me and get the poor guys thrown out. Without fail, a bouncer or bartender would offer me a ride back to campus in case the dejected boys were waiting for me outside. Back on campus, I'd let the kind bartender walk me to my suite to make sure I made it home okay. I'd invite him in and fuck his brains out on my roommate's bed. I never tired of these games because I was having a great time as a Big Time Sinner.

The only thing threatening to interfere with my career as a full-time sinner was that annoying little thing known as class work. I decided not to study for an upcoming audiology exam because I knew unless God performed a miracle, which wasn't likely given my ratio of sins to good deeds, there was no way I could pass it. Instead of putting forth any effort to learn the material, I called my professor, in very convincing tears, and told him my brother had just been killed. I described in detail how he'd been crushed by a crane while working at Kodak. I'd miss the exam, of course, because I needed to go home to be with my family. Through heartfelt tears, my professor said he'd keep my family in his prayers and would give me an A in his class. He ended our conversation with the Lord's Prayer.

I hung up feeling victorious. I didn't have to study and would receive an A in a class in which I deserved a D, at best. While I celebrated my triumph, something unexpected and awful happened. I received an abrupt call from my conscience. I hadn't heard from it in so long I barely recognized its voice, but its mere presence caused discomfort.

Sermons about fire and brimstone heard during my years of Catholic indoctrination came flooding to the surface. Guilt eliminated my appetite, and given the enormity of my ass, that was of great significance. Unable to concentrate on sinning, I stopped partying, having sex and getting drunk. My guilt was so heavy, it kept me awake for days. Every time I closed my eyes I heard my professor crying and praying with me.

I contemplated my recent behavior and was disgusted. I knew I was a better person than the one I was showing Geneseo State and thought about how disappointed my Godmother would be if she knew how I was conducting myself. Suddenly homesick, I needed to hear her voice. Using the phone hanging on the wall of the common room, I called my aunt.

"Aye?" she answered on the first ring.

"Aunt Elizabeth, it's me." Tears were threatening to interfere with my ability to carry on a normal conversation.

"Aye, I knew it would be. Somethin' told me ye'd be ringing. What's wrong, love?" she asked.

The sound of her thick brogue in my ear was as comforting as it was heart-breaking. I missed her dearly.

"I don't know. I just feel sad."

"Ach, yer finally away from that arse weed of a Mum, what do you have to be sad about? Somebody botherin' ye?" she asked, probably ready to jump in the old Caddy and drive to Geneseo and knock out somebody's teeth.

"No, nobody's bothering me. I told a lie to one of my teacher's and I'm feeling so guilty it's making me sick."

"Well, then, ye better get yer keister over to Confession. I shouldn't have to tell ye that. Don't start actin' the maggot just 'cuz I'm not there to box yer ears!"

"I will, I promise. Aunt Elizabeth, can I ask you a favor?" I asked.

"Aye."

"Will you please come up this weekend? I miss you." I was crying.

"Ach, now now, wee doll. Yer too big for tears. I miss ye powerful and will be there first thing Saturday morning. See if there's a game of footy we can watch on Sunday. Since ye up and left for university, I lost me footy partner," said my aunt.

"Yay! Sounds good. We'll watch football and eat crappy food. Thanks, Aunt Elizabeth. I can't wait to see you."

"Me too, wee doll. Me too. Don't let me get there and find ye haven't been to Confession!" she said before hanging up.

Dressing in the cleanest dirty clothes I found lying on the floor, I walked two miles to St. Mary's Catholic Church. When I left the farm, I never thought I'd willingly choose to go to Confession. I didn't believe in Confession. *Or do I?*

I waited nervously for a Confessional to empty and tried to calm down. I was more afraid than when I made my first Confession almost nine years ago, which was surprising considering I had two major sins to confess that day. *I shouldn't be so nervous. It's not like I need to confess killing an uncle again.*

I entered the Confessional, which was more modern than the ones at Nativity. Rather than being separated from the priest by an ornately carved wooden screen, this arrangement placed the priest and sinner facing each other in two nicely stuffed chairs. I preferred the old fashioned style because it felt more familiar, more legitimate and more fundamental.

I sat in the chair facing a priest I'd never met, with whom I had no history. This man was unaware of my family story, my past sins and my character. Quite unforeseen, I wished to be back at Nativity confessing to kind old Father Lyntz. *What's wrong with me?*

It suddenly stuck me the man before me wasn't a priest. He wore jeans, a polo shirt and Nikes. *Nikes on a priest?* If this guy could break with tradition, then I could as well. Extending my hand toward him, I said "Father?" trailing off, to imply I was confirming his occupation. He nodded but didn't speak.

"Hmm, I've never seen a priest dressed like that."

"Nor have I ever seen anyone dressed like you," he said, taking in my less-than-runway-quality outfit.

"Well, I'm a poor college student," I answered, more than a little embarrassed by my dirty, wrinkled clothes.

"I myself have taken a vow of poverty but not one of slovenliness."

Wow. This guy's a total dick. "Forgive me Father, for I have sinned. It's been over a year since my last Confession."

I stopped speaking, unsure how to continue. I looked at the priest, expecting him to provide some guidance. He only looked at me and I interpreted his manner as unfeeling, but perhaps it was because he was so unfamiliar.

"I lied to a professor to get out of an exam and he was so kind and comforting, the guilt is unbearable. That's why I'm here." The priest remained silent, his expression unchanged. *A little help here, pal, would be nice.* "I told him my brother was killed and he, um, he cried."

Hearing the words out loud, I realized they were uglier and more vile than when they'd been running around my head. I cried, unable to hold in the anguish any longer.

"And?" said Father, handing me a box of tissues.

"He told me he'd give me an A, although I didn't deserve to pass," I said, wondering if he could understand my words blanketed in sobs. "He even prayed with me. He said an Our Father." My shoulders heaved and, although embarrassed at my outpouring of emotion, I was unable to stem the tide. After several minutes, I gained a small measure of composure and the priest spoke.

"You disgust me."

Huh? Say what?

"You come crawling in here, whining and sniveling, gambling that the simple act of Confession will cleanse your unfit soul of your evil doings. People like you do whatever they want to whomever they want and think it's my job to clean up the mess. Well, let me tell you something, you won't get off that easily!"

Shit, is this guy ever gonna come up for air?

"You're the worst kind of person there is! You told a tremendously disgusting lie to avoid studying, because it would have interrupted your sleep and TV watching, and your poor, God-fearing professor believed you! Unlike you, he has a heart and his heart is with God! Where is your heart? In a six pack of beer or a box of condoms?"

Just one minute, Padre, you don't even know me! "What's that supposed to mean?" I asked, completely taken aback by his aggressive and assuming demeanor.

"You know exactly what I mean! You care only about yourself. You've put drinking and sex above Our Lord for too long and now that your conscience has the better of you, you come crawling here expecting me to tell you it's okay. Well guess what? It's not! You're a horrible human being!"

This guy's gonna pop a nut if he doesn't calm down! "I know what I did was wrong, but you have no right to make assumptions about me. Why are you talking about drinking and sex?"

"Silence!" he shouted.

If this guy had a moustache, I could easily be convinced he's Sister Fatass.

"As your penance, you will go see this professor face to face. You will describe for him, in excruciating detail, your wicked behavior. Do you understand?"

"Yes," I said, quietly. The tears were making a strong comeback.

"If you do so, which I suspect you won't because you lack dignity and contrition," Father said sternly, "it's unlikely you'll ever escape the fiery depths of Hell."

I contemplated his enlightening words of wisdom and asked for clarification. "So even if confess to my professor, I still won't be worthy in God's eyes? I'll still go to Hell?"

"That's correct. Your soul is probably scarred beyond repair."

I stood and said, "Well, then fuck this shit." I walked home with my burden lifted.

23 THE FAMILY SECRET

I adored Scott's wife, Berta, and usually introduced her as my sister and Scott as my brother-in-law. It really irritated the hell out of him, which encouraged me to do it more and more. Berta was the best sister I could have asked for and I admired her for so many things. She was beautiful, humorous, playful and generous with an amazing set of pipes to boot. That girl could sing!

About seventeen years after their marriage, things between Scott and Berta got a little rocky. When I first became aware there were problems, their daughters were ages eight, twelve and thirteen.

Neither Scott nor Berta shared the details with anyone, they simply said they were in marriage counseling. An uncomfortable feeling stirred in my gut, but I decided to ignore it. Their problems were theirs alone and I didn't want to be involved, other than to help with the girls whenever possible.

On a rare trip back to the farm, Scott and Berta were there with their daughters. They'd been to Buffalo for a wedding and drove to Mom and Dad's to spend a couple days with them. It was an impromptu family reunion of sorts and my parents enjoyed the company.

"I wasn't expecting to feed such a big crowd! Don't get wrong, I'm glad you're here, but I need to go the grocery store if we're ever gonna eat tonight," said Mom.

"Berta and I will go for you, Mom. You stay here," I offered, taking the shopping list from her.

"I'll come with you," said Scott.

"Why don't you stay here so your Mom doesn't have to watch the girls? She's been running all day," countered Berta, grabbing her purse.

"Why don't you stay and I'll go with Patti Anne?"

"What's the big deal, Scott?" I said, rather annoyed. "Just stay here. I'd like five minutes alone with Berta anyway. I never get her to myself."

"Why do you need to be alone? What's the big secret?" he asked, standing in front of the door to block our exit.

"Quit being a dick, Scott, and get outta the way! Come on Berta, let's take your car. Mine's full of dog hair," I said, giving Scott a one-fingered salute. My black lab had accompanied me to New York and car rides made him nervous. Well, actually, everything made him nervous and he'd shed enough hair to weave a Cher wig.

"Geez, Berta. What's Scott's problem?" I asked as we hopped in their minivan.

"He doesn't want us to be alone because he's afraid I'll tell you why we're in marriage counseling," said Berta, pulling out of the driveway.

"He's such an ass. So tell me. What's going on?"

"I can't. I promised him I wouldn't tell anyone," she said.

I could tell she wanted to talk about it and she looked like she was about to let the proverbial cat out of its bag, but no matter how hard I tried to get it out of her, she just wouldn't budge. *Silly goose. Keeping promises to her husband. What a boob.*

"Just tell me this: does it have anything to do with little girls?" I heard myself say. I was uncomfortable opening that door, but I had a nasty feeling in the pit of my stomach and that feeling was usually spot-on. Berta almost drove their minivan into an oncoming car.

"What the hell would make you ask that?" The tears in her eyes told me I'd hit close to home.

"Scott started to molest me when I was four," I said, as quickly possible, because I didn't like the taste of the words on my tongue.

Too embarrassed to make eye contact, I looked out the window at the old homes topped with cupolas that lined Main Street. Embarrassment was soon followed by regret. *I haven't talked to anyone about this since I was four years old. Why in the hell am I talking about it now?*

"Oh, Patti Anne, I'm so sorry," said Berta, taking my hand. We drove in silence the rest of the way to the grocery store. I was embarrassed by my confession and I guess it gave poor Berta quite a shock. When she parked the minivan, she leaned over and hugged me. Seeing tears in her eyes, I couldn't help but join in.

As we cried in the Wegman's parking lot, she asked, "Did you ever tell anyone?"

"Yeah, I told Mom."

"What did she do?" she asked, wiping tears off her cheeks.

"Nothing," I replied in a small voice, barely recognizable as my own. "She gave me Vaseline to soothe the parts that hurt. Apparently, a lot of people are wasting good money on therapy for sexual abuse when they could just slather Vaseline on themselves. It cures all wounds and it's much cheaper," I said sarcastically.

My tears came harder, along with a few heavy sobs. I thought I'd buried this a very long time ago. I'd put those memories and feelings in a place so deep, I never had to look at them. I buried and left them there, until now.

"Please don't tell anyone about this, okay?" I asked my sister-in-law.

"Of course I won't, I promise," she assured me. "I can't tell you what's going on between me and Scott, but I can tell you it has nothing to do with little girls."

Well, that's a relief. "I'm sorry to shock you, but I had to ask because my gut's been telling me to. I guess my gut was wrong. I'm glad it was." *I wonder why it failed me? It's never has before.*

Berta remained silent, biting her lip. I couldn't read her expression but it made me uncomfortable.

I was making a pan of lasagna and singing along with Buck Owens when the phone rang. "Hello?" I said, turning down the CD player on the counter.

"Hey, Patti Anne, it's your favorite brother," Scott said.

"Oh, hi Peter," I replied.

"You're almost as funny as Elizabeth," came his sarcastic reply. "Hey listen, I told you I go to counseling, right?"

"Yeah, why?" I rolled my eyes because I didn't really care. I wanted to go back to singing with Buck, who was much more entertaining. He was also better looking.

"Well, my counselor said as part of my treatment, I have to contact my family members and close friends to tell them about me."

"Okay..." *There goes my stomach.*

There was a long pause before Scott confessed, "I'm a pedophile."

You don't say? What a surprise. "Um, yeah, I know," I said with a cringe. *What a stupid thing to say!*

"Well, actually you don't. I'm not interested in little girls."

Oh god, I'm gonna puke. "Have you told Mom and Dad?" I asked, trying to mask the utter horror and disgust that threatened to make me empty the contents of my stomach.

"Yeah, I called them first. It was one of the hardest things I've ever done," he said through his tears.

"Um, I gotta go. There's someone at the door," I said, hanging up the phone.

I just couldn't continue the conversation. Shaking with anger and disgust, I sat on the floor and hugged my knees. Memories I'd tried to erase from my mind came flooding back, unwanted and unrelenting. I cried for myself, my family and the innocent children whose lives had been poisoned by my brother's horrible actions.

I tried to imagine how my parents reacted to Scott's call. My saintly Dad was already in the throes of Alzheimer's and that little piece of information was probably more than his struggling brain could process. Dad never asked about Scott or discussed him again, at least in my presence. In typical Catholic fashion, if we don't talk about it, then it never happened. What an approach! Too bad it doesn't work for global warming, starvation and AIDS.

Scott and Berta became legally separated and each maintained their own household. The girls stayed with Berta and Scott moved into an apartment about twenty minutes away. He continued to go to individual counseling and Berta, God bless her kind soul, continued to accompany him to marriage counseling. She was trying to find a way to forgive my brother and save their marriage, in spite of his problems. *She's a far better person than I'll ever be.*

My husband and I tried to be supportive, not only of Berta and the girls but of my brother as well. I wasn't thrilled about having a pedophile in the house, but if Berta was trying to make it work, I figured I needed to do the same.

"What do you think about inviting Scott to spend Christmas with us?" I asked my husband, Wally.

Not one to respond quickly to any question because he analyzed every possible angle before speaking, he finally said, "I guess it's alright, but I need to have a talk with him when he gets here."

Wally greeted Scott at the door with a forty-five. "If you even think about going near a child in this neighborhood, I will shoot you. Do you understand?" Wally's eyes were bugging out of their sockets and his face said he wasn't bullshitting.

"He's not kidding and he'll no doubt aim for your balls," I said. I wasn't joking.

Scott was speechless. He finally managed a small nod 'yes', and Wally let him in. There wasn't any more discussion about shooting or children and the guys got along just fine. We had a very enjoyable Christmas and Santa left a few gifts for my brother under our tree. It was obvious he enjoyed himself and I tried not to think about the past or the fact that he was a pedophile.

Shortly before packing his car to head home, Scott handed me a legal-sized sealed envelope.

"What's this?" I asked.

"It's full of homework from my counseling sessions. I don't want it lying around the apartment, in case the girls find it," he explained. "Will you hold on to it for me, until I need it again?"

"Sure, whatever," I replied without an ounce of concern.

"Please keep it sealed. I don't want anyone to read it."

"Yeah, I get it. Don't worry about it," I assured him.

When he was gone, I filed it in my desk and forgot about it.

Life continued as usual and I stopped thinking so much about Scott. I'd grown tired of feeling consumed by him and his problems, so I threw myself into anything that would keep my mind busy. An occupied mind doesn't have time to dwell on things it can't change. It worked for the most part until that nagging feeling crept into my gut again.

I called my sister-in-law. "Hi Bertie!" I said, hoping to sound upbeat. "How are you and the girls, and I'm not talking about your jugs!" I joked, hoping to make her smile.

She was crying. *Oh, come on. It was a little funny.* "What's wrong?"

"Scott was arrested for having child pornography on his computer at work. He's been taken into custody," she sobbed. *Too bad my gut can't pick lottery numbers.*

"Oh shit, Bertie. I'm so sorry you have to go through this. Do the girls know?"

"No, I haven't told them anything yet," she said, sniffing, "but I'm gonna have to tell them soon. This is a small town, it'll be all over the news and they'll hear about it at school."

How do you tell your young children their father is going to jail for fucking little kids? Unfortunately, Bertie was right, if she didn't tell them someone else would.

"He was dumb enough to have that crap on his computer at work?" I asked, very surprised. My brother was a dick but he was pretty intelligent, although his recent arrest would make him seem otherwise.

"Apparently, there was a lot of it and some of it was really, really bad. The police searched his apartment, too. His laptop was loaded with the same type of shit," she cried so hard I could barely understand what she said.

"So, this entire time he's been going to counseling and telling everyone he's 'sober', he's been looking at disgusting pictures of innocent children?" I asked, getting more angry by the second.

"I guess so. He insisted he hadn't engaged in any type of inappropriate behavior since he started going to counseling months ago, but he lied. Some of the stuff on the computer was very recently downloaded," Berta said.

I told Bertie to call me anytime, day or night, and offered to be there when she told my nieces about their Dad. I would have done anything in my power to lighten the heartache they were about to bear.

I shared with Wally everything Berta told me. He hugged me tightly while I cried.

"Oh shit!" I said. "What about that envelop he left here? You know, the one he said had homework in it?"

"Yeah, and?" my husband said, looking unsettled.

"What if there's stuff in there about a child he hurt or was planning to hurt?"

"So open it and find out."

That's what I was hoping you'd say. Everyone likes an accomplice and having my husband as mine eased my Catholic Guilt that still reared its ugly head on occasion.

The envelope contained the sexual fantasies and actions of a very sick man. It was incomprehensible that my own flesh and blood could have thought about and performed the things described on those pages. It read like a horror story. My stomach and bowels threatened to release.

"Trust me, Wally, you don't want to read this," I said, maintaining a safe distance in the event of projectile vomiting.

"No, I'm sure I don't, but you better call our attorney and get his advice about what to do with it." That's my Wally, always thinking.

I spoke with my attorney, shared the details of my brother's arrest and described the contents of the envelope. He told me to get that shit out of my possession as soon as possible and may have mentioned a hot fire. *Why didn't I think of that?* I tossed my brother's sick confessions into the fireplace and watched it burn to ashes, just like the futures of my sister-in-law and nieces.

As I watched the embers of Scott's twisted fantasies die, Mom called to talk about his arrest, her voice breaking as she held back tears. My Mom was not a crier. I watched my father cry at Grama's funeral, but except for a tear when Heidi and Dildo, I mean Max, were taken away, I'd never even seen my Mother get misty.

"I just can't believe this. I just can't believe he's so sick," she said.

What a minute, Scott's sick? I thought he was a pedophile! I went along to see where she was headed. "What do you mean he's sick?" I could hardly wait to hear her reply.

"It's a disease, Pat. He can't help it."

"Mom, he made choices! He has children of his own, yet he chose to abuse innocent boys!" I was more than a little pissed at her for defending him. "Besides, it doesn't exactly come as a surprise, does it?"

"What are you talking about?" she asked, as if she really didn't know.

"Oh, come on, Mom. You know Scott abused me when I was little," I said, prodding her memory.

"What are you talking about?"

"I told you when I was about four he was abusing me and it went on a lot longer than you ever knew."

"No, you did not! You never told me anything like that!"

"Um, yeah, I did. You handed me a jar of Vaseline and walked away," I reminded her. Not only was I pissed, I was hurt. Was it possible she somehow could have forgotten her four year old daughter told her it hurt when she peed? *Maybe that Alzheimer's thing is catching.*

"I don't remember anything like that!" she spat. In ultimate Catholic fashion she said, "Well, at least you didn't have it as bad as I did."

Oh Jesus. What in God's name is she talking about now? "What does that mean?" I asked.

"My father abused me from the time I was about fifteen until I left home to be married."

That's a very disturbing bombshell, Mom, but at least things are starting to make more sense. At least in a sick and twisted sort of way. "Abused you how?" I nudged, although I really didn't want to know.

"He would come into my bedroom when my Mom was away at a meeting or after she'd gone to sleep," she said. "He'd make me touch him and...do things."

She wasn't crying as she spoke. She sounded as if she were reciting her grocery list, without emotion.

"Oh, Mom, I'm so sorry. That's disgusting. Did Gram know?"

"Maybe she did, I don't know. I guess she was so relieved he wasn't bothering her, she didn't worry about it."

Talk about sick. My grandfather was getting his jollies with my mother and my grandmother may have known about it but chose to ignore it because it meant he left her alone? Well, isn't that just great? We're the spitting image of the Walton's.

Suddenly, I felt the earth stop spinning. "Um, Mom," I asked tentatively, "if you'd been abused, why did you let it happen to me? Why didn't you stop it?"

"I don't know what you're talking about."

"Well, I mean since it happened to you, shouldn't you have been more aware? Wouldn't you have been on the lookout for signs of something going on so you could prevent your child from going through what you did?"

"You never told me anything was wrong. I did everything I could to take care of all you kids."

I simply couldn't understand my Mom's perspective. Because she had been sexually abused by her father, she seemed unable or unwilling to sympathize with me even though I was a victim, too.

While Scott did time in the pokey, he felt the need to correspond with me. I never replied because I could hear my Godmother saying, "If ye can't say something nice, then shet yer pie hole." Nothing I had to say fell into the nice category, so I resisted the urge to tell him what a selfish fucking pig he was.

In one of his letters, Scott said he forgave me. *What?* I had to read it again, three or four times, to be sure I understood correctly. *You forgive me? For what?* Scott's letter went on to say Berta told him I'd read the contents of the envelope he'd given me to keep hidden and, although it took him a long time, he forgave me. *What a guy. The very image of Jesus H. Christ.*

Scott wrote to some of our cousins in Canada he hadn't seen or spoken to in almost twenty years. I guess he was trying to drum up sympathy or line up potential contacts for his eventual release from the big house. Originally sentenced to ten years, he only served six because he provided testimony about some other kid fuckers. Some brilliant government asshole decided his assistance warranted a reduction in his debt to society. I, on the other hand, was a proponent of increasing his sentence. Scott possessed information about those scumbags prior to his arrest, but he didn't share it with the authorities until he could personally gain from doing so. Imagine the number of children who could have been protected and spared the nightmare if he had spoken up earlier. *His Confessions must take hours and hours.*

While Scott served his six years, my parents did their best to keep his arrest and imprisonment a secret. Even from her siblings and mother, my mom kept Scott's situation hidden. My brothers and I were forbidden to tell anyone what happened, although I didn't understand why.

"What Scott chose to do is not a reflection of you and Dad. Why are you working so hard to keep this big family secret?" I asked, during one of our many long phone conversations about Scott.

"Because it's nobody's business, that's why. I don't need them talking about us behind our backs and that's just what they'll do."

She had a point, they were Catholics so of course they'd gossip and say hurtful things behind our backs. That's what we would do if one of them went to jail for being a kid fucker.

"But they're your family, Mom! You need their support."

"They won't give me support and I don't need it! I don't want anything from any of those people!"

"Those people? They're your flesh and blood," I reminded her, sad that she seemed alone.

"Coulda fooled me. They never call, drop by to visit or invite us to dinner. I never hear from any of them."

"Do you call them?" I asked. "Do you invite them to the farm for dinner?"

Mom didn't answer. I'd heard this complaint before. She didn't pick up the phone to call her brothers or sisters-in-law; she expected them to come to her. Keeping in touch was solely their responsibility.

"You're telling me, if you told Gram that Scott was arrested, she wouldn't feel badly for you? Don't you think she'd try to comfort you?" I asked. "She's your mother, for God's sake."

"She'll tell my brothers who will tell their wives, and if there's one thing I will not put up with, it's my sister-in-law sticking her big fat nose in this family's business. She always thought she was better than me, and there's nothing she would love more than rub this in my face."

"So, you're ashamed of Scott," I pointed out, matter-of-factly.

"I am not."

"Then why do you care about them rubbing it in your face? If you're not ashamed, then it wouldn't matter." I knew my Dad wouldn't approve of the way I argued with my mother, but I couldn't stop myself.

"I'm done talking about this! Promise me you won't tell anyone about Scott. I've spent my whole life taking care of you kids and sacrificing to give you what I never had. Scott has a disease and can't help it. I don't want anyone finding out about him," pleaded my Mom.

"I'm not gonna lie for him. If someone asks me a direct question, I will give them a direct answer."

"Then I have nothing else to say to you," she said and the phone went dead.

Although I was irritated with her, I also sympathized with her given the situation she faced. Moms defend their children and love them no matter what. By keeping Scott's arrest secret, she was doing her job as a parent. However, I wasn't Scott's parent nor did I feel the slightest bit obligated to defend him or lie to protect him.

My other brothers and I tossed around theories about why Scott is a pedophile. Some people claim you're born that way while others, like my Mom, say it's a disease. Personally, I don't give a damn why anyone decides they want to fuck little kids. They should be responsible and kill themselves as soon as they sense the urge.

Peter and I are convinced Scott was sexually abused by a priest while serving as an altar boy at Nativity. Father Burte was well-liked by the parishioners for both his boyish sense of humor and friendly nature. He was charismatic and put people at ease, which made him a favorite with the ladies of the congregation. The parishioners really appreciated the effort he put into encouraging young boys to become altar servers. No matter when we stopped by the rectory to drop off a casserole or buy a Mass card, there were always a couple teenage boys hanging around. I don't think my Mom ever thought twice about it.

"What a nice man," she'd say. "Father spends more time with those boys than their parents do. Some people just shouldn't have kids!"

Hello Betty. Wake up and smell the lubricating gel.

Father Burte had a cottage on Conesus Lake, where he frequently took four or five altar boys for the weekend. To the parish, he couched the trips as mini retreats and opportunities for the boys to fish, water ski and enjoy the great outdoors. Living on one-hundred-thirty acres sure made it hard for Scott to find the great outdoors.

Evenings at the lake were spent playing cards. Father would start up a game of euchre and offer various incentives for beating him at his favorite game. The ultimate prize? The winner earned a place in Father Burte's bed for the night. He had a separate bedroom, complete with a solid oak door. Something tells me Father and the lucky winner weren't going through the Stations of the Cross.

As Peter and I talked about Scott's group of altar boys, we realized with great horror every single one of them had either committed suicide, suffered from severe drug or alcohol problems, or was in therapy for some sort of serious, social disorder. Was there something in the holy water?

24 DAD

My Dad changed in small but odd ways. He seemed easily confused about things he once could have done blindfolded. His emotions were different as well and I suspected the worst. I suggested to Mom it might be a good idea to have him tested for Alzheimer's disease. Epic failure. Based on her reaction, you'd think I suggested they invite a black family over for dinner or become Methodist. Mom went loony tunes, insisting he most certainly did not have Alzheimer's. Because she's a medical professional.

"How can you even make such a suggestion? You never come home and have no idea what your Father is like," she said.

She had a point because I only went home about once a year. It was all I could handle. My Mom and I were on each other's nerves within an hour of my arrival and I quickly grew tired of her constant nagging of my Dad and relentless bitching about my Godmother.

"That woman never lets up! I swear she lives just to irritate the hell outta me!" That was Mom's general assessment of Elizabeth and she vocalized it often.

It was true I didn't see my Dad very often, but that made the changes in his behavior so much more obvious to me than to those who saw him every day. Trying to explain that to Betty was like talking to Helen Keller.

Five years later, Dad was diagnosed with Alzheimer's. *Wow. Wish I'd suggested he get tested sooner.* He was put on medication to slow the progression of the disease but I don't think it made a difference. Maybe if he'd been taken for an evaluation five years earlier, the drugs would have been more successful but placing blame wasn't going to cure my Dad.

My father's confusion grew and before long, he was unable to tell time or figure out how much to leave for a tip. Getting dressed became a humorous challenge. Well, at least I found humor in it.

Walking out of his room wearing only his fruit of the looms, Dad held a pair of pants in his hand. To say I was shocked is grossly insufficient. My Father was very shy and didn't even let me see him in an undershirt and pants. He never left the bedroom with being fully dressed. My eyes couldn't accept he stood before me wearing nothing but underwear.

"I know I'm supposed to put these on," he said, pointing to the pants, "but I don't know where they go!"

I laughed out loud and he did too. *If I don't laugh, I'll cry.*

My Dad spent more and more time in his favorite chair, looking off in the distance wearing a vacant, sad expression. No doubt scared of the future and frustrated by his confusion about nearly everything, Mom barked out orders, telling him how to eat, walk and sit. His reaction was not surprising. He crawled inside himself and pretty much stayed there.

When my Dad tried to help by drying dishes and putting them away, he didn't measure up to Mom's standards. "Mac, that doesn't go there! How long have you lived here? For Pete's sake we've never put that bowl in the closet!"

*What does it fucking matter where he puts the mashed potato bowl?
Let the poor guy feel useful.* For whatever reason, Mom couldn't
overlook his forgetfulness so Dad gave up trying to help. He did what he
was told to do, when he was told to do it. I suspect he felt like he was
back in Catholic school.

A couple years after the diagnosis of Alzheimer's, Dad fell in the kitchen
after breakfast and was unable to stand. It was an annoying Life Alert
commercial come to life. Mom wasn't able to help him to his feet and
called 9-1-1. When the EMTs arrived, they asked Dad how he felt.

"Just fine," he said.

"Mac, how do you really feel?" asked one of the guys who knew my
parents fairly well.

"Like shit," he replied.

That said it all. My Dad didn't swear in front of my mother and he never
complained about his health. He never missed work for any reason
other than when he was hospitalized after being pierced through the
gut by a metal rod, while on the job at Kodak. I, on the other hand,
have called in sick because the Syfi Channel was doing a Ghost Hunters
marathon.

Dad spent a couple weeks in the hospital recovering from pneumonia,
although he didn't have any outward symptoms like a cough. The
diagnosis was a complete surprise to both of my parents. While
hospitalized, his Alzheimer's kicked into high gear, which it usually did
whenever he was ill but it typically receded as he regained his strength.
During his hospitalization, he was extremely disoriented and difficult to
understand. As the antibiotics worked their magic and Dad became
properly hydrated, the fog cleared and he was less confused.

On the morning he was scheduled to be released, Dad had a seizure.
The medical staff was stumped, unable to find a clear cause, and my
Dad continued having several mini seizures a day. As I listened to my

Mom explain my father's situation over the phone, I knew I needed to get to the airport right away.

I flew to my hometown to get some answers because, although my Mom was good at giving orders to my Dad, she didn't know how to assert herself with anyone of authority. From her perspective, doctors, police and priests were infallible and not to be questioned. I realized if anything was going to get done, it was up to me.

I landed at the airport, about a thirty minute drive from the family farm, and was greeted by wonderful, warm spring weather. I rented a car and drove straight to the hospital to check on my Dad. Tucked into his hospital bed, he looked like he'd aged five years over the past three months.

"Hi Dad," I said, leaning over the metal railing to hug his large, farmer frame.

"Oh, hi there," he said, without opening his eyes.

"Open your eyes, Dad."

"They are open," he responded, eyes still closed.

"Mac! Open your eyes. There's someone here to see you!" ordered my Mom, but she looked worried in spite of her gruff demeanor.

"Do you know who I am?" I asked, almost dreading his response.

"Yes, you're George," he responded, quite seriously.

"George? Is my face as hairy as George's?" I asked, laughing.

"No, but your ass is," replied my Dad, with only the slightest hint of a smile.

I looked at my Mom and George in complete and utter disbelief. I looked back at my Dad, now wearing a smile and the four of us laughed. There could be no doubt, it was indeed funny, but very uncharacteristic of Dad and his eyes were still closed. *Wow. Dad never talks like that in front of me or Mom. Why the hell won't he open his eyes?*

Able to engage in conversation about basic things like his name and his hometown, Dad didn't know the year or the name of the president. The last two didn't really bother me because half the time, I didn't know what year it was and most of the time I tried to forget who's President.

In spite of countless attempts to get Dad to open his hazel eyes, they remained closed. Over the course of the next few days, his spoke less often and I sensed him slipping away. He only perked up if a doctor or nurse came into the room, especially a nurse.

"Good Morning, Mac," said one of the nurses, coming in to check on my Dad. "How are you feeling this morning?"

"Oh, just fine," he answered, turning his head in the direction of her voice.

"That's good to hear. Who are your visitors?" she asked, giving us a knowing wink.

"Oh, they're, well, um...," he stammered.

"Why don't you open your eyes and see who they are?" she suggested. Dad didn't reply and his eyes remained closed.

The next ten days brought several mini-seizures. Completely unresponsive, Dad stopped eating and drinking. He no longer spoke or turned his head to listen to the movements of the hospital staff as they buzzed around, performing their duties. Despite the excellent care he received, Dad was ridden with bed sores on his butt and the bottoms of his feet, which the nursing staff treated and covered with clear, adhesive tape. They worked diligently to keep him clean and rotated his muscular frame frequently, but in spite of their valiant efforts, the bed sores refused to forfeit their real estate.

Realizing there was nothing more they could do, the hospital staff moved my father into the attached nursing home. Beikirch Nursing Home was the Buckingham Palace of nursing homes with a staff-to-patient ratio that most people would kill for. It was clean, bright and didn't smell like piss.

I made arrangements with my husband and my work to stay in New York indefinitely. Common sense told me Dad wouldn't live much longer and I wanted to stay with him until the end. *How long can a person survive without food or water?*

Mom and I arranged flowers and placed framed photos near Dad's bed, probably more for ourselves than him because my father never opened his eyes. While we fussed, his doctor came in.

"How's the patient?" he asked, as if he didn't know.

"Unchanged," I replied. "I'd like you to help manage my Mom's expectations," I said, noting her facial expression was difficult to read. "How long can she expect my Dad to live, given he's not taking food or water?" There was no need to beat around the proverbial bush. We were all adults and knew he was dying.

"Unless you plan to request an IV or feeding tube, I'd say less than a week. I'm sorry, but I think it's best to be honest," said the doctor, sounding genuinely sympathetic.

"Dad doesn't want any sort of intervention, right Mom?" I asked. She nodded in agreement.

"I think that's the best course of action, given the circumstances. We'll do our best to keep him comfortable." The doctor shook hands and excused himself to see to other patients.

The next few days ran together. I stayed with Dad while Mom went to Mass, ran errands, attended meetings and did her best to maintain a normal schedule. It was obvious she had difficulty excepting what was clearly imminent. Our gentle giant was dying and nothing could prevent it.

"It's really sweet of you to spend so much time with your Dad," said one of his nurses, interrupting the magazine article I was reading to my father. "I'm sure it's a comfort to him."

"He'd do it for me," I replied, grateful for a two-way conversation.

"I know you want to be here when he passes," she said, resting her hand on my shoulder, "but I think you should know most of our residents manage to slip away when their family members go to the bathroom or the cafeteria. It's almost as if they wait until they're alone to die."

"Well, then, I guess I won't leave him alone," I said, my mind made up.

Later that afternoon, the caring and kind nursing staff moved another bed into Dad's room, giving me a more comfortable place to sleep. The kinks in my neck and shoulders from sleeping in the insufficiently padded armchair were very grateful. When the staff delivered meals to other residents, they dropped off sandwiches and cookies to me, reminding me how important it was to keep my strength. *If Mom sees these cookies, she won't let me eat them. Shit, how old am I?*

Mindful of the warning that residents frequently check out while their family members are on the crapper, I left the door to Dad's john open and talked to him incessantly while taking care of business. I was determined to be by his side when he died, not wiping my backside in another room.

"I haven't left, Dad," I warned, should his saintly soul consider making a dash for the Pearly Gates, "I'm right here watching you in the mirror, so you better not even think about dying. I'll be right out." I didn't know if my nonsense made any difference to Dad, but it helped keep the mood light. Nothing says downer like a death bed.

George came to check on Dad every evening after work, but it didn't make sense for him to sit there, falling asleep in the chair. After an hour or so each night, I sent him home, promising to call if anything changed. George was hurting badly because Dad was his hero. He's not much of a talker but it was easy to see his heart was breaking. Scott was in prison and Peter had a wife and five kids that needed him. My Mom came and went. She seemed to have difficulty sitting there, seeing her once strong husband lying in a bed, unresponsive. She found reasons to keep her distance and I tried to understand.

"I have to let Jasper out. It's not fair to leave him in the house all day," she explained. I've never had an unkind feeling toward any pet but I hated that dog. He failed obedience school and my parents found it endearing and humorous. Without their children living at home Jasper became their child, and unlike their human children, Mom and Dad spoiled him rotten. Rules out the window, Jasper had free reign. He jumped, barked and humped at will.

In addition to Jasper, Mom's time was in demand by the numerous boards and organizations to which she was dedicated. *Fine with me. I can't talk to Dad the way I want to when Mom's here because she wouldn't understand.* Conversation and companionship were the only things I could give him. When Mom wasn't there, I talked to Dad for hours on end. I read from books and magazines, and told stories from my childhood. Convinced he could hear me, I hoped my diarrhea of the mouth was bringing him some measure of comfort.

"If you want me to stop talking, Dad, you have to open your eyes," I said, offering him an escape from my blabbering. His eyes remained shut so my mouth kept flapping.

As I settled into as comfortable of a routine one can have while keeping a death-bed vigil, Mom surprised me with a one-two punch that damn near forced me to take her out of this world. In complete secrecy, she spoke with Dad's doctor. While I sat bedside, reading the Farmer's Almanac aloud to Dad, Mom cornered the doctor in the hall and told him the family wanted a feeding tube.

"So your mother tells me the family has elected for a feeding tube?" said Dad's doctor, eyebrows slightly raised, as he checked my Dad's unchanging condition.

Excuse me? What did this guy just say? "Absolutely not! Why would we prolong this?" I asked, gesturing to the body lying in bed. "My Dad's not going to get better and, truth be told, he's already gone. This isn't my Dad," I said, holding back tears.

"Well, I admit, I was surprised. I'll honor the wishes of the family, of course, but a feeding tube seems unusual in your Dad's case."

"So, then why'd you bring it up?" Somehow I knew what he was going to say, but it didn't make it any less shocking.

"Well, your mother said the family changed its mind," said the doctor, looking me in the eye.

"That couldn't be further from the truth. Whatever you do, don't let anyone put anything in my Dad. That's not what he wanted. I'll take care of my mother." *What the hell is wrong with her!*

The sympathetic doctor agreed to hold off on any procedures until we spoke again. *He must know Mom is off her cracker. What the fuck was she thinking? I know she's traumatized but Dad hasn't opened his eyes or spoken in weeks. Why would anyone consider prolonging that kind of an existence?*

I called my parent's house and Mom answered on the second ring. "I won't let you do this, Mom. Dad didn't want any kind of life support and you know it," I barked, not wasting time on greetings or other pleasantries.

"He's my husband."

"He's my father and you have no right to keep him living like he is now. He's ready to die!" I bellowed, wishing I could speak more calmly. I could hear Dad saying, "You catch more flies with sugar than vinegar."

"How do you know he's ready to die? Has he told you that?" she asked, being absolutely ridiculous. "I talked to your brothers and they said they want him to have a feeding tube, too."

My bullshit alarm sounded loudly. "Hold on. Did they tell you they want Dad to have a tube or did you tell them you were going to have one installed and they didn't argue?" I wondered if "installed" was the proper term. It's not something I discussed very often.

"What's the difference?" she asked.

"There's a huge difference, Mom! They aren't going to tell you 'no' because they're trying not to upset you, but I'm telling you there's no way in hell you're going through with this. I don't care if I upset you. I won't allow you to make Dad suffer any longer than he has to."

She was silent, but I was pissed and ready for battle. "I'll settle this once and for all," I told her.

Promising to call back, I hung up and called each of my un-incarcerated brothers. I relayed to each the facts regarding Dad's medical condition and the prognosis for recovery, which was zilch. They didn't think a feeding tube was a good idea, but they didn't want to fight with Betty. *Big Surprise.*

I called Mom again but she didn't answer. I left a message, speaking as calmly as I could and informed her the vote was three against one. No feeding tube. As gently as possible, I told her the doctors and nursing staff were aware of our wishes. Dad was going to be left as is. After Mom's sneaky little fiasco, I was more determined than ever to stay by Dad's side, in the unlikely event she tried to convince the doctors to do something stupid.

To the amazement of the medical staff, Dad was going on two weeks without food or water. His doctor expected him to last less than a week, but my Dad was so strong he just kept going. *How can he still be alive? I can't stand to see him like this.* Apparently it is indeed possible for a human to live two weeks without water, but it's not a pretty sight. The only hydration my Dad received was from a small sponge on a stick I used to swab his mouth and wet his lips, which were cracked and bleeding. I kept them smeared with Chap Stick but it wasn't enough. I was completely helpless and my thoughts turned to Christopher.

My Catholic foundation getting the better of me, I called my former Holy Crush, who was a well-established pastor in a nearby parish.

"Christopher? Dad's dying and needs Last Rites. There's no one in this world I'd rather have bless him than you." It was the honest truth and untainted with ulterior motives. My sexual attraction to Christopher died years before.

I called Mom and George to let them know Christopher would be there about eight o'clock that night to administer Dad's last and final Holy Sacrament. I knew they'd both want to be there. I was about to call my Godmother but remembered she was in Ireland. I knew she'd be disappointed when she got home and heard about her brother's condition.

Shortly before eight, I went outside Beikirch Nursing Home to wait for Christopher. Realizing that unlike the rest of my family, I never called him Father, I considered trying to do so. Maybe next time. I heard his crappy winter-beater coming long before he pulled into the parking lot. He drove the same jalopy he had when I put my innocent hand in his crotch and asked whether or not he intended to fuck me. As a smile hit my lips, I wondered if Christopher remembered that day, but recalling what was bringing us together again chased away thoughts of everything except my Dad.

Embracing me tightly, Christopher said, "I do wish we were seeing each other again under different circumstances."

"Me too, but thanks for coming. I wouldn't trust anyone else to do this," I said, kissing his cheek.

"That's high praise coming from you, especially since you've decided Catholicism is a bunch of hocus-pocus...or have recent events caused you to embrace your faith once again?"

"Oh Christopher, you know damn well I think it's a bunch of crap, but my Dad doesn't and that's why I need you. If anyone's going to prepare my Father's soul for Heaven, which by the way I do believe in, I want it to be you. You're the only priest I trust," I explained, as we walked arm-in-arm through the hallway towards the death bed.

After exchanging pleasantries with my Mom and George, Christopher took out his tools of the trade and arranged them on the bedside table. Making the sign of the cross, he said a short prayer. With his bottle of Oleum Infirmorum, or Oil of the Sick, Christopher blessed Dad's eyelids saying, "By this holy unction and His own most gracious mercy, may the Lord pardon you whatever sin you have committed by sight." Anointing Dad's ears, nose, lips, hands and feet, Christopher said a similar prayer, replacing "sight" with the appropriate word for that particular body part. *Don't forget to bless his arse, 'cuz he sure did lay some farts that qualified as sinful.*

I moved closer to my Mom and wrapped my arm around her, noticing how small she suddenly seemed. It struck me how dramatically her posture changed over the past few weeks from an upright, commanding one to that of an almost frail, slightly bent, older woman. The tears flowed freely from everyone's eyes, including Christopher's, I noticed.

"By the Sacred mysteries of man's redemption, may almighty God remit to you all penalties of the present life and of the life to come: may He open to you the gates of paradise and lead you to joys everlasting," Christopher said. The rest of us "Amened" as the ritual dictated. "May almighty God bless you," Christopher continued, making the sign of the cross, "in the name of the Father, the Son and the Holy Spirit". Again, we "Amened" in unison.

Mom and George thanked Christopher for coming and he wished them

God's peace. Kissing my father's forehead, he took my hand and we walked away, leaving my family to their tears and private thoughts.

Standing next to Christopher's car, I confessed, "I just want him to die. I just want him to go home." I knew Christopher would understand. I loved my Dad and wished he was well, but the man who'd been my Father stopped living weeks ago. It seemed unfair that his body wouldn't let go, although his mind had already done so.

Christopher hugged me one more time and told me to call him for anything. Thinking what I would have done to hear him say that when I was sixteen made me smile. I waved goodbye to my friend, thankful to have him in my life.

After saying goodnight to Mom and George, I watched the nurses administer morphine and rearrange Dad's unresponsive body. I kissed him goodnight and said, "I love you, Dad. Should you feel the need to die tonight, please wake me, okay?" He didn't answer so I crawled into my bed, just inches away and fell instantly to sleep.

About six o'clock the following morning, I was awakened by my father's grossly labored breathing. It sounded like he was drowning. I rushed out to the nurse's station and came back with a wonderfully kind woman who listened to Dad's breathing for about two seconds before dashing out of the room. She returned, pushing a machine of some sort and said she wouldn't normally allow a family member to watch this procedure, but there wasn't time to waste.

Shoving a tube down Dad's throat and into his lungs, she flipped a switch. The sickening sound of mucus being vacuumed from my Dad's lungs threatened to purge my stomach. Based on the contortions of my Dad's face and body, the experience was very painful. Although it seemed like hours until the nurse flipped off the machine and removed the tube, it was probably only a matter of minutes. After checking his pulse and blood pressure she administered morphine, patted me on the back and went back to her station.

So this is what death looks like. I was unable to help him or ease his pain. Before me was a man who'd sacrificed countless times to make my life more comfortable. A man who lived for his family and who was dying a slow, painful death.

Dad continued to run a high fever so I cooled his forehead with a wet washcloth. Taking in his unhealthy shade of red, and sensing the incredible heat pouring off his body, I heard the disquieting gurgling sounds from earlier begin again. It started slowly and quickly grew to a deafening roar. I high-tailed it to the nurse's station and we repeated the ugly dance we'd performed earlier. Within an hour, it happened a third time. More vacuuming and more intense pain for my poor father.

When the nurse was gone, I sat as close to my Dad as possible. Taking his gigantic farmer hand in mine, I began my speech. "Dad, it's time for you to let go. It's time to die. Don't worry, we'll be okay. We'll take care of Mom but you have to go now."

Maybe Dad won't die until he says goodbye to Peter and Scott. Peter couldn't get away from family and work obligations and Scott was in prison. Somehow, I needed to help my Dad finish his business, allow him to leave his pain behind and move onto whatever came next.

"Dad, I don't know if you were awake or not, but Peter was here," I lied. "He came to say goodbye yesterday. He sat with you for a few hours and told you he loved you. He had to go back home to take care of Samantha and the kids." I hoped he'd believe me. *Is it a sin to lie to dying person who's been given Last Rites?*

"You know Scott can't be here because he's locked up in the pokey, but he sent you a letter," I lied again. I continued talking out loud, pretending to read a non-existent letter in which Scott apologized to Dad for all the pain he caused. He apologized for life choices that ultimately led to a prison sentence. The letter expressed his love and said goodbye.

Unable to determine if my lies made a difference, I prayed out loud to all the dead people I knew, imploring them to call my Dad home. One by one, I called out their names.

"Gramma, Grampa, Tim, Uncle Patrick, Jimmy, Aunt Hazel, Uncle Dave, Aunt Audrey, RoseMary, Uncle Gordy, Uncle Eddie, Uncle Jeff, please call my Dad home. It's time. Please call him," I begged through tears.

I repeated my request, adding names of the deceased as they came to me. My Dad remained motionless, eyes closed until the gruesome gurgling sounds of drowning began again. *What should I do?*

I could get a nurse to shove the hose into his lungs again, causing great pain and prolonging death, or I could do nothing and leave it in the hands of Dad's maker. I sobbed, struggling with the desire to ease his pain while realizing he needed to die. I held his enormous hand, hot with fever, and asked the dead to call him home.

Seated to Dad's left, I watched in disbelief as his head turned away from me toward his right, and his eyes opened for the first time in weeks. Hot tears ran down my face and onto his bed sheets. I squeezed his giant hand between the two of mine as I watched him glance around the room, as if looking at faces in a crowd. His eyes rested here and there, momentarily, as if gazing upon the faces of people gathered behind me. Tears filled my eyes, threatening to blind me from a sight I wasn't sure I wanted to see. Blinking hard to clear them, I saw Dad's head turn toward me and our eyes met.

"Oh, Dad. I'm so sorry..." His breathing was extremely labored and I was scared. The drowning sound grew louder and more awful. "I love you, Dad. You need to let go. It's time to go home." Holding my gaze, Dad gave me a small smile, although it was obvious he was in pain and unable to breath. "I'm sorry, Dad. I love you."

The noise stopped. Dad's eyes and mouth were open, his tongue hanging limp, while his color rapidly changed from bright red to grey. It was 8:05am.

I looked back and forth from my Dad to the institutional clock on the wall. Putting my hand over his pace maker, I felt it stop and start a few times. After three minutes without ticking, I walked out of the room and toward the nurse's station. The nurse who'd suctioned Dad's lungs walked toward me, clean linens in hand.

"What's wrong?" she asked with real concern.

"Nothing," I replied, "he's gone."

"What? Are you sure? Come on," she said, hooking my arm as we walked toward Dad's room.

Crossing the threshold, she looked at Dad and said, "Oh, I'm so sorry. We need to open the window so his soul can escape. Is that okay?"

I nodded and she opened the window, leaving it so. "I guess it's silly, but we get a little superstitious here. If you don't mind let's leave it open for awhile." She seemed concerned I might think she had a screw loose.

"Do whatever you need to do, but he's already in Heaven."

"You're a wonderful daughter. You obviously loved your Dad very much," she said, while removing the morphine feed. "We were all impressed with how you fought for him and never left his side. When my time comes, I'll be happy if my kids spend half the amount of time with me as you did with him."

"Thanks. He deserved better than this," I said, pointing to my Dad. "I'm glad he's gone now, though." I hoped she understood I wasn't glad my Dad was dead, but if he had to die, I didn't want him to continue suffering. "My Mom will probably show up after Mass and I don't want her to see him like this."

She gave me a quick hug and disappeared. Within moments, she returned with another nurse and together, they gently bathed my Dad as if he were still alive. The nurses must have questioned my mental stability as I said things like, "You did it, Dad!"and "I'm proud of you." Perhaps I went temporarily insane, but the tears were gone and I was happy he wasn't hurting or drowning any more. The nurses arranged my Dad as nicely as they could, closed the privacy curtain around the side of his bed facing the door and left me to my thoughts.

I called George. "Hello?" He knew what my call meant.

"Dad's gone. He died a few minutes ago. I was with him." George was silent and I knew he was crying. I took charge for what would be the first of many times that week. "I don't want Mom to show up and find him dead. Will you wait for her out front so she doesn't just walk in? I think we should tell her what happened before she walks in and sees him."

He agreed to intercept Mom and I took care of the rest. I called Peter, trying to find a comforting way to tell him our Dad was dead. He cried and promised to come home for the funeral. After telling Peter I loved him, I called the funeral home.

Waiting for Fred the mortician to answer, I thought about how he'd known my Dad for most of his life. I flashed back to a conversation we'd had earlier in the week, when I went with Mom and George to pick out Dad's casket. I didn't trust Fred, because he tried selling my Mom stuff she couldn't afford and Dad wouldn't have wanted. I put the kibosh on the extras and told Fred we wanted the most basic casket without any frills. *The man would be dead when we put him in it, right? Why throw his hard-earned money in the ground with him?*

Fred's voice brought me back to the moment at hand. "Hi Fred, it's Patti Anne. Dad died this morning." The man was an undertaker so there was no need sugarcoat it.

"What? Are you sure?" he asked. *Umm...yeah, Fred, I'm looking at the dead body as we speak.*

"Fred, the man is dead. Can you come with the death mobile, or not?"

"The hearse? Of course I'll be there, but I was sure Mac would live for years. This is gonna be real hard on your Mom...," observed Fred. *Good thing Fred is here to point these things out.*

"Okay, well, Mom's still at Mass and I don't want her showing up to find an empty bed. As much as she makes me fucking crazy, I'm not gonna move Dad until she has a chance to see him. I'll call you soon."

I packed the few personal things Dad had in the room, but since he never wore anything but a hospital gown, there wasn't much. I folded up a couple shirts hanging in the armoire. It must have given Mom comfort to think he might actually put one on and come back home. Endlessly sentimental, I pulled off my T-shirt and pulled Dad's green polo shirt over my head instead. It had "Mac" embroidered over the spot his heart would have been. It made me feel better.

I found Dad's shaving kit and thought briefly about shaving him so he'd look more like himself in the casket. Images of my Dad's face with pieces of tissue covering bloody nicks on his cheeks and neck came to mind. *What the hell do I know about shaving a man's whiskers? I'll probably botch the job and leave him looking like a badly carved hunk of meat.* I decided to leave it to Fred, the undertaker.

In the mirror over the dresser, I watched George step cautiously into the room. *Geez, he's dead, you know. He's not hiding behind the curtain waiting to jump out and scare you.* I kept my thoughts private, realizing he hadn't spent the past hour or so with our dead father and didn't share my level of comfort. Not knowing what waited on the other side of the curtain, George seemed unsure what to do, so I took his arm and lead him to our father's bedside. I told him some of the details of Dad's death, leaving out the part where I purposely let him die. He cried while we waited for the arrival of our Mother.

We heard Mom coming down the hall long before we saw her. Her walk was hard to miss. She walked with purpose and wouldn't have made a good ninja. George and I stepped outside the door.

"Mom, don't go in yet," I said, as I took her arm. Immediately on the defense, she pulled away and demanded to know why.

"Because Dad died this morning," I whispered. How does one tell their mother that their father is dead? As much as I wanted to lay this responsibility in my brother's lap, I knew I owned it. I was there when he left this world and I had to be the one to tell her, but I wouldn't tell her everything. Only I would know I was responsible for his death.

Her face contorted into something awful and she moaned out a very painfully sad "no". I held her close as she sobbed. It was over as quickly as it began, and within moments, she regained her composure. As her heart of ice regained control, she pulled away and pawed through her purse, frantically searching for something.

"Mom, what are you doing?" I asked.

"I'm calling your brothers. I'm sure you two didn't do it." *Oh, ye of little faith.* I told her I'd already called Peter and he would be here in a few days. "What about Scott?" she asked.

Looking at George for backup, I stammered, "Umm...he's in jail. I didn't know he could take calls." George nodded.

"Don't be an ass, Pat," said Mom, dialing like a woman possessed. I didn't know what that meant, but considering it was about Scott, I didn't really give a shit.

"Do you want to see Dad?" I asked, as gently as I could.

"No. I don't," she snapped, not making eye contact. *That was certainly unexpected. You couldn't tear me away from this room without seeing him if I were you.* I assured Mom the nurses had bathed Dad and he looked peaceful. I wasn't craving a bedside spectacle, but I wanted her to understand this opportunity wouldn't present itself again. If she said she didn't want to see Dad's body, then I needed to call Fred. The nurses needed to disinfect the bed for the next poor bastard in need of a place to die.

Mom made very clear she had no intention of looking at her dead husband, so I asked George to take her home. I told them I'd wait for Fred to collect Dad and I'd be home. Mom walked away without a word. I'd never understood my Mother and at that moment, I wondered if I ever would.

Fred arrived within fifteen minutes and the look on his face was one of utter shock. This guy sees dead people all day long, for Christ's sake. It's his job. My hardened heart softened a bit towards Fred. It was obvious he was fond of my Dad.

"I couldn't believe when you called me this morning. I never thought this man could die."

Wow. Way to help me keep it together, Fred. Back to business. "We want to have viewing hours on Thursday and Friday and the funeral Mass and burial on Saturday, okay?" I asked.

"That'll be fine," Fred said quietly, looking at my Dad.

"I want to be there when you prepare Dad's body."

"What?" asked the undertaker.

"You know, when you drain his blood and remove his organs? *Remember that part?"* Duh, Fred. *You do know what you're doing, right?*

"Absolutely not!"

"Fred, I know Dad's dead, but I need to be there to make sure his body is treated with respect." I imagined someone tossing him around on a cold metal table like a side of beef.

"I assure you, I will personally take care of your Father and there's no way you will be there with me. No way in hell." It was obvious Fred wasn't gonna budge, so I finally let it go.

Standing to the side of the hearse, I watched Fred and his brother load my Dad's body into the back. Fred gave a solemn wave as they pulled away. Driving back to the farm, I was angered to see people riding bikes and playing in sprinklers as if the world hadn't changed. My Dad's body was growing cold and the entire town was enjoying a beautiful day as if his death didn't matter. I tried to focus on the positive. Dad was in Heaven rather than drowning in a nursing home, but I wanted to run over some of those happy fuckers anyway.

Without really deciding to do so, I drove to my Godmother's house. Considering she was Dad's only living sibling and my Godmother, I felt like I should be the person to break the news of his death. I should have let someone else tell her.

Ringing the doorbell, I walked in. Elizabeth hadn't locked her door for as long as I could remember. I supposed it saved her the trouble of locating the proper key when she was full of Arthur's Guinness. Shouting her name to avoid scaring the shit out of her, I followed the sound of her singing and found her ironing in the kitchen.

"How's the big size of ye?" she asked, which was one of her more endearing ways of asking how I was doing. I never liked it. The whole "big size" thing put me off.

The look on my face spoke volumes to the woman who knew me so well. "Ach, is it yer Pap?"

"I'm sorry, Aunt Elizabeth. He died this morning," I said softly, as I embraced her. She smelled like ivory soap and corned beef with a light dusting of whiskey.

"Yer acting the maggot," she said, reaching behind her for a flask.

"No, I'm not kidding. He's gone," I insisted. *First Fred and now Elizabeth. Why doesn't anyone believe me?*

"And ye were there when his saintly soul departed?" she asked after draining her signature whiskey container.

Tone down the drama. "Yes, just me and Dad," I said, fighting tears. It was still so fresh in my mind.

"Aww naw! Aye right. Away and wash the back of yer bollox!"

Cleary, she still didn't believe me. *Why the hell would I make this up?* The tears halted momentarily as my blood pressure rose. "Do you need to see a body or what? He's dead!"

"Aww feck! Ye killed again! I'll knack yer melt in, wee doll!"

In my family, them's fightin' words, so I high-tailed it out of my aunt's kitchen and jumped in the car. As I drove away, spewing gravel in every corner of her manger scene, she stood in her door shouting something I couldn't understand, but I got the general gist of what she said. She accused me of killing again.

I made arrangements with Fred to go to the funeral home to see Dad before anyone else. I wanted to make sure he looked like himself and not some stranger. I'd been afraid of dead bodies in the past, always a little worried they might sit up in the casket or suddenly open their eyes as I looked down at them, but I wasn't afraid of my Dad. Not too much.

My husband and George tagged along. I suspect their motive for doing so was to get a break from Mom rather than the urge to see a dead guy.

The body in the casket didn't look like Mac. Dad was a farmer and always sported a red, sun-kissed complexion, but the dead guy before me was whitish grey and sickly looking. Fred had royally fucked up Dad's hair, so I borrowed George's comb.

Poised above the casket, ready to touch my dead father, I said, "Dad, if you sit up or open your eyes, I'm going to kill you."

"Too late for that," remarked Wally.

I managed to get Dad's hair combed properly but he still didn't look right. *Oh, his glasses are missing!*

"Fred, where are Dad's glasses? You didn't put them on another body, did you?"

"Of course not! Check his pocket," said Fred, shaking his head at the thought of mixing up his dead clients' belongings.

I found them inside his suit pocket and placed them on his nose. Dad looked more like himself but still not right.

I don't think Fred crammed enough cotton into Dad's mouth and he super-glued his lips into the wrong shape. I considered trying to fix it, but the image of me draped over my father's dead body, prying open his mouth stopped me. It might offend.

Day one of funeral fun arrived. *Let the good times roll!* The sun shone brightly and the weather was perfect for spending the day outside rather than in a dark, drab funeral home with a dead guy. As we crossed the hearth of the funeral home, the sun taunted and teased. I thought briefly about sneaking out the back door and picking up Barbara Ann and Proud Mary for a trip to the beach, but I figured my absence would be noticed. Besides, Dad needed me. I knew he was dead but I still talked to him as if he could hear me. Crazy runs in my family. *If I'm not careful, I'll end up fucking whacko like Elizabeth and Mom.*

Gently taking Mom's arm, I walked her to Dad's casket. She cried but not the way I expected. I didn't know if she was in denial or fear, but she seemed to be holding up just fine. As I decided we just might get through this without excessive drama, Elizabeth walked in. Fred greeted her at the entrance to the viewing room.

"How's yer onions, sir?" she asked Fred, who tried to maintain his composure while interpreting her greeting. A look of disbelief spread across his face as he realized she'd inquired about his balls. Poor Fred smiled and gestured her into the room. I saw beads of perspiration gathered on his forehead.

Elizabeth staggered to the casket, making use of pieces of furniture to keep her upright and mostly on course. It was pretty obvious she'd been living in a whiskey bottle since I'd broken the news of her brother's death. She wasn't taking it well and my heart hurt for her.

Elizabeth put her hand on my Dad's forehead. Her hat was so large, it nearly shaded his entire body. "Ach, would ye look at the hack of him," she said, commenting on his appearance. Pulling her ever-present flask from her purse, she tried putting it in Dad's hands, which were crossed over his chest with a rosary draped between them. Dad was dead and not cooperating with his sister.

"May I be of assistance?" Fred hadn't taken his eyes off her and wanted to prevent her from messing up the painstaking work he'd performed on Dad's body.

"Not on yer Nelly. I haven't a baldy notion why ye didn't dress him up with a flask," chastised my whiskey-loving Godmother.

As Elizabeth tried forcing the flask into Dad's uncooperative hands, Fred took it gently from her and rearranged the rosary as the rest of us looked on. I knew this was only the preview. We were in for a three day show and unfortunately, I had a front row seat and back stage pass.

Elizabeth and Fred compromised and placed the flask in the casket near my Dad's elbow. It looked ridiculous and I made a mental note to remove it when my aunt wasn't looking. My Godmother pulled a second flask from her oversized purse, took a long pull and shoved it back where it came from. Turning on her heel, she clapped her hands and made an announcement. "Mac's been kilt. She done it once and she done it again," accused my aunt, pointing at me. "Have a jook at her. Ye can see it on her dial!"

She's so drunk she probably doesn't know my name. I was confident my

Mom or one of my brothers would speak up in my defense. *Silly me. Where do I get these crazy notions?* No one argued with Elizabeth, instead they just looked at me.

"Aunt Elizabeth, please don't make this harder than it has to be," I pleaded. My family continued to stare at me, as though considering a lynching. Thankfully, my husband walked in behind the group and stopped squarely in front of Elizabeth.

"If you have accusations to make against my wife, then you better go to the police and make them. Otherwise you will shut your mouth and not do another thing to upset this family. Do you understand?" asked Wally.

Elizabeth wasn't used to being told to do anything, much less to shut up. Although I loved her dearly, it was a refreshing change. "Does it look like a came up the lagan in a bubble?" she asked.

"I have no idea what the hell that means, but I'm telling you to pull your head out of your ass and be nice."

Wally continued to glare at Elizabeth until she shook her head and walked away mumbling something about a fecking eejit. I beamed at my husband as he walked across the room to join me.

"Don't worry, I won't let her start that shit again," he whispered as he hugged me tightly. "You have enough stress without that crazy old bitch adding to it."

"She doesn't mean it, she's just drunk and upset," I said, coming to my Godmother's defense.

I was thankful for my husband. I knew he meant every word and he'd keep an eye on her. I could forget about Elizabeth's rage and focus on what was really important. If only I could get rid of the nagging feeling that maybe she was partly right. I knew I didn't have a hand in Patrick's death because I'd been an infant when he died, but this was different. I could have gotten help and had my Dad's lungs suctioned again, but I chose not to. I sat back and let him drown in his own mucus.

On my way to the ladies room a couple hours later, I walked by another viewing room. It was arranged with chairs, boxes of tissues and such, but was empty except for the dead person at the far end and the woman standing over the casket. *My eyes must be playing tricks on me. The lady combing the dead guy's hair looks like Elizabeth. Holy shit! It is Elizabeth!*

I tiptoed into the viewing room feeling like a teenager sneaking into her parents' liquor cabinet. I knew I didn't belong there. "What the hell are you doing, Aunt Elizabeth?"

She spun around so fast she almost fell on the floor. The comb fell into the casket with its occupant. "Are ye startin' then? Cuz I'll set," she slurred and struggled to focus her eyes.

"I don't wanna fight with you. What are you doing in here?"

"I see that yer wheel is running but the hamster's dead. Ye don't even know yer poor Pap, then, is that it?" she asked, taking another long drag from her flask.

What the hell is this crazy woman talking about? "Um...this may come as a surprise to you, but this isn't Mac," I said, pointing to the dead stranger.

"Eh? Stop actin' the maggot and help me fix his gob. They made a bags of doin' his hair." My aunt took another drink and rested the flask on the dead guy's chest while she dug around the casket for her misplaced comb.

Why me? "Aunt Elizabeth, this isn't Dad and we don't belong in here. This guy belongs to a different family. Let's go," I said, holding out my hand.

"Aye right. Ye kilt him and now you pretend ye don't even know him."

Elizabeth bent over the deceased and finally retrieved her comb. As she tried to make the complete stranger look like my Dad, the whiskey got the upper hand and she lost her balance. I tried to catch her, but she pulled her arm away and her upper half fell on top of the corpse. She swatted at me with her flask as tried to extricate herself from the dead guy's coffin.

Maybe I should shove the rest of her in and close the lid.

Our ridiculous battle was interrupted by Fred's most unhappy voice. "Ladies, what is going on in here?" He looked like he might have a stroke.

Elizabeth managed to pull herself off the corpse's chest and turned to look at the poor, unfortunately soul who'd raised his voice to her. Taking one look at Fred, she began to laugh. She laughed like someone who'd been on a three-day bender.

I imagined how this scene must look to Fred. A drunken Irish woman and her niece, fighting over the open casket of a stranger, flask in hand. The poor guy's hair was completely fucked up and his hands had been rearranged as well. I looked away from the corpse to poor Fred who was shaking in disbelief. I couldn't help myself and laughed, too. Tears rolled down my face and I thought I just might piss on Fred's funeral home carpeting.

My Godmother stopped laughing and looked at me like I was kooky. "I'm ready for the funny farm with ye," she said. She straightened her dress and walked out.

"Fred..." I needed to explain.

"I don't want to know," he interrupted, "Please go back to your Dad's viewing."

I tried pulling myself together, but the hilarity of the whole scene was too much. Stumbling away from the dead stranger, I snorted with laughter. At the viewing room's door I looked back at Fred who shook his head in disbelief at the mess we'd carelessly made of the dead stranger and I peed in my pin-striped suit.

The second day of calling hours was even harder and Elizabeth's drinking didn't help. Arriving mostly sober, she was slurring and surly within an hour. To ease my burden, Wally packed my tipsy aunt in our car and took her to a bar for the rest of the viewing. When he brought her back to the farm at supper time, she could barely walk. He parked her on the davenport with a pillow and she drifted off to sleep.

On burial day, we arrived at the funeral home for a private family service before trudging to Nativity for the Mass. Elizabeth was wearing an enormous black hat covered in ugly flowers that looked positively ridiculous. When Fred offered to take it from her, she slapped his hand and told him to back off. I couldn't tell if she was walking crooked because she was already drunk or if it was just the hat throwing her off balance. Whatever the cause, she couldn't walk a straight line, stumbled into a folding chair and fell on the floor.

"Who tripped me?" she demanded to know.

"No one touched you. You tripped over a chair," I explained, offering her my hand.

"Houl yer wheest! Are ye tryin' to put me in the ground beside my dearly departed brother?"

Well, now that you mention it..."Geez. Forget it." I walked away before she could see my tears. It hurt that my Godmother, who was normally so loving, was treating me so badly. I knew she couldn't help it but the tears came anyway.

Somehow, we managed to get through the service. Wally made sure Elizabeth was seated next to Mom in church. He knew they'd drive each other crazy. *Good. Serves them both right.*

When Elizabeth went up for Communion, she skipped the wafer altogether. She went straight for the wine and drained the cup. The Eucharistic minister didn't know what to do until Elizabeth prodded her. "Ye got any more in the back?"

I laughed out loud, as did everyone within ear shot, except the priest. Apparently he failed to see the humor. He must not have been Irish.

The funeral procession prepared to leave Nativity for the short drive to Mount Olivet, the cemetery behind my childhood home. I was alone in the car with my husband, grateful for his calming presence, and noticed Mom and Elizabeth standing in the grass a few car lengths ahead. They were supposed to drive with George and Peter, but instead of climbing into the car, they exchanged big arm gestures. *Uh oh.* I hopped out to watch the fireworks. Wally suggested I stay put and let them work it out, but I never did listen very well.

"You aren't riding with Mac! If anyone rides with him, it'll be me!" my Mom snapped at her sister-in-law.

"Houl yer horses, Betty. Ye don't belong with Mac. Ye never were the full shilling and he knew it!"

"How dare you talk to me like that! Get out of my way. I'm riding in the hearse!" Mom yelled, trying to move Elizabeth's well-proportioned figure out of the way.

Elizabeth held her ground and crossed her arms. "Jesus, Mary and wee Alex Diver. That's jam on yer egg!"

"For God's sake, Elizabeth! You've lived in America for how many years? Why don't you try speaking English and get the hell outta my way while you're at it!"

I watched this play out, refraining from interfering because I was having the most fun I'd had since before Dad went into the hospital. They deserved each other and I wanted to let them knock the snot out of each other, but we needed to get this goddamned thing over and done with. I needed a drink.

"Why don't you both ride with Dad? There's plenty of room," I suggested, opening the front passenger door, motioning them to slide in. Both Mom and Elizabeth shot me death stares but neither gave in. As they crammed into the front seat with the hearse driver, I noticed he looked almost as pissed as they did. I smiled big and waved before walking back to my car.

"That wasn't very nice," Wally said, "but those two had it coming. I love you, babe."

Holding my hand all the way to the cemetery, my kind husband tried to talk about anything other than my dead father. I wanted to drive home and forget about my daughterly responsibilities, but there remained one very large chore to be accomplished. We still had to plant my Dad.

My parents owned a burial plot at the top of Mount Olivet, which meant my childhood playground was getting a new resident. *I hope no one ever poops on his grave.* A tent had been erected and filled with a few rows of folding chairs. The wind blew like hell and the pleasant warmth that had tempted me to skip out of the funeral home only a few days earlier, was replaced by an angry grey sky. It was bitterly cold and within minutes I shivered.

As we walked to the gravesite, Mom complained about Elizabeth, the eulogy, the size of hearse and the anticipated cost of the reception. *Her husband, my father, is about to be put in the ground and all she can do is bitch about things that don't matter.* "If you don't shut up, I'm gonna shove you in the hole with Dad!" I shouted over the gusting wind.

"I don't think she's kidding, Betty," warned my husband. "I'd give her some space if I were you." Wally took my hand and led me to one of the chairs in front of the casket, which was now closed. Standing behind me, my husband tried to protect me from the wind or perhaps my Mom. Both could be painful to experience.

Elizabeth sat next to me and almost took out my eye with her fucking hat. Before I could tell her to put the goddamned thing under her chair, or in the trashcan, the wind whipped around and lifted it off her head. She let out a squeal as she jumped to grab it. I watched it spin around, gaining altitude faster than a 747. It found a lovely resting place near the top of a hundred foot tall evergreen.

"Ah feck," she grumbled, "Tis me best hat."

25 WEE DOLL

Three months after Dad died, I was back in town for a close friend's wedding. On my way from the church to the reception, I passed my Godmother's house and knew Dad would want me to stop, even though I dreaded the thought. Memories of my most recent encounter with Elizabeth, during which she accused me of killing my Dad, were fresh and raw. I knew she was right and I didn't want to face her again.

Feeling Dad's calming presence, I pulled into Elizabeth's drive and noticed the statues in the manger hadn't been moved since the last time I was there to tell her about Dad's death. *That's weird. She moves them around every few days so they don't get bored.*

As usual, I rang the bell and walked in. The house seemed unusually still. Missing from the background were the sounds of my aunt busying herself in the kitchen, cooking or ironing, while singing folk songs from her beloved Ireland. My gut sent me signals I didn't want to receive so I tuned them out.

"Aunt Elizabeth?" I called. "It's me, Patti Anne."

I listened but the house remained silent, as if keeping a dark secret. The house that had always felt welcoming and familiar took on a strange and menacing air. I wanted to run out and forget I'd been there, but I was supposed to be a grown up, so I called out again.

"Hello? Are you home?"

I heard a muffled response from upstairs and with trepidation, started up the old oak staircase. I noticed the rail and stairs were dusty, as if no one had touched them for days. *I don't like this.*

"Aunt Elizabeth, where are you?" I asked, walking toward her bedroom. The door was ajar and I could see her lying in her antique, four poster bed. In spite of the summer heat, she was piled with quilts.

Walking into her room, I took in the unkempt state of things. My Godmother was an excellent housekeeper and, normally, there wasn't a dust bunny to be found under a bed or behind a dresser. I went to her bed and sat on the edge.

"Aunt Elizabeth, are you okay?" I asked, disturbed by her uncharacteristically grey skin. Even her fiercely red, curly hair seemed dull. It was like she was fading. "What's wrong?"

"Ach, me wee doll," she croaked, her voice dry and unfamiliar. "I'm so glad yer here. There's something I want to tell ye before I join yer Pap and the rest of me family." Her eyes were dim and watery. Nothing about the woman lying before me looked right. Aunt Elizabeth had always been bigger-than-life, vibrant and strong. My heart broke as I took her hand.

"Please don't talk like that. You're not going anywhere. When's the last time you ate?"

"Hold yer wheest, before I bust ye on the dial," she responded, lacking her usual oomph. "I'm dyin' and I know it, so listen to me while ye can." She closed her eyes and I thought maybe I'd come too late, but they opened again and she continued, although she sounded thoroughly exhausted. "I've done me best to keep ye on the path to Heaven, though we all know ye tried me patience more in once, ye did."

I smiled at the memory of my Godmother busting into my Confessional to tell Father John I'd knocked over gravestones in the cemetery. "I'm sorry I was such a bad kid."

"Ach, ye weren't so bad. I'm sorry yer Mum doesn't have the sense the Good Lord gave a turnip, and she had no right to dress ye like a boy all those years, but listen good. She loves ye, me wee doll, and ye've got to be a better daughter," said my wise Godmother. I didn't want to hear this conversation and the expression on my face must have said so.

"Don't look at me like that, I can still take ye over me knee. Yer not the easiest person to love but that's 'cuz no one taught you proper. I'm sorry I couldn't do more."

"Oh, Aunt Elizabeth," I said, tears streaming down my cheeks, "you've been the best aunt I could have asked for. You stood up to my parents and teachers in my defense more than once. Shit, you knocked out my seventh grade teacher's teeth!"

"Aye. Ugliest woman I ever saw, that one."

"No one else would have done that for me. I don't think I ever thanked you, so I'm thanking you now. Thank you, Aunt Elizabeth for loving me, defending me and making me laugh for the past forty years."

"Yer me wee doll and I love ye, child."

"I love you, too." My tears were flowing freely and my chest ached. I can't let her die.

"Yer Mum's never been the full shilling, that's no secret. But she's yer Mum and ye need to love her before it's too late." I knew she was right.

"I will do better, I promise," I answered, determined to make good on my promise. "Are you in pain? Can I get you anything?"

"Sing to me. Sing one of my songs, love." She closed her eyes. I struggled to hold back my tears long enough to grant one, last favor for the woman I knew I was about to lose. *Why do I get all the deathbed scenes?*

I sang quietly, hoping to do the song justice.

"In Dublin's fair city, where the girls are so pretty

I first set my eyes on sweet Molly Malone

As she wheeled her wheelbarrow through streets broad and narrow

Crying cockles and mussels alive a-live O!

A-live a-live O! A-live a-live O!

Crying cockles and mussels alive a-live O!

She was a fishmonger and sure it was no wonder

For so were her father and mother before

And they both wheeled their barrows through streets broad and narrow

Crying cockles and mussels alive a-live O!

A-live a-live O! A-live a-live O!

Crying cockles and mussels alive a-live O! "

Aunt Elizabeth's eyes never opened again.

26 NUNS

For most of my adulthood, a movie played in my mind. In truth I've had several but this is the only one that's G-rated. In the movie, a few close friends and I dress as nuns and ride bikes through the wine country of western New York, along Seneca Lake.

Can you picture it? Mid-fall, trees at their peak, dressed in leaves of bright gold, glorious red and warm orange. Enter stage left, five nuns in long black habits sporting head pieces. They peddle old Schwinn bicycles along a winding road through grape country. The afternoon sun plays in the ancient maples, spilling long shadows across the dirt road.

The images ran rampant in my head and became more elaborate over time. I saw nuns enjoying an afternoon bike ride and taking in God's great bounty in the form of delicious New York wines, crusty baguettes and local cheeses. After a tasting at one winery, they'd climb aboard their conveyances and peddle off to the next. It wouldn't take long before they'd be a bit wobbly from too much wine and too little bread.

They'd break into songs from "The Sound of Music" and maybe a few favorite hymns from their Catholic school days. When a nun has to make water, the rest of the group is forced to pull over, dismount and create a human wall to shield her from passing traffic while she recycles her wine. These were kind and happy nuns who loved to laugh. These nuns were like dear old Sister Mary Margaret rather than that hairy-lipped duo, Sisters Constance Joseph and Carol Fatass.

The scenes had danced through my imagination for far too many years when I finally decided to do something about it. Hell-bent to see this movie become a reality, I pitched the idea to Barbara Ann, because I knew if I could convince anyone to join me in this charade, it would be her. Aside from her propensity for the unusual, there's no one else I'd prefer as a member of my convent. There are only a precious few who understand and accept my humor and far fewer who share it. Barbara Ann, thank God, does all three.

While describing my plan to my best friend, I strived for Catholic Guilt. "If we don't do it now, Barbara Ann, when will we?" I asked. "Do you wanna wake up one day to realize you're an old woman and it's too late for this kind of fun? Would you really deny me this one request?" My Mom couldn't have done better.

She loved the idea but family obligations, young children and work apparently make it difficult for a grown woman to spend four days dressed as a nun, drinking wine all day. Who knew? After several months of groveling and, yes, perhaps even shaming her into it, she agreed to accept a leading role in what promised to be an award-winning movie. With Barbara Ann on board, we tackled the seemingly impossible task of convincing others to join us. Three, four or five nuns are always better than two. I think I read that in the Book of Matthew.

I hadn't given my husband many details about our "girl's weekend", because I didn't think he'd understand the humor. He's a very serious man and dishes out laughter in small chunks. I knew he wouldn't waste a ration of belly laughing on the notion of me dressing as a nun while tipping back wine with my childhood friends.

However, when FedEx delivered a nun habit, he had some questions.

"Do I need to be worried about this?" he asked. "Is this a cry for help?"

"What are you talking about?"

"Well, you've told me stories of your hellacious years of Catholic School, you resent being raised in the faith, your Dad and Elizabeth just died and now you want to dress like a nun and drink wine on a bike?" asked Wally, as if it was unusual.

"Yeah, so?" I may have been defensive.

"You don't see anything odd with your plan?"

"Um, no. Not at all. Can you help me get this habit on?" I asked, trying to figure out how to work the head gear.

"I swear, if you get as loony as Elizabeth, I'll shoot you myself," said Wally, taking the habit out of the box.

Miraculously, Barbara Ann and I convinced three other girls to join our escapade. We'd been friends since middle school and they were intimately familiar with our humor. Setting a date for a long weekend in September, I scoured the internet for the best possible place to serve as our temporary convent. I figured we wouldn't spend a lot of time in it, but knew we'd be there long enough to prepare a few meals, play games and laugh until we wet our habits. I found a little compound directly on Seneca Lake and reserved a yurt.

A traditional Mongolian yurt is a round, portable, wood lattice-framed dwelling used by nomads in Central Asia. Yurts are more home-like than tents in both shape and build and have thicker walls. The one we rented was a permanent dwelling with running water, indoor plumbing and a heater. It had a decent kitchen and two "bedrooms" that were without doors, but had mosquito netting, which offered a small measure of privacy.

The bathroom door was no more than a heavy curtain and some members of our convent were rather shy. To protect everyone's privacy, we agreed that if a nun had to do more than tinkle, she need only tell the other members of the convent it was prayer time, and they'd exit the yurt until prayer time was over. Our plan was rather ineffective because the walls of the yurt were so thin, everything that happened on the inside could be heard from the outside. It turns out nuns fart.

Getting from the main road to the yurt required a four-wheel-drive vehicle. The dirt lane down to the lake was quite steep, full of gaping holes and knotted tree roots. Once at the bottom, the dirt path to our yurt was even steeper and slightly muddy. Based on the looks of those staying in nearby yurts, you've seen it all once you've seen a bunch of nuns in full habits slinging mud in their SUV. I wonder what they thought when they heard us belting out the 'F' word on a regular basis.

After dropping off some groceries, clothes and an espresso machine at the yurt (one nun actually brought an enormous espresso machine, so much for a vow of poverty), we set out to partake of the best New York State had to offer.

When we arrived at the first winery, a couple members of our convent became uneasy because every head in the room turned to take us in. Barbara Ann and I flourish in that type of setting, and find attention only serves to improve our performance. However, our compadres had yet to acquire an appreciation for being on display. Trying to hide behind us, my shy friends found ample coverage behind my backside which looks even bigger in a habit. Barbara Ann and I reminded our reserved friends this was all in good fun as we approached the serving area with grace and poise, slightly inclining our heads down and forward in what felt like the posture of a holy sister. We were greeted with warmth, if not a bit of reservation. The hosts seemed hesitant and unsure what to serve six women of the cloth.

Sister Barbara Ann belted out, "Line 'em up. We're thirsty from prayer." That seemed a suitable icebreaker and we sampled wines of the Great Lakes.

After tasting and re-tasting everything the first winery had to offer, we crammed into the van, one nun after another. Other visitors to the winery followed us outside to watch our departure. Several shook their heads in disbelief while sending us off with vigorous arm waves. We only drove a short distance before pulling into the next winery and our reception was quite similar, except the gracious hosts at the second winery donated two bottles of wine for us to take back to our parish as altar wine.

"How very generous of you," I said, "On behalf of the Sisters of Constant Flatulence, I thank you very kindly." I bowed slightly and smiled.

Our hosts smiled sweetly at first and then looked a bit confused as they processed the name of our convent. After a moment or two, they laughed out loud. Exceptionally good sports, they told us to keep the wine, in spite of our little prank. To show our appreciation for their good humor, we bought another two bottles, along with bread and cheese. We wandered outside, found a picnic table in the afternoon sun and sat down to enjoy the moment.

I stepped back to take in the scene and compare it to my mental movie. There sat four beautiful nuns, each with a glass of wine. They talked and laughed in the fall sunshine while enjoying God's bounty in the form of fresh bread and local cheese. It was damn near perfect, especially when one of the innocent nuns broke wind as she struggled to uncork a bottle. I rejoined my convent, happy for such good friends.

I hope Elizabeth is watching from above.

I truly felt as if God was laughing, enjoying our little prank. To show his appreciation for our humor, he put wonderful people in our path and gave us a glorious day to share our fellowship. I believe God has a sense of humor and I think he'd enjoy dressing like a nun, too. But that's just me.

With fully tummies and empty wine bottles, we crammed ourselves back into the van and headed to the next watering hole. It had a lovely, hillside garden, which we decided would be the perfect spot for some group pictures.

A tour bus driver watched our antics from a few feet away in the parking lot. Unable to resist the urge to get a better look at our motley crew, he walked over and offered his photographic assistance. We were only too happy to accept. The bus driver took pictures with each nun's camera, chuckling every time he clicked the shutter.

When he snapped a picture with the last nun's camera, he wished us a wonderful day and turned for the parking lot.

"Wait, don't leave yet!" shouted Sister Barbara Ann. "We need a picture of you!"

The rest of the convent cheered.

"What's your name?" Sister Christine asked the hefty black bus driver.

"Well, my wife calls me 'Pookey Bear' most of the time," he said sheepishly.

The nuns sang out in unison, "Pookey Bear?" I thought I might piss myself.

We insisted Pookey Bear join us on the bench for one last picture. He laughed out loud and if it's possible for a large, imposing black man to blush, he did. Nestled between two angelic nuns, Pookey Bear looked completely out of place.

Imagine Mr. Bear's surprise when Sister Samantha put her hand on his inner thigh as the nuns chimed "cheese" for the camera. I thought he might come unglued. Despite his generously-sized frame, he jumped off the bench and sprinted for his bus. Once safely aboard, he shut the folding door to prevent evil Sister Samantha, that hussy, from following him.

We blew him kisses as we tumbled into the van, one nun after the other. He looked on in horror while we laughed until we cried.

Two years after the nun escapade, the same group went back to Seneca Lake. This time, however, the habits stayed in our closets. My wonderful friends indulged me once but said that was enough for one lifetime. I still take my habit out on occasion, put it on and wander around the house with a glass of wine. It keeps Wally on his toes.

I'm not really evil, but no matter how old I get I sometimes still enjoy acting like a complete and utter ass. Thankfully, Barbara Ann shares my illness, which explains why we've been friends for almost fifty years. We love to laugh to the point of vomiting and blowing snot in our hair. Watching each other fall down or staple a finger to a piece of paper provides endless satisfaction. We see humor in almost everything. Some people call it immaturity or irreverence. I call it a gift.

I hope you'll accept my gift and join me in laughing at my Confessions. All of them, good and bad, make me who I am. The way I look at it, I can't be blamed for drinking to excess, laughing at other people when they fall down or telling people exactly what I think of them. It's in my blood. It could be worse; I could be a pedophile or have a heart of ice.

If there's one thing my strict Catholic upbringing taught me, it's religion doesn't make you a good person. Going to church doesn't mean shit when you come right down to it. Sacraments are fine for those who want to keep with tradition, but they don't make the people who believe in them any more worthy than those who don't. What matters is the kind of person you are and how you treat those around you. It's something I continue to struggle with, but I no longer succumb to Catholic Guilt, nor do I fear my poor attendance at Mass will send me to Hell. Those childhood fears are behind me and this book is my last Confession. I am in a state of grace.

Where's me flask?

About the Author

Patti Lavell lives in the Florida Keys with her husband and their daughter, two dogs, two cats, and a turtle. Their son is in the Navy's Nuclear Power Program and the couple couldn't be more proud of both children.

Made in the USA
Charleston, SC
05 January 2013